MATRIX OF MAN

MATRIX OF MAN

An Illustrated History of Urban Environment

SIBYL MOHOLY-NAGY

FREDERICK A. PRAEGER, *Publishers*
New York • *Washington* • *London*

FREDERICK A. PRAEGER, *Publishers*
111 Fourth Avenue, New York, N.Y. 10003, U.S.A.
5, Cromwell Place, London S.W.7, England

Published in the United States of America in 1968
by Frederick A. Praeger, Inc., Publishers

Second printing, 1969

© 1968, by Sibyl Moholy-Nagy

To Manhattan Island
my inspiration and my love

Research for and illustration of this book were greatly aided by a grant from the Arnold W. Brunner Fellowship Fund of the Architectural League of New York.

CONTENTS

MATRIX OF MAN

INTRODUCTION

This is a book about faith in the historical city. Although towns are inanimate, they assume the characteristics of their creators. Men create and destroy values with equal intensity. As the only creature with a historical memory, man reveres the past, yet he ignores or denies it in the name of an utterly unknowable future. He thrives equally on intraspecific cooperation and internecine competition.

Cities, like men, are embodiments of the past and mirages of unfulfilled dreams. They thrive on economy and waste, on exploitation and charity, on the initiative of the ego and the solidarity of the group. They stagnate and ultimately die under imposed standardization, homogenized equality, and a minimum denominator of man-made environment. Most decisive of all, cities, like mankind, renew themselves unit by unit in a slow, time-bound metabolic process.

City personality does not rest on material progress but on historical options faced by a specific town and no other. If this were not so, we would all move to Oak Ridge, Tennessee. The constancy of urban change derives its dynamism from an eternally evolving imagination kindled by the coexistence of past and present. The deafening banality that Rome is not Paris, Kalamazoo not New Haven, is too low-keyed to penetrate the minds and influence the activities of the urban specialists, a new species, who maintain a perpetual momentum of urban crisis. Their most popular spokesmen have declared all cities moribund. Our "urban nightmares" can only be saved by "universal planning principles and over-all solutions." Popular success on the civic wailing wall depends on the carrying power of piercing Cassandra cries that time is running out. It never does.

Human existence is a continuous regrouping of matter and ideas. All nonpersonalistic religions knew the truth of the Eternal Return long before the invention of the Last Judgment menace. Everything is still possible, because the energy inherent in all things does not diminish. The endless flux of time can only be understood through the visible interaction of this energy with the material substance of the perceptible world. The twentieth century is going through a decisive reordering of this energy-and-matter relationship because new energetic factors have come into play: population increase, mechanization, mass distribution of goods and services, mass communication and education, secularization, and the separation of man from the processes of nature. This regrouping of things and meanings is most visible at their densest points of concentration—the cities. But even a casual historical comparison with former intensifications of change should make it clear that the upheaval in our environmental structure is no stronger than the first impact of wheeled traffic, banking economy, firearms, or the collapse of divine kingship and the ecumenical church.

The current "urban crisis," and its pessimistic, self-destructive diagnosis, differs from previous environmental revolutions in its contextual misdirection. We have developed a stupendous ability for incongruous comparisons. Twentieth-century man is drunk with achievements in one single field of human endeavor: science. Full of self-adoration because he has created a technological-industrial discipline without precedent, he thinks he has severed his ties with historical continuity. In the manner of an adolescent, blissfully ignorant of the fact that the first intimations of adulthood are generic rather than individual, scientific man fancies himself his own beginning. His best claim is the scientific process which is made to furnish standards for all human activities and problems. To be unscientific is to be inferior.

The disastrous results of misapplied laboratory techniques in sociology, psychology, and education are just starting to show. In city planning and architecture, the "scientific outlook" still has the romantic glow of the untried dream. The technocratic illusion that man-made environment can ever be the image of a permanent scientific order is blind to the historical evidence that cities are governed by a tacit agreement on multiplicity, contradiction, tenacious tradition, reckless progress, and a limitless tolerance for individual values. Science must be specialized, isolating, value-indifferent, and purely quantitative. With our capacity for incongruous comparisons, we try to solve qualitative problems of racial and social relationships with quantitative statistics; we attach significance to the ratio of old slum units to new slum units because the scientific determinism of the last century postulated that man is the product of his physical environment. The qualitative aspect of the city is the content of this environment, which is nonscientific, because its single definable denominator is social and spiritual self-preservation at

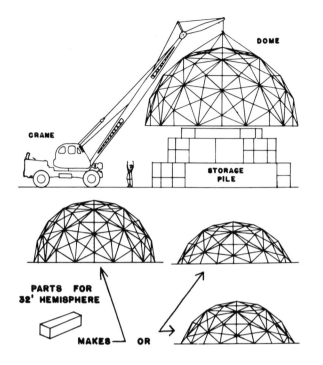

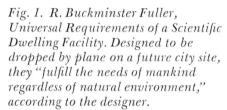

*Fig. 1. R. Buckminster Fuller,
Universal Requirements of a Scientific
Dwelling Facility. Designed to be
dropped by plane on a future city site,
they "fulfill the needs of mankind
regardless of natural environment,"
according to the designer.*

maximum well-being. No other epoch has received more persuasive proof of the split between human content and ahuman objectivity than ours. The blind logic of science takes its course regardless of the effects of air, water, and food pollution, drugs, chemical and nuclear weapons, speed and the combustion engine. But in architecture and planning, only that is good which serves the human condition at a particular stage of existence.

Man learns by observing, imitating, and adapting. This process can only be maintained if that which is observed, imitated, and adapted constitutes a potential contribution to the most desirable end. A lion tamer does not train in a flea circus.

The Frequency Modulations and the Angular Modifications employable by man may be applied by him to local sub-system interactions of energetic universe. The local transformations thus integrated ever reactively (indirectly-inadvertently) accelerate irreversible total transformations of universe.*

Such an idea might produce geodesic domes (*Fig. 1*); it will never produce cities.

Neither will cities be built or replanned according to codified

* R. Buckminster Fuller, "Considerations for a Curriculum," *University of North Carolina Bulletin,* Vol. IV, No. 3 (1954).

data fed into computers (*Fig. 2*). No matter how progressive the replacement of content by scientific control may sound, the reaction to any medium is founded in comparative content values. The city is the symbolic configuration of a place in history and a place on the surface of the globe. Prescientific eras had no difficulty in distilling from the accumulated evidence of this twofold sense of place a knowledge of urban well-being.

Toward the middle of the twentieth century, planning and architecture were persuaded by an artificially induced inferiority complex to submit to the criteria of "controlled laboratory conditions" for the transfiguration of the human habitat, despite the *caveats* nailed on the laboratory door by the scientists themselves. "Science is limited to regularities of unsurpassed exactness and objectivity of description," wrote Niels Bohr, "which can only be achieved by including in the account of the phenomenon explicit reference to purely experimental conditions." And in an interview in *Fortune,* in May, 1965, Vanevar Bush cautioned, "It is earlier than we think. . . . Science proves noth-

Fig. 2. Three sets of similar symbols represent problem solutions relating to totally dissimilar levels of human experience. Set (A) exemplifies the origin of spermatazoa and ovum; set (B) demonstrates Christopher Alexander's momentous discovery that "a city is not a tree"; and set (C) is Constantine Doxiades' attempt to hide an age-old platitude behind a spurious scientific façade.

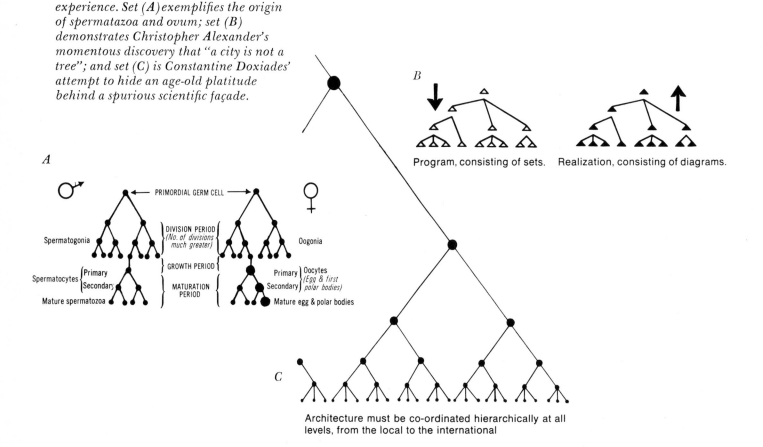

B

Program, consisting of sets.   Realization, consisting of diagrams.

A

PRIMORDIAL GERM CELL

Spermatogonia

DIVISION PERIOD
(No. of divisions much greater)

Oogonia

GROWTH PERIOD

Spermatocytes { Primary / Secondary

MATURATION PERIOD

Primary / Secondary } Oocytes *(Egg & first polar bodies)*

Mature spermatozoa

Mature egg & polar bodies

C

Architecture must be co-ordinated hierarchically at all levels, from the local to the international

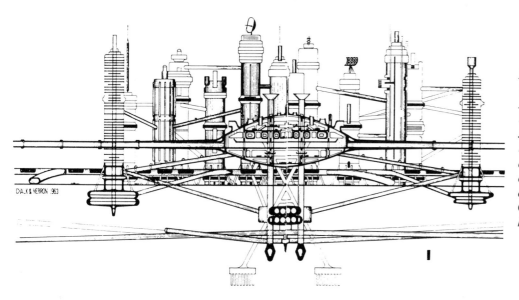

Fig. 3. Plug-in City, developed by Chalk and Herron of the British Archigram group. The similarity between fascist systems—which subject each individual to the brutalizing regimentation of centralized dictatorship—and a computer-controlled environment system makes Orwell's 1984 look positively humanistic.

ing absolutely. On the most vital questions it does not even produce evidence."

It must be assumed that man's shelter on earth is one of the vital questions that cannot be solved by scientific evidence. Experiments are by nature ephemeral; cities are by nature permanent. Yet we spend millions on "systems research," symposia, and publications to promote "a metabolic system organized by High Technology [with] totally integrated enclosure, transportation and communication subsystems . . . plug-in, infra and metabolic cities taking their rightful place among the hardware of the world" *(Fig. 3).**

The irony is that the "postarchitectural" system-makers are the irrational dreamers of today, whose creations have become the comic strips of professional publications, while the "hard-headed realists" are the planners and architects who know that man's reaction to his environment is largely arational, determined by purely emotional identifications with religion, wealth, education, art, amusement, charity, and family life. The logical response to these purely human ingredients that make the city is their constantly evolving historical genesis.

There is no progress in the realization of man's urban dream, only in mechanical equipment. Resistance against discontinuous "progress" is a generic trait of the species; the evidence of

* *Architectural Forum* (October, 1966).

15

environmental realizations is a permanent textbook. Villages, towns, and cities are the only continuous, visually extant testimony of the human condition. Only in his communities does man reconcile the schizophrenic contradictions of his existence through a multiplicity of solutions. The city, as the highest product of this catalytic process, is man's salvation and his demon, his instrument and the *deus ex machina* that rewards or condemns its creator.

Among the many absurd assumptions of the scientific approach to urban problems, none is more superficial than that our problems and attempted solutions are unique. The traffic problem, for example, started in earnest in the sixteenth century, and wheeled congestion was far more deadly when uncontrollable animals and unregulated pedestrians met head on (*Fig. 4*).

Fig. 4. Ludgate Hill Viaduct, 1870, by Gustave Doré illustrates the fearful mixture of humans and animals drawing wagons, omnibus, and hearse, uncontrolled by traffic lights.

Fig. 5. Medieval street in Perugia, Italy. Its charms are obvious only to the passing tourist.

Second-century Roman slums, overpopulation, windfall speculators, and venal city governments described by Juvenal dwarfed
anything the twentieth century possesses, and the medieval city,
that favorite dream of churchmen, was dank, dark, ugly, and
unsanitary away from its cathedral plazas (*Fig. 5*).

External organization is the tangible symbol of man's need
for tradition. We share with all past community builders certain basic approaches, conditioned by eternally recurrent constellations of matrix and content based on the interaction of
climate, land, race, tradition, economics, and resulting in conceptually related plans and buildings. These archetypes can be

17

grouped together according to their most distinctive patterns as

geomorphic
concentric
orthogonal-connective ⎫
orthogonal-modular ⎬ the linear cities
    and ⎭
clustered (*Figs. 6A–6E*).

It is the purpose of this inquiry into urban origins to seek out examples of and define these five settlement configurations, which occur the world over, and to set spinning a kaleidoscopic view of their images.

Rightly or wrongly, it is assumed that in the building of communities, as in many other human endeavors, the strongest, most convincing solutions were achieved in the beginning. A new approach promises most for the future when the challenge flung at that which no longer satisfies is still unimpaired by compromise. Beginnings are more potent than completions. Only the imperfect is productive. Prehuman chaos produced matter, but only man's unfulfilled vision of order produced form.

A history of urban origins is a history of design imagination. It is not mentioned in better scientific planning circles that man-made environment, whether good or mediocre, is the product of architecture, envisioning form-producing order. Even so unlikely an architectural critic as Karl Marx recognized this when he wrote in *Das Capital:*

A bee puts to shame many an architect in the construction of her cells. But what distinguishes the worst architect from the best of bees is this, that the architect raises his structure in imagination before he erects it in reality. At the end of every labor process we get a result that already existed in the imagination of the laborer at its beginning.

In the following history there are no footnotes to absolve the author from criticism by proving that his statements were made before with greater authority, or that what he has to say has various degrees of relevance. Verifiable sources have been mentioned in context. The need for additional information depends on an unforeseeable variety of interests. For these, a short bibliography has been appended, but it is not a substitute for the excellent card catalogues that are widely available.

A

B

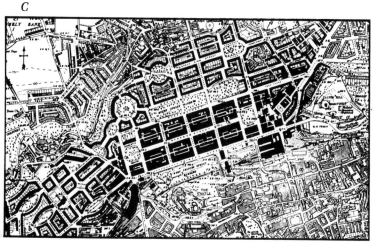

C

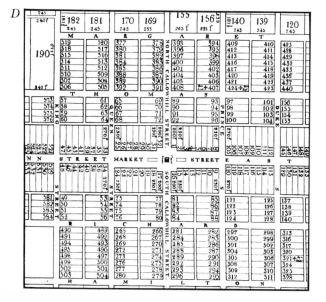

D

Fig. 6.

A) The Greek island of Serifos exemplifies the beauty and limitations of geomorphic building. The rock face, the steep summit carrying the church, the natural lookout toward the sea from which comes the livelihood of the community, are all combined into an interacting organism. Photo: Wilm Hofmann.

B) Cracow in the fourteenth century. This concentric city intelligently combines three factors: the slope, the river, and the central power symbol of the castle summit.

C) The orthogonal-connective plan is exemplified in Craig's replanning of Edinburgh, beginning in 1767. The new-town sector cuts through the concentric medieval town, and makes the linear street, the rectangular bloc, and circular public plazas the urban determinants.

D) In the orthogonal-modular plan of Reading, Pennsylvania, 1747, streets are less lines of communication than dividers of lots, and public spaces are not designed environment but voids between house modules.

E) Neubühl near Zürich, Switzerland. The emphasis in cluster plans is residential. House groups are set into the landscape with no relation to roads or to public buildings that would focus commercial, religious, educational, and recreational community interests.

E

The search for applicable meaning in geomorphic, concentric, orthogonal-connective, orthogonal-modular, and clustered prototypes was guided by available documentation, as well as by intuitive and visual recognition. The only reason for undergoing the ordeal of writing a book is to exert some influence on present and future reality. To achieve this influence, only an heuristic instinct for the human image in the environmental configuration can serve. "Life is for action," said Cardinal Newman. "If we insist on proof for everything, we shall come to no action. To act you must assume, and the assumption is faith."

GEOMORPHIC ENVIRONMENT

In a recent book, an architect postulated, "every reasonably sensitive and experienced architect knows what architecture is. . . . It is the creation of a microcosm of Nature, of truth by arrangement of functional and material components of buildings."*

For the sake of cities, it must be hoped that every reasonably logical architect and planner knows that architecture is nothing of the sort. Of all human activities, the making of a designed environment on any level of sophistication is the antithesis of a "microcosm of Nature." Buildings stand in the same relationship to natural environment as mailed armor stands to the human skin or a water cooler to the hump of a camel. Even at its most complex, science derives from natural laws. Human settlements, on the other hand, derive from man's determination to make himself independent of the cyclic provisions of nature and the purely generic defense mechanisms of the herd.

In its formative stage, this determination to provide for himself and his brood artificial walls, artificial spaces, artificial heat, light, and food storage was geomorphic in orientation. The adjective, formed from words meaning "earth" and "form," implies that the human settlement was determined by the shape and the climatic conditions of the earth. But settlements always occupied a selected environment in which the most advantageous location was chosen to bring nature under the control of man.

When man settled down from the nomadic existence of hunter and food gatherer to cultivate the soil and raise livestock, he developed a triad of geomorphic planning: village, rural town, and citadel.

In textbooks, establishment of village society is termed a characteristic of the Neolithic Age—roughly, the period between 8000 and 4000 B.C. This is rather misleading because the founding of village communities is perpetuated into the twentieth

* Robin Boyd, *The Puzzle of Architecture* (New York, 1966).

Fig. 7. Farm in the
Housatonic Valley,
Connecticut.

Fig. 8. Farmhand
cottages built as
granaries, Zacatecas
highlands of Mexico.
Despite their remoteness
from each other in
distance, climate, and
ethnology, both
examples obey the same
laws of geomorphic
adjustment and
functional typification.

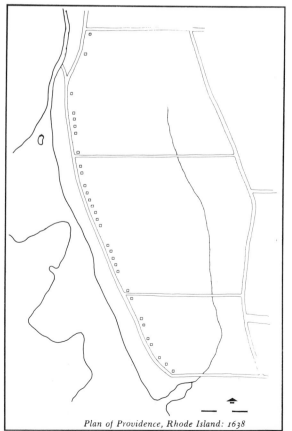

Fig. 9. *A German* Wurt *in the tidewaters of the North Sea in the early Middle Ages. These artificially expanded islands were a perfect response of human cunning to the limited provisions of nature. They offered safety, sustenance from the sea, and some crop raising far beyond the natural conditions.*

century, as seen in the kibbutzim of Israel and the resettlement of Sudanese villages in Egypt. Agriculturalists, whether they live singly or in groups, depend fatalistically on the recurrent cycles of cultivating, sowing, harvesting, storing, and livestock breeding, regardless of hand labor or mechanical equipment. The purely expedient nonsymbolic character of geomorphic shelter has produced basic shapes, invariable within the conditions of a region, and outside the formal variations of individuality and taste (*Figs. 7, 8*). It is easily possible to read from a geomorphic plan the predominant mode of nonspecialized labor. The *Wurten*, artificially enlarged sandspits, along the coast of the North Sea were settlements whose purpose was to provide security, livelihood through fishing, and sanitation in one compact plan (*Fig. 9*). They have survived in the *Halligen*, the small islands of the Frisian coast. In Central Europe, cattle and horse breeders clustered their farms around spaces, forming a village corral protected by house walls. Crop raising, as exploitation of

Fig. 11. *Original plan of Providence, Rhode Island, 1638. It is based on the medieval toft and croft (cottage and field) tradition. The land was soon exhausted, leading to an exodus of disgruntled farmers at the end of the seventeenth century, and to a switch from farming to seafaring and later to industry.*

Fig. 10. *Germanic* Waldhufendorf, *or woodland village. Each family worked a strip of mixed land for their own use, sustained and protected by the chieftain or lord of the manor, who was in charge of the surrounding "Mark" and guaranteed seed and help in time of crop failure.*

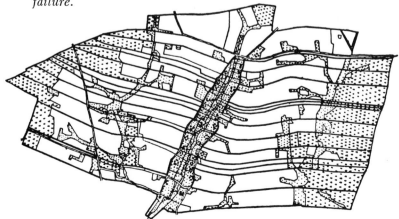

Plan of Providence, Rhode Island: 1638

nature, led to the Germanic *Hufendorf,** usually strung out at the bottom of a natural valley (*Fig. 10*). Each village farm cultivated a long narrow field for family use and the wider vicinity of cleared land for the overlord.

It was one of the peculiar tragedies of America that this type of geomorphic settlement was the predominant concept introduced into New England by seventeenth-century settlers (*Fig. 11*). From the earliest times, Germanic society had been feudalistic, meaning that a hereditary chieftain, who later became lord of the manor, took a proprietary interest in the flourishing of the holdings, called in England the toft (dwelling) and croft (enclosed field) system. Without this centralized control of tithes and subsidies, distribution and allotments, the villages of New England soon collapsed, losing their settlers to seafaring and manufacturing or to isolated homesteads.

Rural towns must be as ancient as villages or at least as old as the concept of barter exchange. An *oppidum,* as the Romans (who invented the complete urban vocabulary still in use today) called it, was as geomorphically conditioned as the villages by which it lived.† The same cycle of harvest and market deter-

* *Hufen,* or "hide," since land was measured with cow hides.
† *Oppidum,* probably from Latin *ob,* "for the purpose," and *edomo,* "to subdue."

Fig. 12. Characteristic Saxon rural town whose inhabitants were called Ackerbürger *(acre citizens). Each house had a generous yard allotment (white area between hatched house lots) to raise small crops and fowl, in addition to working fields belonging to the proprietary lord, whose castle and storage buildings (black area) dominate the plan.*

Fig. 13. Cap Haitien, Haiti, a fine example of the continuous street elevation as casa mura, *or dwelling as a defensive wall system. Elevations are similar but not identical.*

Fig. 14. Fairfield, Connecticut, an American sprawl town. Gray areas are old holdings, spreading irregularly from main street (a); *black areas are subdivisions built since World War II on former farmland. After Christopher Tunnard and Boris Pushkarev,* Man-Made America: Chaos or Control *(1963).*

mined its society, which was augmented by the retired farmer, carrying his lifelong habits of uniformity and functionality into his old age. The market town stood in the same proprietary relationship to the manor or the castle as the village and, therefore, followed identical rules of uniformity (*Fig. 12*). The main distinctions were the emphasis in the *oppidum* on temple or church as shared symbol of religious faith and the continuous street elevation along the lines of traffic leading to the market.

The unified market town was introduced into the Americas where it flourished under the colonial feudalism of Central and South America (*Fig. 13*). In North America, the Germans and the Dutch knew how to build uniform market towns, but English and Scottish settlers adhered to dispersed village planning, even in town foundations with purely urban character, resulting in the ragged subdivision lots of modern times (*Fig. 14*).

In addition to village and market town, the third achievement of man's mastery over geomorphic environment was the fortified settlement or citadel. Its origin is as inextricably connected with sedentary living and the accumulation of wealth as the village.

25

Cleared land, livestock, and human labor were the desired aims of warfare and domination. The geomorphic requirements of the fortress were as unchangeable as those of the village and resulted in generic types. Mountain or hilltop citadels far outnumber the fortified control points on waterways and roads, but, in every case, the common characteristic remains the full exploitation of natural advantages. There is barely any difference between the oldest excavated Helladic fortress of Dimini, in Thessaly, and the Celtic *Steinsburg*, in North Germany (*Fig. 15*). Troy, in all its successive stages from the late third millennium B.C. to the close of the second, received its unalterable shape from the fortress mound, and so did Mycenae and Tiryns of the early Greek Achaeans. It is an amusing sidelight on the limited freedom of geomorphic planning that the approach to the citadel of Carchemish in Syria, dating from the second millennium B.C., and the famed Spanish Steps of Rome, designed by Specchi and De Sanctis in 1721, show almost identical concepts (*Fig. 16*).

The most interesting aspect of the fortified high place as geomorphic settlement lies in its historical function as nucleus of the Greek polis. Like all invaders, the Ionians and Achaeans, and the Dorians later, maintained their hold on a subjugated people by planting strongholds, which later grew into cities. The *acro polis,* or "high town," was the nucleus of every Greek settle-

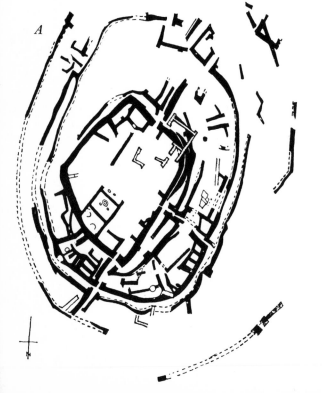

Fig. 15. *The chalcolithic (Copper Age, fourth millennium, B.C.) fortress of Dimini (A) and a Celtic stronghold called* Steinsburg *(B), 2,000 years younger and thousands of miles to the north, show related plans for mountaintop citadels.*

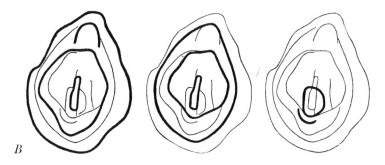

26

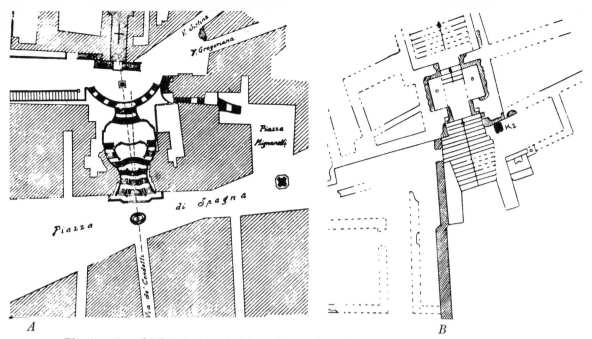

A   B

Fig. 16. Even highly designed approaches such as the
sophisticated Spanish Steps in Rome, from 1721 (A),
are mere variations of the primitive geomorphic
response that produced an almost similar solution
3,500 years earlier in Syrian Carchemish (B). The
chronological links to Baroque Rome are Hellenistic
Cos (see Fig. 109B) an island sanctuary, and Roman
Praenaste, built by Sulla in the first century B.C.

Fig. 17. The theater of the Sacred Precinct
at Delphi, a spectacular fifth-century
example of Greek geomorphic genius. The
ruggedness of the mountain backdrop is
emphasized by the linear precision of the
auditorium. The geometric craftsmanship
enhances the unformed substance of nature.

ment. It is tempting to speculate what would have happened
to the Greeks and to academic art history if the migrating hordes
had terminated their wanderings, say, between Chicago and
Omaha or between Berlin and Magdeburg instead of on the
cliff-studded massif of the Balkan Mountains. Theories about
Hellenic genius in siting temples and devising intricate perspectives toward female mountain clefts and male mountain
peaks would never have arisen. As it was, the Greeks developed
a keen eye for spectacular geomorphism. The natural rock carried the state temple, as in Athens, the citadel, as in Corinth,
and accommodated the theater (Fig. 17). The rest of the city, as
it gradually accumulated, remained unplanned.

The purest example of geomorphic settlement was achieved
neither in Europe nor in Asia but in the inappropriately called
New World of South America. An endemic mixture of latent
guilt and European snobbism have made it difficult to admit
that Meso-America and South America offer examples of his-

Fig. 18. Machu Picchu, holy city of the Peruvian Incas, rises 1,400 feet above the Urubamba River valley. The geomorphic adjustment is ritualistic, leading from terrace to terrace to intihuatana—*the place where the Inca each year tied the sun to a stone pillar to secure the maize crop.*

torical and modern architecture and an ancient tradition of imaginative planning that equal and, in pretechnological examples, often surpass the designs of the Old World. The highly diverse pre-Columbian cultures, which we deign to lump together as "Indian," created lasting prototypes in geomorphic, concentric, orthogonal-linear, orthogonal-modular, and clustered plans. Machu Picchu (*Fig. 18*), the work of Inca builders on a remote mountain peak of the Andes, achieves a total accord with the given environment because the sun worshipers conceived the city as a crown of nature, and nature as the crown of the city. A diagonal path rises over five terraces to the sacred plaza of the *intihuatana*, the phallic rock image at the highest point of the town where the Inca tied the sun each winter solstice to assure its shining on the maize crop. The unity of contrasts achieved between the sacred focus and artfully emphasized vistas, alternating between masonry treating stone as if it were mosaic and natural rock formations, between huge hierarchic structures and secular dwellings melting almost into the virgin landscape (*Fig. 19*), has no counterpart in Greek acropolis design except in Athens.

Emperors, crusaders, rebels, and conquistadors had cooper-

Fig. 19. Secular dwellings outside the holy precinct at Machu Picchu are embedded into the terraced mountainside like natural growth.

ated with nature for geomorphic protection (*Fig. 20*). The end of such cooperation came with the introduction of firearms, which spread throughout the Western world in the fourteenth and fifteenth centuries. The photogenic ruffles that the French field marshal and engineer the Marquis de Vauban (1633–1707) put into three *systèmes* around cities (*Fig. 71*) obviated geomorphic selection for aggression or defense.

Fig. 20. The Crak des Chevaliers in Syria, built by French crusaders at the close of the twelfth century A.D. Like all fortresses of its type, it is an extension of the mountaintop and controls the valley below.

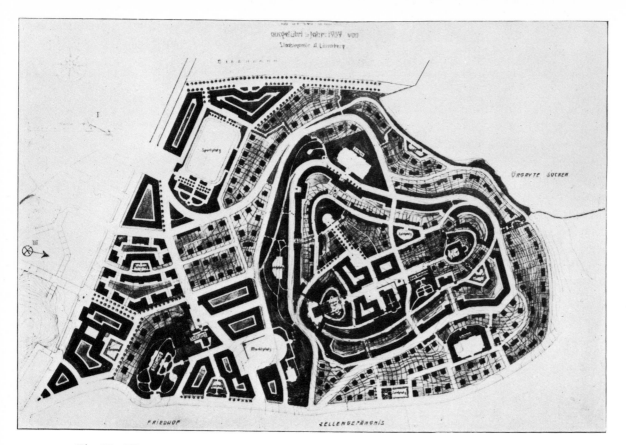

Fig. 21. The new town sector of Gotenburg, Sweden, planned in 1909 by the architect Lilienberg. It was an attempt early in the twentieth century to return to geomorphic planning. Streets are wrapped around a natural hillside, leading to the summit where church and town hall face each other across a wide, landscaped mall.

No concept of man-made environment ever dies and none ever becomes obsolete. Since the basic relationships of man to earth and man to man are unchangeable and nonprogressive, he must return at some junctures in his social consciousness to certain environmental ideals. After several hundred years, during which concentric and orthogonal planning obscured other solutions, protest against the increasing alienation of man from his natural origins instigated a geomorphic revival in the twentieth century. Aside from individual houses designed within a geomorphic context by Frank Lloyd Wright and his followers, which cannot occupy us now, there were renewed attempts at a bulldozerless approach to community planning. Lilienberg's new town sector of Gotenburg, in Sweden, designed in 1909, went beyond lip service to "organic planning" by garden-city reformers (*Fig. 21*). In the center section of one of the oldest and boldest urban renewals of the twentieth century, the main road winds around a hillside without destroying the continuity of street elevations. With the double focus of church and town hall on the mountain terrace, New Gotenburg is a true *Stadt-*

krone, a crown of the city, as the German architect Bruno Taut was to name this type of plan in 1913. A Greek or Etruscan would have felt instantly at home on this acropolis.

In the brief romantic spring of moral renewal that followed World War I, architects dreamed of lifting liberated mankind high above the iniquity and chaos that had previously marked cities. Bruno Taut, leader of the *Glaskette* design group in Berlin, proposed shaping from an Alpine peak a symbolic "crystal city" that would be a guiding beacon for the excruciating efforts to build a new urban world (*Fig. 22*).*

In 1946, after another world war, a similar though much weaker spirit of delivery and new commitment gave to Patrick

* See Bruno Taut, *Die Stadtkrone* (Jena, 1919).

Fig. 22. Bruno Taut's prototypical Stadtkrone, *proposed in 1919. It was to be sculpted from the Matterhorn massif, to shine as inspiration before planners of a new urban world, where man and earth would complement each other.*

Neighbourhood Unit No. 3

plan to show contours

FEET 100 0   500   1000   1500   2000 FEET

Fig. 23. In the same optimistic spirit that had vowed a better world after the peace of 1918, British planners Abercrombie and Matthews designed Clyde Valley New Town in 1946, combining contour planning according to the lay of the land with the new concept of socially cohesive neighborhoods. Like Taut's dream of a renewed compact between man and nature, the geomorphic revival of Clyde Valley had no sequel. As prosperity spread, renewal agencies and developers discovered that the shortest distance between investment and profit is the bulldozer track.

Fig. 24. Paul Rudolph, Married
Student Housing, built against hillside.
Yale University, New Haven,
Connecticut (1960).

Abercrombie and Matthews in London an opportunity to design
a government-sponsored geomorphic town in Wales (*Fig. 23*).
Although the cohesion of land and layout is shown to be viable
and organic, no further attempts at new land-integrated towns
were made, because planning commissions found level ground
or bulldozers more convenient.

Fig. 25. *The resort community of the
Italian architects Bellante and Di Carlo
on an ancient site, Tiberius' Cave, in
the Gulf of Naples. The timelessness
of man-site cooperation, and the
progressive technology of
prefabrication are combined into a
successful entity.*

Fig. 26. Haystack Village by Bruce Graham and Norman Jaffe. It molds an elegant ski resort along the ridges of Vermont's Green Mountains, which are popular because they are mostly white. Only the affluent can afford today what the earliest discoverers of man's ability to master and exploit the earth had taken for granted.

This attitude has become the planning determinant of new communities. Examples of geomorphic sensitivity, such as Paul Rudolph's Married Student Housing, at Yale University, integrating a multiple, continuous residential unit with the hillside, are considered extravagant (*Fig. 24*). Ironically, only luxury building, such as Bellante and Di Carlo's resort community around the Rock of Tiberius, jutting out into the Mediterranean (*Fig. 25*), or Bruce Graham's Haystack Ski Village, in Vermont (*Fig. 26*), have been able to avoid the leveling of distinctive geographic features and, thus, have rediscovered the oldest, most primitive response of man, the environment builder, to the challenges posed by the earth.

CONCENTRIC SETTLEMENTS

Despite evidence to the contrary, man is not an ape who lost his tail so that he could sit behind a steering wheel, nor did he develop speech in order to produce TV commercials. Anthropoid and hominoid share a common ancestor from which evolved two separate species, differing in essential characteristics. Analogically, modern cities are not villages that have progressed into "machines for living," and citizens are not peasants grown sophisticated in search of profitable shelter. All permanent human communities share a common ancestor in the cave and the primeval hut, but their basic types differ in all essential

A

Coupe AB

Millet-thrashing floor

Tree where millet is dried

Wood pile

Chief's peanut storehouse

Barn

Hut of chief's younger son

Chief's millet storehouse

Chief's hut

Goat stable

Water tank

Oldest son's second wife

Peanut barn

Stable for son's calves

Chief's storehouse

Oldest son's storehouse

Hut of the chief's son's first wife

Stable

Millet pounding floor

Kitchen

Chief's cattle barn

Women's hut

Storage hut

Chief's millet storehouse

Kitchen

Meadow

Meadow

Hut

Hut

Hut

Hut

Hut

Hut

Meadow

Hut

Hut

Hut

Hut

B

Fig. 27.

A) A contemporary village in Cameroon, Africa. The tribal chief occupies a central cluster of dwelling, granary, and stable, surrounded by the identical circular huts of wives, children, retainers, and animals.

B) Neolithic village in the Federsee moor district of Germany. Oval huts (Hütten) with a central hearth are placed at random on a pasture (Wiese), leaving ample open spaces for livestock and work. The concept of the geomorphic village community has remained unchanged despite chronological and geographic distances.

characteristics. Archaeologists have maintained that an orderly evolution, covering some 4,000 years (from 5000 to 1000 B.C.) led from postnomadic settlements to Neolithic villages and Bronze Age cities. Recent archaeological finds make it unlikely that in the oldest known civilizations of Anatolia, Palestine, and the islands of the eastern Mediterranean there existed no distinction between urban and agricultural communities. As far back as the seventh millennium B.C., Neolithic villages, as distant from each other as Khirokitia on Cyprus and the moor settlements of southern Germany, had all the geomorphic characteristics already described. Their building plans were uniform and single or double celled, with a preference for round and oval shapes where rubble, mud, or wattle was the available material, and angular where tree trunks were easily procured. Ample space between each homestead gave outdoor working space, and the absence of a planned focal plaza indicated no separation of religious cult from nature. A comparison between a Neolithic settlement and a twentieth-century African village shows the constancy of form and function in the geomorphic planning concept (*Fig. 27*).

Within the last twenty years, archaeological progress has mapped at least two sites, Jericho in Palestine and Çatal Hüyük in Anatolia, which can only be called incipient cities. The concept of their layouts is radically different from the organically accumulated village community. In the seventh millennium B.C., Jericho was enclosed by a free-standing wall of coursed stone (which is still standing, in places 11 feet high). Above it rose a stone tower 28 feet wide and, after 8,000 years, still 21½ feet high. The twenty-eight steps of this tower are formed from single stone slabs that have outlasted twenty-two subsequent building periods.*

Jericho was not a freak, a singular mirage of the future. This became evident when Çatal Hüyük in Anatolia was excavated by James Mellaart (*Fig. 28*). The town had been laid out as an integrated unit, sharply separated from the surrounding land by continuous walls and accessible only by ladders from above. With its high density and flat uniform roofs, Çatal Hüyük, as reconstructed by James Mellaart, shows a surprising similarity to the contemporary mountain town below the Crak des Chevaliers in northern Syria (*Fig. 29*). The most urban aspect of Çatal

---

* All preclassical data follow *Relative Chronologies in Old World Archaeology*, edited by Robert W. Ehrich (Chicago, 1954).

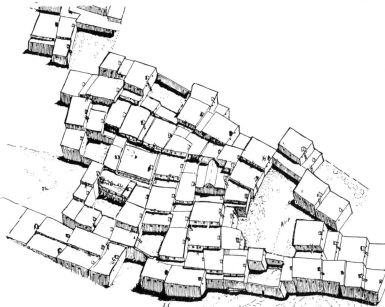

Fig. 28. Bird's-eye view of one sector of the Neolithic town of Çatal Hüyük in Anatolia, as excavated and reconstructed by James Mellaart. Each sector had an open public plaza and continuous house wall, acting as buttress for the soft unburned mud-brick. Despite the simple over-all scheme, there is great variety in space, shapes, and dimensions.

Hüyük is the clear distinction between public streets and plazas, and interior spaces of a great variety of shapes and purposes. A high degree of specialization becomes evident from the number of space functions: shrines with altars and idols, living quarters, and storehouses. The assortment of tools, weapons, and refined artifacts such as fabric, jewelry, and polished obsidian mirrors, furnish proof of a wealthy exchange economy. The citizens could afford to barter the products of native industry—chiefly

Fig. 29. Modern Syrian village at the base of Crak des Chevaliers, as seen from the castle's ramparts. There is considerable resemblance to Çatal Hüyük (see Fig. 28), the 8,000-year-old Anatolian town, though the older town was a good deal more sophisticated, artistic, and wealthy than its modern counterpart.

obsidian, the steel of protohistoric man—for luxury items from far away trade centers. Perhaps the most telling evidence of the differentiated urban community are the terra-cotta plaques that identified each house by a singular unrepeated design (*Fig. 30*).*

The historical puzzle of the earliest nongeomorphic town foundation is compounded by a lapse of 2,000 years—more time than separates us from the Roman Empire—before we can continue to trace the development of urban history as the dominant factor in the evaluation of human development. No history was made in villages. At the beginning of the fourth millennium B.C., the scene shifted from the fertile regions of Anatolia to the alternately flooded and parched "land between the rivers" in southern Iraq. The ancient land of Mesopotamia, with its twin river highways, the Tigris and Euphrates, connected the vast Asiatic land mass with the Mediterranean. Before 4000 B.C. a people known only through archaeological finds at such sites as Al Ubaid in Iraq, built temples on city terraces surrounded by dwellings (*Fig. 31*). They left an abundance of fine artifacts proving the existence of a specialized artisan class and of ritualistic religion. Around 3500 B.C. a cultural and urban explosion took place in the delta area, caused by "the black-headed people"—the Sumerians. Most archaeologists conjecture that they were immigrants who came from a homeland

* James Mellaart, *Çatal Hüyük, a Neolithic City in Anatolia* (London, 1967).

Fig. 30. House plaques from Çatal Hüyük, late seventh millennium B.C. Until the Romans invented house numbers, a perceptive postman could identify each addressee from his abstract identification sign.

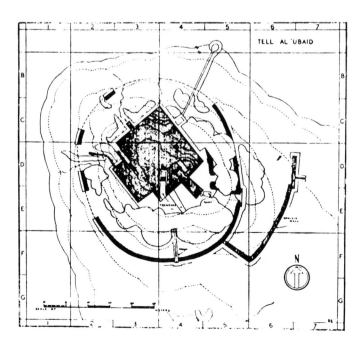

TELL AL 'UBAID

Fig. 31. The city mound of Al Ubaid in southern Mesopotamia. As in the case of Çatal Hüyük, the "first" commercial town, the concentric, single-focused layout of Al Ubaid is so perfect that one must assume a lost prototype from which this plan developed in a long, gradual evolution. The city terrace rises above the grade lines of the natural hill, or tell, in geometric precision. Remnants of roads point like arrows toward the heart of the city.

in the green Iranian highlands. Their appearance in history coincides with the invention of bronze, which terminated the exclusive reliance on copper, wooden, and clay objects. One might assume, therefore, that the same two magnets, sea trade and metal, drove the clever Sumerians from agricultural security into the unstable twin river delta, which later coaxed the Greek tribes out of the primordial forests of Europe, and after still more millennia cost uncounted Europeans their lives in the conquest of the Americas. The new demand for copper and tin and the many uses to which their alloy, bronze, could be adapted must have ruined the Neolithic obsidian industry.

The Sumerians found as little ore in southern Mesopotamia as did the Greeks on the craggy slopes of the Peloponnesus and the Dutch, French, and English in North America. Like all un-invited newcomers, they founded tightly organized settlements and produced goods in exchange for metal. Sumerian urban-ization arose when human intelligence discovered that there are easier and more diverse methods by which to make a living than the labors of the peasant. With their innate genius for producing and trading, they distributed glazed, wheel-turned pottery, cylinder seals with hieroglyphic writing and numerical notations, wheeled vehicles (*Fig. 32*), shipbuilding, and the carving of idols in the image of man throughout the early Bronze Age world.

It has been recognized that the urbanization of the Indus Valley, seen in the Harappa culture, from about 2800 to 1800 B.C., that of the Chinese Chou Dynasty from around 1027 to 450 B.C., and the architectural concepts of the Egyptian Old Kingdom (*ca.* 2800 to *ca.* 2100 B.C.), were influenced by Sumerian civiliza-tion. Sumerian city-states were literate (having invented writing as an indispensable tool of private property), socially mobile and diversified, metal oriented, professionally specialized, com-petitive, and religiously anthropomorphic. All these character-istics we still call urban. Rural societies were and have remained iconographic, land-locked, socially homogeneous, land-value oriented, unspecialized, cooperative, and crypto-animistic.

The map (*Fig. 33*) shows the principal urban regions men-tioned in this book. The numbers on Figure 33 indicate the thirty-six areas of maximum metropolitan density throughout the world 5,000 years after urbanization had become an estab-lished historical fact. The conclusions to be drawn from an examination of this map are obvious: there are city-bearing and noncity-bearing regions, depending on access to, or sepa-

Fig. 32. Oldest presentation of a wheeled vehicle drawn by harnessed animals, from Sumer. Clay tablet engraving, ca. 2800 B.C.

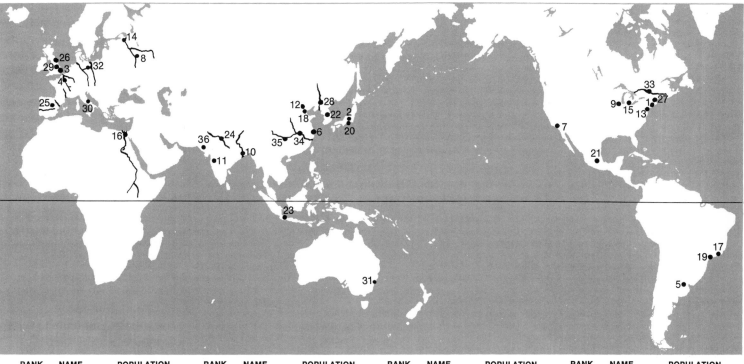

RANK	NAME	POPULATION	RANK	NAME	POPULATION	RANK	NAME	POPULATION	RANK	NAME	POPULATION
1	NEW YORK	14,114,927	10	CALCUTTA	4,518,655	19	SAO PAULO	3,164,804	28	SHENYANG (MUKDEN)	2,411,000
2	TOKYO	10,177,000	11	BOMBAY	4,422,165	20	OSAKA	3,151,000	29	BIRMINGHAM	2,377,230
3	LONDON	8,176,810	12	PEKING	4,010,000	21	MEXICO CITY	3,050,723	30	ROME	2,278,882
4	PARIS	7,369,387	13	PHILADELPHIA	3,635,228	22	SEOUL	2,983,324	31	SYDNEY	2,215,97
5	BUENOS AIRES	7,000,000	14	LENINGRAD	3,552,000	23	DJAKARTA	2,906,533	32	WEST BERLIN	2,176,612
6	SHANGHAI	6,900,000	15	DETROIT	3,537,309	24	DELHI	2,549,162	33	MONTREAL	2,156,000
7	LOS ANGELES	6,488,791	16	CAIRO	3,418,400	25	MADRID	2,443,152	34	WUHAN	2,146,000
8	MOSCOW	6,354,000	17	RIO DE JANEIRO	3,223,408	26	MANCHESTER	2,442,090	35	CHUNGKING	2,121,000
9	CHICAGO	5,959,213	18	TIENTSIN	3,220,000	27	BOSTON	2,413,236	36	KARACHI	2,060,000

ration from, coasts and major waterways. Trade, not piety, was the impetus that built cities.

Lewis Mumford declared, "every feature of the early city revealed the belief that man was created for no other purpose than to magnify and serve his gods. That was the city's ultimate reason for being."* As proof of these pious intentions, he cites the Assyrians who studded Assur, their capital, with several hundred gorgeous temples. Interestingly enough, no other people has left such an unabashed record of the unspeakable atrocities committed on conquered cities. The Sultan Tepe tablets, composed by Shalmanassur relate:

With the full force of my manly vigor I trampled on his land like a

*Lewis Mumford, *The City in History* (New York, 1961).

Fig. 33. Map showing the thirty-six largest metropolitan regions of the twentieth century. With a few strategic or dynastic exceptions, such as Madrid or Delhi, all major cities are located on coasts or major waterways, proving that communication and trade determined the location of major cities. From Kingsley Davis, "The Urbanization of the Human Population," Scientific American *(September, 1965).*

A

B

Fig. 34. *The city, showcase of power and wealth, as eternal death trap. To the ancient illustrations of the surrender of a Syrian city (A) and a European merchant city of the sixteenth century (B) could be added Coventry, Dresden, and Hiroshima.*

wild bull and turned his cities into ruins. I piled up hills of heads beside the city gates. I impaled all their young men and young women by the heaps. Then I departed from Arzashu [royal city of the Urartians] and climbed this mountain. I made for myself a royal stele and inscribed on it my deeds in praise of Assur, my Lord, and the power of my might.*

This document and the fate of cities throughout history identify their very existence with sheer power obsession. To have cities and to destroy others characterizes the drive toward urbanization that gripped mankind in the third millennium B.C. as one of the arational impulses in human history. City life meant separation from natural resources, defenses, and escape routes. It meant passive exposure to famine, epidemic, conflagration, earthquake, and assault by sword, later by cannon, and ulti-

* W. G. Lambert, in *Anatolian Studies,* Vol. XI (1961).

mately by airborne weapons (*Fig. 34*). The conspicuous display of urban wealth, and the concentration of administrative power in monumental buildings, had a magic attraction for the have-nots who attacked with monotonous regularity the cities, "because this is where the money is." And like ants, who cannot remember the boot that crushed their hill, the Sumerians, and all city dwellers after them, rebuilt on the same spot with even greater splendor and more vaunted claims to superior achievements, inspiring the next wave of attackers with even fiercer greed.

Man has built and loved cities because in the urban form he constructs the superimage of his ideal self. The common denominator of cities, from Nineveh to New York, is a collective idol worship, praying for power over nature, destiny, knowledge, and wealth. The gods of cities are supermen, of whom Don Marquis wrote:

> And he clothes them with thunder and beauty,
> He clothes them with music and fire;
> Seeing not as he bows by their altars
> That he worships his own desire.

Prophets of divine over human power have fared badly in cities—witness Lot, Confucius, Jesus, Savonarola, Joseph Smith, as well as the first Sumerian victim, Urukagina, who lived in the middle of the third millennium B.C. Like all early Sumerian rulers, he was elected governor, or *ensi,* from among the free citizens of Lagash. With courage and vision, Urukagina carried out the first recorded urban reform.* He established written law applicable to all, more than 500 years before the famous code of Hammurabi. He insisted on equality of welfare, suppression of graft, on the restriction of priestly wealth and privileges. It is in his clay records that the word "freedom" (*amargi*) is first recorded in the annals of mankind. In Sumerian, the term is synonymous with "return to the mother," establishing man's right to be free as his birthright. When the unreformed neighboring city-state of Umma threatened an attack, Urukagina reassured the men of Lagash that their archenemy would be destroyed because the city god would not fail to reward his people for the re-establishment of piety and justice. He did. Lagash was wiped out, which goes to show what happens to an *ensi* who takes his Mumford straight.

* See Samuel Noah Kramer, *The Sumerians* (Chicago, 1963).

41

The testing of the city gods was severe. Only those survived as candidates for a cultural career who were of significant service to man, who were at the center of interest of a social group and were associated with the fulfillment of socially approved desires.*

The constant factor among these socially approved desires was success. The mountain climber meets the challenge of inaccessible height with all his resources; and a special breed of elderly men insist on crossing oceans in unsuitable boats. But after they have spent their strength, the mountain and the sea are the same. The dream of cities rose from the obsession to cause change, to influence destiny, to wield power. This is why the great waves of city-destroying nomads, the Sea-People, the Goths,

* Eustace Haydon, *Biography of the Gods* (New York, 1941).

Fig. 35. Ziggurat (an artificial world mountain of mud-brick and bitumen) and foundations of the Appearance Temple, where the priest held his briefing sessions with the city god, in the ancient Sumerian city of Uruk (Warka), ca. 3000 B.C. The 20-foot base was erected on the highest point of a natural hill (tell), surrounded by the town. From J. Jordan, Uruk-Warka, *(1928).*

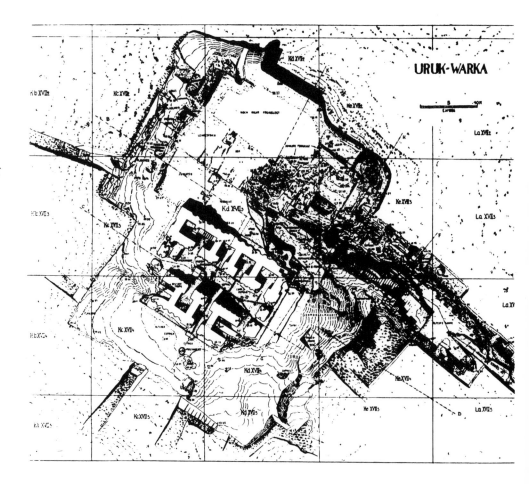

the Seljuks, and Mongols claimed a mandate from their tribal gods for the destruction of cities as oppressive power images.

The Sumerian city-states of the predynastic fourth millennium gave to each human ambition a divine image. The sum of human potential was the urban gods. They dwelled in the temple atop the ziggurat, or "world mountain," from where their wisely invisible presences, through the priests, arbitrated the disputes of a democratic society (*Fig. 35*). Every citizen was equidistant from the source of spiritual, social, and economic order, and equally close to the protection of the sacred enclosure in times of war. This is why the oldest cities, of which we have reliable records, were concentric, single-focused, and centrifugal, spreading outward from the visual proof of their reason for being. Anonymous dwellings in hivelike continuity clung to the flanks of the natural tell or hill that carried the *Stadtkrone,* crown of the city. Communication, both spiritual and physical, was single-directed: from house to temenos (sacred precinct), where all economic transactions were administered by the priests; from city to open land, which was owned and worked by individual citizens; and from man to idol, who was the intermediary between human ambition and a divine bicameral system. There was an upper house of "creating gods" and a lower one of "executive deities," implementing the divine decisions. The Sumerian pantheon was an idealized projection of civic government in the early Sumerian polis.

The Sumerians could never have come as far or achieved as much either spiritually or materially, had it not been for one very special psychological drive which motivated their behavior and deeply colored their way of life—the ambitious, competitive, aggressive and seemingly far from ethical drive for pre-eminence and prestige, for victory and success.*

The city was the existential anchor of each life, the here and now of achievement or failure. There was no Sumerian heaven to promise a transsubstantiated glory. Gilgamesh, the hero and incarnation of the Sumerian self-image, concluded bitterly after his lifelong search for immortality had failed, "When God created man, he withheld eternity for himself and let death be man's lot."†

From its inception, the city was dichotomous, embodying a superhuman scale in its monuments and a pragmatic, human

* Kramer, *op. cit.*
† *Ibid.*

43

scale as anonymous-collective backdrop. Dynamic energy was generated by opposites of good and evil, personified in gods and their quarrels. In the epic, *Inanni and Enki: The Transfer of the Arts of Civilization,* as translated by Samuel Kramer from Sumerian tablets of the third millennium, Inanni, the deity of the city of Erech, contrives to wrest kingship from the ancient city Eridu, that was before the Flood, thus taking away its name and fame. Enki, the Lord of Wisdom, finally reveals the more than 100 divine decrees which are fundamental to all civilizations; among the essentials listed are leadership and libel, power and envy, prostitution and marriage, falsehood and truth, the destruction of cities and their holy purification.

The *imago profanis* of the city, free of any pretense to being a shrine of otherworldly aspirations was, next to the invention of writing, the greatest innovation of the Sumerians. Their specific brand of urban piety consisted of the claim to having created a microcosm on a par with the galaxies. The construction of a ziggurat, despite excruciatingly difficult handicaps of materials and skills, established a city-state in the dead center of earth and sky. It did not matter that these axial exclamation marks were often in view of each other. Man in the center of the universe was not a geographical fact but a truth. Once a city had been founded and dedicated to a god representing its ideal and no other, it could not be moved to a different location. Because of this identity of place and symbol, the exile of populations was the most degrading punishment of the vanquished. Where subsistence was marginal, as in the jungles of Central America, entailing wide population dispersion, or where the deified ruler held a position of absolute power that demanded his magic presence during ceaseless conquests, as in India, Persia, and Cambodia, a ceremonial capital, uninhabited except by priests, had to be maintained as gigantic symbol of the stake each anonymous citizen held in the power structure *(Figs. 36, 44).*

It is the despair of students in a democratic society and the triumph of city-of-God advocates that only temples and palaces have survived from the first and second urban age. But the essence of symbolic self-glorification is that it demands of public structures a fabric and monumental scale surpassing in durability and size mundane shelters. Ziggurats, pyramids, temples, basilicas, cathedrals, and palaces never had "human scale"; this is the impotent outcry of an age that no longer knows the difference between bigness and greatness. Commemorative and associative monumentality had meaning only in relationship

44

Fig. 36. Above the Indian town of Palitana on the Gulf of Cambai rises Satrunjaya, 2,000 feet above sea level. It is the city of the Jain gods, and comprises nine walled, many-gated separate towns for the departed Tirtankharas (wise men). Each enclosure is a complete urban unit with a chief temple in the center and subsidiary chapels, spacious plazas, connecting roads and many-celled cloisters. No one lives there. From the eleventh century onward, powerful Jain rulers, rich merchants, and artistic monks built this symbol of their faith and their authority.

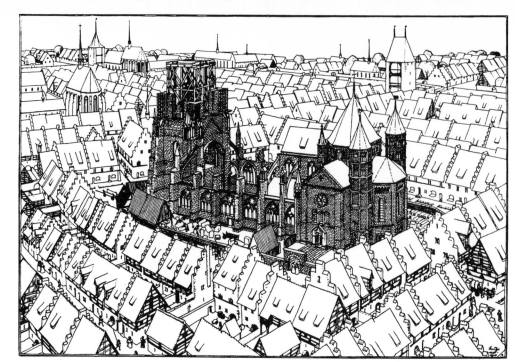

Fig. 37. A medieval cathedral rising above the anonymous city which depends on it for identification, just as the Sumerian city had depended on the ziggurat, and Greek and Mayan cities on the acropolis. From Gruber, Gesicht der Deutschen Stadt.

to the anonymous backdrop of the image seekers (*Fig. 37*). Any public building deprived of the contrast and support of the background community which it serves is like an actor rejected by his audience because he has played his part badly (*Fig. 38*).

This anonymous backdrop of the city was for 2,000 years a dense mass of energy concentrated within a city's walls (*Fig. 39*).

A

Fig. 38.
A) This view shows the superbly urban effect of a public building among its satellites.
B) The destruction of urban meaning is sadly apparent from this view of Strickland's Commercial Exchange Building in Philadelphia's "National Monument Park." The maniacs of urban removal decided in 1960 on "the destruction of all nonhistoric buildings" in the area, reducing a few architectural gems to vulgar gold teeth in poorly recapped mouths.

B

Fig. 40. Folded corners at entrance to main plaza of palace compound at Mari, Mesopotamia, late third millennium B.C. Protection of the friable mud-brick structure is pleasantly combined with a horizontal-vertical light-shadow articulation.

Designed street elevations first appear in Western civilization only with the rise of an urban middle class in late Hellenistic and Roman cities. In Mesopotamia, the street served for communication from anonymous cell to anonymous cell; to the fields and pastures beyond the city gate, which were largely individually owned; and from the river or seaport to the economic center in the temple enclosure and, later, to the huge palace yards. The dichotomy between the city as symbol and the city as the stage of human aspirations was already fully expressed when archaeology stumbled on Sumerian and Akkadian city plans—the carefully designed entrance to the vast palace plaza at Mari, for instance, served as activity center for the city *(Fig 40)*. Street elevations were staggered, zigzagging along the main roads to adjust to the curve of the concentric city plan *(Fig. 41)*. In 1966, this aesthetic-expedient concept proved its undiminishing validity in an excellent example of a rebuilt city block in Hanover, West Germany. Dieter Oesterlen's Hanover Historical Museum has the same staggered exterior walls facing the cur-

47

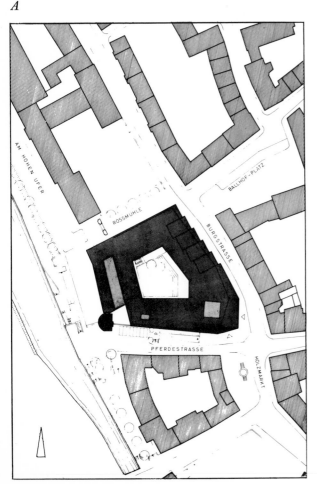

Fig. 41. *Palace and Gimilsin Temple of Eshnunna, ca. 2200 B.C. The staggered elevation of the palace toward the street takes account of curvature inherent in the concentric plan.*

vature of a medieval street with overshot half-timber houses (*Figs. 42A, 42B*).

Behind the forbidding *casa mura* (wall house) tradition lay an understanding of the necessary separation of private from public sphere. A residential section of the Mesopotamian city of Ur, from the early third millennium B.C., shows that the urban hive, whose density derived from the mutual buttressing of continuous mud-brick structures, was shot through with

A

Fig. 42. *The timelessness of urban concepts is well illustrated by the plan and elevation (A, B) of the Historical Museum in Hanover, Germany, built in 1964 by Dieter Oesterlen. The curved street pattern and the staggered elevations of old half-timber houses evoked a sympathetic response in a new medium that underlines historical continuity and the reverence of man for his past.*

B

courtlike bubbles (*Fig. 43*). In addition, there were small local shrines serving specific district deities, like the *pieves*, or parish districts, of Italian cities. Temple courts were places of assembly, trading, and debate, while the patio belonged to the family, where the tensions of politics and competition were excluded.

The unalterable demands of human nature assured the survival of the introverted patio house in the Orient and in all Latin countries. Four human requirements could only be met by the house built around a court: physical elimination, well water, the barred gate, and the enclosing wall, which had been man's claim to territoriality since the first sedentary husbandman marked off his pasture from that of his neighbor.

Plutarch defined kingship as government of one man by the consent of the governed (in contrast to tyranny as the will of one man over the wills of the governed). The Sumerians never lost the original concept of kingship, which was a contributing factor to the gradual extinction of the concentric city-states. At the spring festival, the king or his representative governor, the *ensi,* was stripped of all garments and insignia, slapped in the face by the priest, and driven outside the city. In his place ruled for one day a man of the people, enjoying all privileges, until the king was invited back. Even after the terrible destruction inflicted on the Sumerians by the Akkadians, a gardener ruled in Nippur during the brief Sumerian revival lasting less than 200 years (*ca.* 2100 to 1900 B.C.) because the rightful king had died during his one day of exile. It is comforting to know that not only tyranny has a historical continuum. From the eighth to the fourteenth century, the citizens of Zaragossa in today's Spain demanded that each new Aragonese king swear an oath protecting urban liberty:

We who are as worthy as you and could do more than you elect you king on condition that you preserve our privileges and liberties, and that between you and us there shall be someone with power greater than yours [the law]. If this shall not be so, we say no.

As the Bronze Age gave way to the Iron Age, the first urban age came to a close. The single-focused attempt of each city-state to secure its place in the cosmos had to give way to the more complex challenge of finding a place in the world. By the middle of the second millennium B.C., the Sumerians and their counterplayers, the Akkadians, started to vanish from history. To the future of mankind they had bequeathed literature, bicameral government, codified law, algebra, monetary economy, irriga-

Fig. 43. Residential section of Ur, Mesopotamia in the third millennium B.C. *Spaces numbered 2 are small local shrines to lesser deities, one of which is neatly fitted into a street intersection* (arrow). *Spaces (3) are residential courts. From Leonard Woolley,* Excavations at Ur *(1926).*

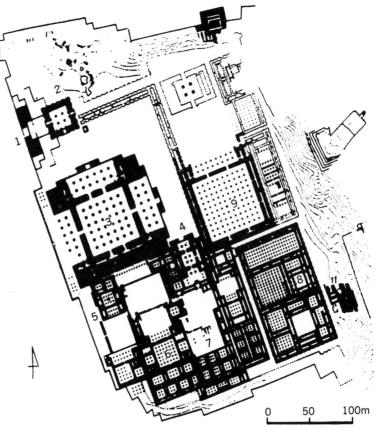

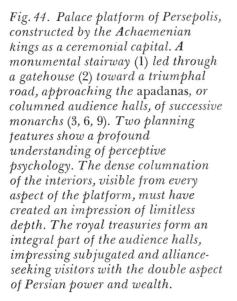

Fig. 44. Palace platform of Persepolis, constructed by the Achaemenian kings as a ceremonial capital. A monumental stairway (1) led through a gatehouse (2) toward a triumphal road, approaching the apadanas, or *columned audience halls, of successive monarchs (3, 6, 9). Two planning features show a profound understanding of perceptive psychology. The dense columnation of the interiors, visible from every aspect of the platform, must have created an impression of limitless depth. The royal treasuries form an integral part of the audience halls, impressing subjugated and alliance-seeking visitors with the double aspect of Persian power and wealth.*

tion, monumental achitecture, anthropomorphic sculpture, and a pragmatic ethics, which sanctioned almost any action in order "to fulfill the divine command against inactivity." This activist principle of Sumer formed the basis of future urban societies. It would henceforth divide Occidental from Oriental cultures. To the westward heirs of Sumer, the Jews, Assyrians, Macedonians, Greeks, Romans and their European-American progeny, doing nothing would not taste like honey, as the Arab proverb says, but would taste like sin.

The gains and curses of the first urban age might have evaporated in the inferno of incessant warfare if they had not proved so persuasive to those who came to destroy them. Like pollen-carrying insects, the invaders of Mesopotamia spread the city-building impulse to emerging societies. Despite uncountable variations of the centrifugal city, two of its features retained their form and their meaning for all time. One was design contrast—the juxtaposition in scale, proportion, placement, and materials of singular monumental architecture and collective anonymous buildings. The second Sumerian planning feature that proved immortal was the city terrace. Its origin was topographical, a refuge from the sudden floods of the unpredictable twin rivers. The water god, Ea, taught his children how to construct platforms from reed and bitumen that could float. The Marsh Arabs of Iraq, who, after all, are partially descendants of the Chaldeans, float their reed houses today on similar platforms. Later, the terrace became the most important feature of the city-state. It was the market place where the priests regulated trade and arbitrated conflicts long before the agora and forum were invented, and it was the sacred ground, on which rose the cosmic symbol of the ziggurat bearing the temple of the city god. No later age invented a finer planning feature to spell out man's existence between earthbound and heavenly aspirations (*Figs. 31, 40*).

Bronze Age palaces in Syria, Iran, and Crete took up the design of terraces, raising their multispaced civic centers above the common ground. The most grandiose terrace realization belongs fittingly to a phantom city—a sort of supersacred precinct of divine kingship: the palaces of Persepolis (*Fig. 44*). Darius the Persian, beginning about 518 B.C., and his successor, Xerxes I, constructed a platform 50 feet high and 1,500 by 900 feet wide, bound with iron clamps into a natural rock promontory. It is now assumed that no one ever lived in these gigantic hypostyle halls of Egyptian derivation and in their modular satellite spaces, but that it was the shrine of the alpha and omega of imperialism. Persepolis was the treasury of the Achaemenian world conquerors. The 2-feet-wide double-run staircase leading to the terrace severed the imperial from the common world. Its sides are covered with reliefs of sculptured tribute bearers whose suggestiveness to the live embassies, ascending to the imperial presence, had the subtlety of planted dollars on a collection plate.

Each city terrace was unique because in a last celebration of geomorphic response each depended on its given site. In Delphi, the drop from the central terrace to the rocks below is steep and shocking (*Fig. 45*); in Pergamon, the terraces unfold like a gracious fan (*Fig. 99*); and in Jerusalem, a modest build-up is enhanced by contrast with the natural ravines around the

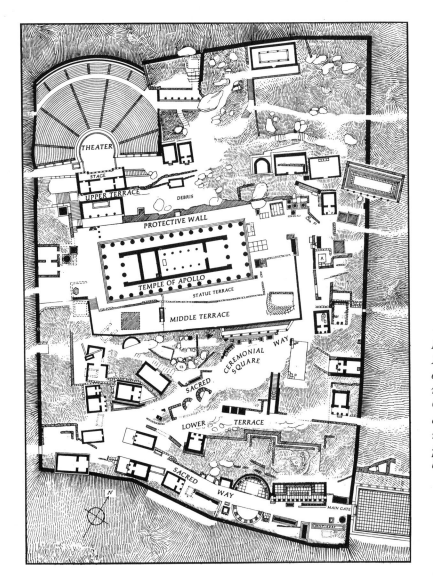

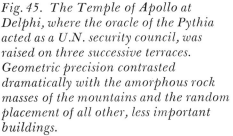

Fig. 45. The Temple of Apollo at Delphi, where the oracle of the Pythia acted as a U.N. security council, was raised on three successive terraces. Geometric precision contrasted dramatically with the amorphous rock masses of the mountains and the random placement of all other, less important buildings.

Haram (*Fig. 46*). Seen from the Jordan Valley below, this platform, quite obviously, is the only site on which the brazen columns of Solomon's Temple could have risen and where "Mohammed was wafted by his mystic steed al-Buraq (lightning) and climbed up to God by way of a ladder placed on the sacred rock."*

The magic of the terraced ascent was rarely understood by Western builders. Its apotheosis came from cultures that had

* Michel Join-Lambert, *Jerusalem* (New York, 1958).

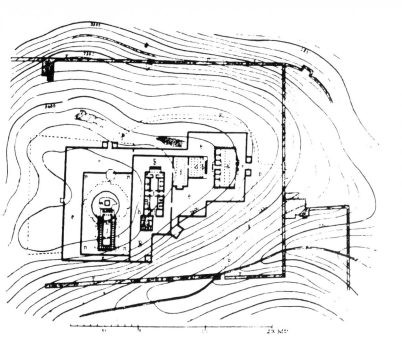

Fig. 46. Haram, the temple district of Jerusalem. The original platform, built by Phoenicians for King Solomon around 1000 B.C., is based on the Sumerian city-terrace tradition. Later conquerors—the Romans, the Moslems, and ultimately the returning Jews—distinguished their cult buildings by slight raises in the terrace level. Despite a very modest differentiation in height, the "raising unto heaven" becomes evident through contrast with the bordering ravine.

Fig. 47. When the steppe nomad Kublai Khan conquered the ancient Chinese capital of Peking, in 1267, he rebuilt it according to traditions going far back into Chinese history. The succession of terraces and open columned halls derived from the temple cities of India, which in turn had adopted enclosing girdle wall, processional axis, and hypostyle halls from the all-pervading Egyptian prototypes.

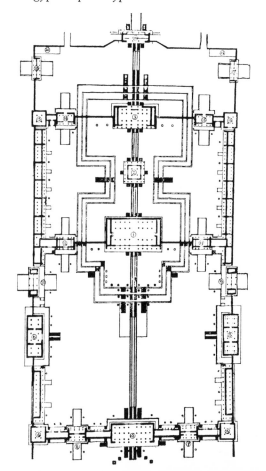

been touched by the cosmic quest of the first ziggurat builders. Asia furnishes two examples showing extremes of overstatement and understatement from which later city designers could have learned much by way of conceptual adaptation. The terraced center section of the great palace axis in Peking is a seventeenth-century re-creation of a traditional design reaching far back into history (*Fig. 47*). The three platforms leading to the T'ai-Ho Tien, the Hall of Supreme Harmony, in the palace city, are separated by no more than three steps each. The effect of separation from the mundane ground comes less from height than from exquisitely carved marble rails delineating each level, and from two intervening halls whose perceptive function is to arrest movement and increase anticipation. As in all Chinese plans, whether of exterior or interior space succession, there is no monumental termination of the central axis. Space "leaks out," to use the rather fatuous art-historical phrase which should be replaced by: space asserts its infinity toward the endless horizon. In the ceremonial center of Peking the impact of the terraces is less physical than symbolic. All major halls occupy the third level, but the Imperial Hall stands higher conceptually because it contains the throne which was the navel of the Realm of the Middle, as the Chinese had styled their empire since the beginning of recorded history.

The diffusion of concepts between the Asian continent and America still meets with skepticism or rejection. Classical

53

archaeology, a discipline founded on the reconstruction of past societies from nondocumentary evidence, is slow to accept visual analogies. Yet, it is the concrete evidence of concentric, single-focused cities that seems to be the strongest proof of conceptual crossfertilization. It is unlikely that the combination of cosmic belief in a vertical world axis and its symbolic location in the center of a seven- or five-tiered "mountain" developed independently in Asia and America. If we compare the sacred district in the ancient Mesopotamian city of Ur as it was completed by the Assyrians and Chaldeans in the seventh and sixth centuries B.C. (*Fig. 48*) with the ceremonial core of the Maya city of Uxmal in Yucatán, Mexico, dating from the tenth century A.D. (*Fig. 49*), the conceptual affinity is obvious.

The Kushans, who were originally steppe nomads of Scythian origin, became the concept carriers between the declining Middle Eastern cultures of the Bronze and Iron Age and the rising medieval cultures of Asia when they conquered India in the first century A.D. Their most remarkable ruler, Kanishka (second century A.D.) maintained the cultural ties his grandfather Kadphises had established in the time of Augustus. In his treasure house at Peshavar were found examples of all art styles of the civilized world as it existed in the first millennium B.C. R. Ghirshman writes:

Merchandise from Egypt and the Roman Mediterranean was loaded in Red Sea ports, arrived at the mouth of the Indus river, went up as far as Peshavar, crossed the Hindu Kush and Pamirs in caravans,

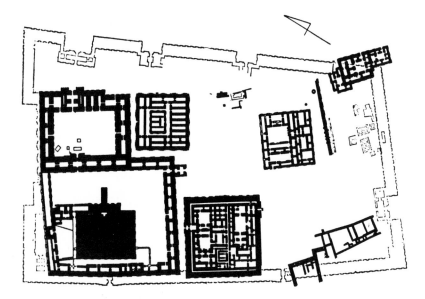

Fig. 48. The ziggurat and city terrace of Ur, Mesopotamia, as regulated according to orthogonal geometry by the Assysians, some 2,500 years after the city was founded by the Sumerians, who constructed it in a curvilinear design. The narrow gates, the intersquared courts, the modular cells, and the oblique building approaches reappear in medieval India and Indian America.

54

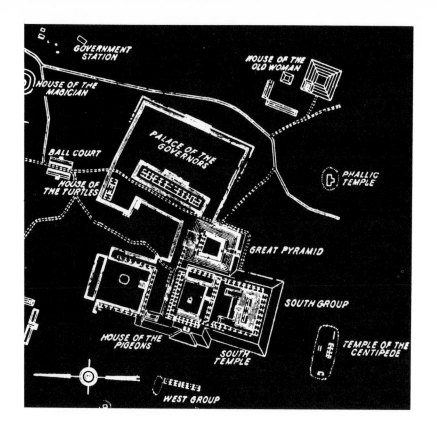

Fig. 49. The Maya city of Uxmal in Yucatán, Mexico, built shortly after A.D. 900. The links to Asiatic planning are a calculatedly oblique approach, religious structures separated by raised terrace courts, modular cell spaces, and a hierarchy of verticality that assigns to the highest structure the contact with the cosmos.

Fig. 50. The causeway circuit of Tikál, Guatemala, reflects the ceremonial causeways of Egypt and the circumambulation routes of the Buddhist sacred districts. From Michael Coe, The Maya, (1966).

and after traversing Chinese Turkestan, reached China. From the beginning of the second century A.D. the Kushans, therefore, controlled the three main stretches of the Silk Route.*

Since the very essence of trade is two-way exchange, Indian and Chinese arts and crafts were diffused through the Mediterranean and vice versa. With material culture went conceptual influence. The missionary since time immemorial has been followed by the trader, and there is no reason to assume that the Chinese and Polynesian boats that reached the American coast a long time before Cortés did not have their priests on board as he had his. Beside the vertical terrace focus of the concentric cosmic city plan, the concept of circumambulation is shared by all. There is no plan of any community that does not include motion patterns. The extent of planned communication and its relationship to buildings distinguish true urbanism from a merely accumulative village pattern. The closed causeway circuit—the *sache*—of the Maya ceremonial center in Tikál, Guatemala (*Fig. 50*), has much in common with the

* R. Ghirshman, *Iran* (Baltimore, 1955).

circumambulation patterns of the Hindu-Buddhist centers. The planners of Copán (*Fig. 51*), midway on the Maya trade route between Chiapas and the Peten, went one step further than their Asiatic and local prototypes. The huge central plaza, level with the river, is separated from the ceremonial acropolis by a most elegant stair arrangement, which—like the Hundred Steps of Versailles—is in itself a ceremonial experience. A thousand years later, in 1965, Mexico City built the largest American housing development over the ruins of the acropolis where the Aztecs made their last stand against the Spaniards. The planners had enough respect for the symbolic logic of historic environment to construct a terraced Plaza of Three Cultures (*Fig. 52*), re-creating a reminiscence of the *forensis dignitas* of public assembly that had been the common heritage of nucleated, concentric cities.

Fig. 51. Model of the city terrace and acropolis of the Maya city of Copán in today's state of Honduras. Neither Egypt nor Greece nor Rome can match in sophistication the oblique approach via grandiose staircases to the ceremonial acropolis and the reciprocal view from above over the vast public plaza, structured by ceremonial subcenters and the ball court.

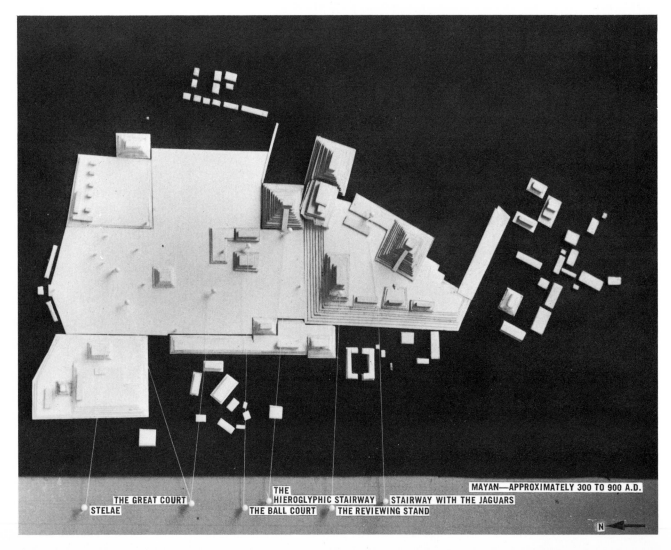

THE GREAT COURT
STELAE
THE HIEROGLYPHIC STAIRWAY
THE BALL COURT
STAIRWAY WITH THE JAGUARS
THE REVIEWING STAND
MAYAN—APPROXIMATELY 300 TO 900 A.D.
N

CONCENTRIC STRATEGY

The continuity of environmental concepts is guaranteed by incessant transformations. Just as the city terraces of America differ in local detail from those in Mesopotamia and the Far East, so the concentric planning concept changed from its cosmological to a practical connotation when the first wave of many successive Indo-European invaders established their rule over Anatolia and Syria. Despite almost continuous barbarian invasions and the assaults of city-state against city-state, the citadel as defensive focus of a city did not appeal to the Sumerians and Akkadians. Their faith in the superiority of cosmologi-

Fig. 52. The satellite town sector of Tlaltelolco in Mexico City, constructed in the 1960's by the architect Mario Pani. The stepped platform covers the Rock of Defeat, where the last Aztec chief was killed by the Spaniards. Tall masts for flags and illumination provide on public fiestas the symbolic transformation of an urban communication link into the city terrace, an ancient tradition of early Mexican cultures.

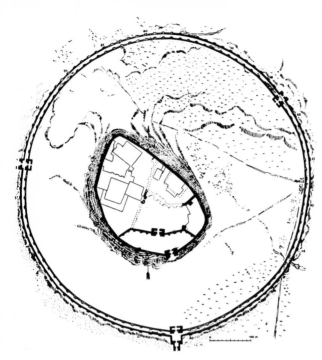

Fig. 53. The Hittite citadel of Cincirli in Anatolia shows the overlapping of two concentric concepts. The core is characteristic for the strategic-defensive wall (burg) of all Indo-Germanic tribes. The perfect circle of the double girdle wall, constructed at the beginning of the first millennium B.C., despite tremendous topographical obstacles, testifies to a symbolic-cosmological influence that reached the mountain chieftains from the ancient cultural centers they had conquered and destroyed.

cal protection, or their resignation to the inevitability of death, must have been profound. In the second millennium B.C., the Hittites, Elamites, Urartians, and others built a different type of city, whose centrifugal core was the fortified citadel. Considering the geomorphic dependence of a maximum security stronghold, it is most surprising that in the early first millennium B.C., Cincirli, the capital of the Neo-Hittite Empire, received a double wall (*Fig. 53*). Disregarding all topographical adjustments, this superbly constructed ring is perfectly circular, overcoming almost inconceivable obstacles in the landscape to achieve geometric perfection and to place three gates at inter-compass points. The only explanation is a new extrageomorphic inspiration which must have penetrated the rather raw animistic religion of the Hittites. This new approach was taken up by the builders of at least a half dozen other citadels who surrounded their old crags with cosmic circles. Herodotus, the Greek traveler and historian of the fifth century B.C., has described Ecbatana, capital of the Iranian Medes, as a perfect circular city, built in 715 B.C., by their first king on the layout of an ancient Elamite settlement. Concentric ring-walls divided the population into seven castes or classes, each occupying one of the rings. The innermost circle belonged to the king and his nobles. In the *Timaeus,* Plato obviously combined the sensationally new knowledge of the Persian capital with Mesopotamian-Indian cosmology, which plays such a great part in his entire work. His ideal island community of Atlantis has a forbidden inner city of seven interwalled circles whose height rises toward the center. Each ring-wall has one of the planetary colors of the Sumerian ziggurat terraces: black for Mercury, red for Mars, purple for Saturn, blue for Venus, and white for Jupiter. In Plato's ideal city, the two innermost enclosures were capped with silver, signifying the moon, and gold, signifying the sun. It would have seemed perfectly logical to the Sumerians that in Plato's microcosm the circle of the sun is occupied by the treasury.

The next chapter of this inquiry into urban origins will relate the ascendancy of orthogonal over concentric city plans without disrupting the historical continuity of the concentric concept. We are dealing here with a canon, not with a linear progression of urban concepts. The self-realization of an urban society in different morphons (forms) is like the harmonizing of a *Leitmotif* in different keys. As urban origins multiply, the chorus will be enriched by more and more variations. None of the voices that had at one time carried the tune was ever silenced.

A new period of concentric city planning started with the Sassanids, who assumed the rule of Persia in A.D. 226, after defeating the Parthians, who had held a precarious caretakership over the indigenous West Asian population and the heirs of Alexander the Great. Alexander's successors, the Seleucids, had tried in vain to turn the basically nomadic, animistic, tribal, and antiurban Iranians into provincial Greeks.

The Sassanids, who were of the same Scythian-Iranian origin as the Parthians, arrived on the Middle Eastern stage when the glamor of Hellenism and Rome started to fail dismally and a return to "the God of our Fathers" seemed advisable. Under King Ardashir I, they staged a Zoroastrian revival and founded, opposite the degenerate Seleucia on the Tigris River, the new capital of Ctesiphon. The new city had a circular plan, though no more than the audience hall with its fabulous *liwan* arch has survived. This multistory arched entrance hall, first built by the Parthians (*Fig. 54*), was derived from the high gate

Fig. 54. Assur: Parthian palace, 100 B.C. The multi-storied arch as entrance to cities and palaces seems to have been one of the rare original inventions of the otherwise thoroughly eclectic Assyrians. It became the most enduring feature of Western architecture, as the subsequent chapter on the Roman Triumph and its influence will prove.

Fig. 55. Court and liwan arch of the Palais Azem in Damascus. Although built in the eighteenth century, it expresses that same pride in wealth and power that had motivated the conquering Assyrians to inflate the modest brick arch of the Sumerians into suprahuman proportions.

of Assyrian palaces; it added a new dimension to the single focused city: the interpenetration of exterior and interior space in the ceremonial core of which the Moslems were later to make such imaginative use in the *liwan* (*Fig. 55*). Another cosmic circle on the far eastern end of the Sassanid realm, Firozabad (Gur) (*Fig. 56*) shows by the similarity of its circular plan that the concentric revival was systematic. The ancient Iranian religion conceived of the universe as a globe divided into two halves. One was dominated by Ormuzd, the god of light and goodness, and the other by Ahriman, the god of darkness and evil. The Persian battlecry, "Here Ormuzd, there Ahriman," was nothing else but a reinterpretation of the Sumerian acceptance of the two natures of man.*

In the unending cycle of rising and falling nations, the Sassanids were defeated by the Arabs, who terminated once and for all the second urban age that had lasted from the beginning of the Iron Age in the early first millennium B.C. to the fall of the Roman Empire at the close of the fifth century A.D. The circular capital Baghdad, which the Abbasid Dynasty laid out in 762 near the ruined Hellenistic and Seleucid cities of Mesopotamia, was as utopian an experiment in "scientific order" as Le Corbusier's *Ville Radieuse* in our time.

The city as concentric world mountain had thrust man into the company of his divine superimage in a fixed, static relationship. The power symbol was absolute and immutable. The astrologically interpreted astronomy of the medieval Arabs

* *Ibid.*

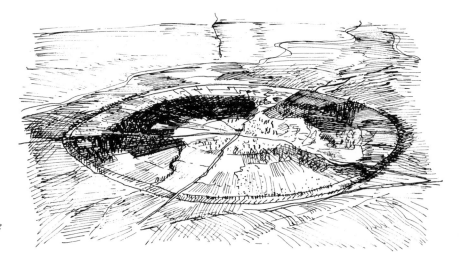

Fig. 56. *The concentric city terrace of Firozabad (Gur) built by Ardashir, founder of the Sassanid Dynasty of Persia in the early third century* B.C. *Crossing main roads were oriented toward the compass points and the twelve city sectors were named after the signs of the zodiac.*

Fig. 57. *Koy-krylgan Kale, Khwarizm (U.S.S.R.), astronomical plan from the second century* B.C. *Khwarizm on the Oxus River developed a high culture from Chinese Han and Greek-Bactrian influences, which vanished under the onslaught of the Mongol and Turkish invasions.*

Fig. 58. *Further proof of the close interrelationship of Asiatic and American cultures is the astrolabic circle with twelve divisions, in the interior of the Inca fortress of Sacsahuaman above Cuzco, built in the fourteenth century* A.D. *From George Kubler,* The Art and Architecture of Ancient America *(1962).*

modified religion through science for the first time in human history. They founded Baghdad as a zodiac, oriented within the astrolabic circle, which would reflect the impartial order of celestial law rather than be at the mercy of whimsical deities.

The Abbassid caliphs must be counted among the exceedingly rare rulers who saved man's cultural achievements by protecting scholars and artists, and who increased the imperishable values that justify human existence by subsidizing creative talent. Arab scientists produced workable astronomical instruments, the astrolabe and alidade, permitting the measurement of celestial distances. They also developed Greek mathematics into systems with transmissible symbols. The great mathematician of the Baghdad school, al-Khwarizmi, who in the ninth century gave algebra its name, its first textbook, and its application to monetary calculations, as his name implies, was a native of Khwarizm, the ancient land of Chorasmia along the Oxus River in today's Uzbekistan. In this remote valley that served as highway between Lake Aral and the European-Asiatic trade bridge of Serindia, flourished a productive and highly original civilization from the fourth century B.C. to its destruction by the Mongols and the Turks. Al-Khwarizmi's exalted position in the Abbassid court indicates a long and close connection between the two centers of learning.

Koy-krylgan Kale was a dynastic sanctuary of the Khwarizm rulers (*Fig. 57*). Its plan was revealed by S. P. Tolstov's excava-

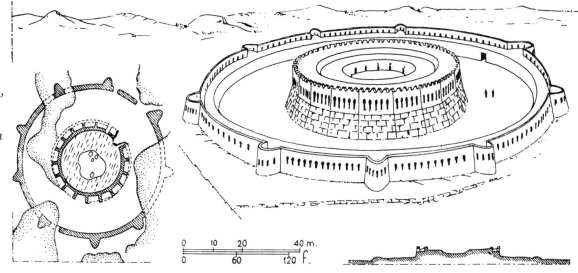

Fig. 59. This reconstruction—by the Russian archaeologist, S. P. Tolstov—of Koy-krylgan Kale, the royal city of Khwarizm, fits the description of Baghdad (see Fig. 61) better than the modern reconstructions.

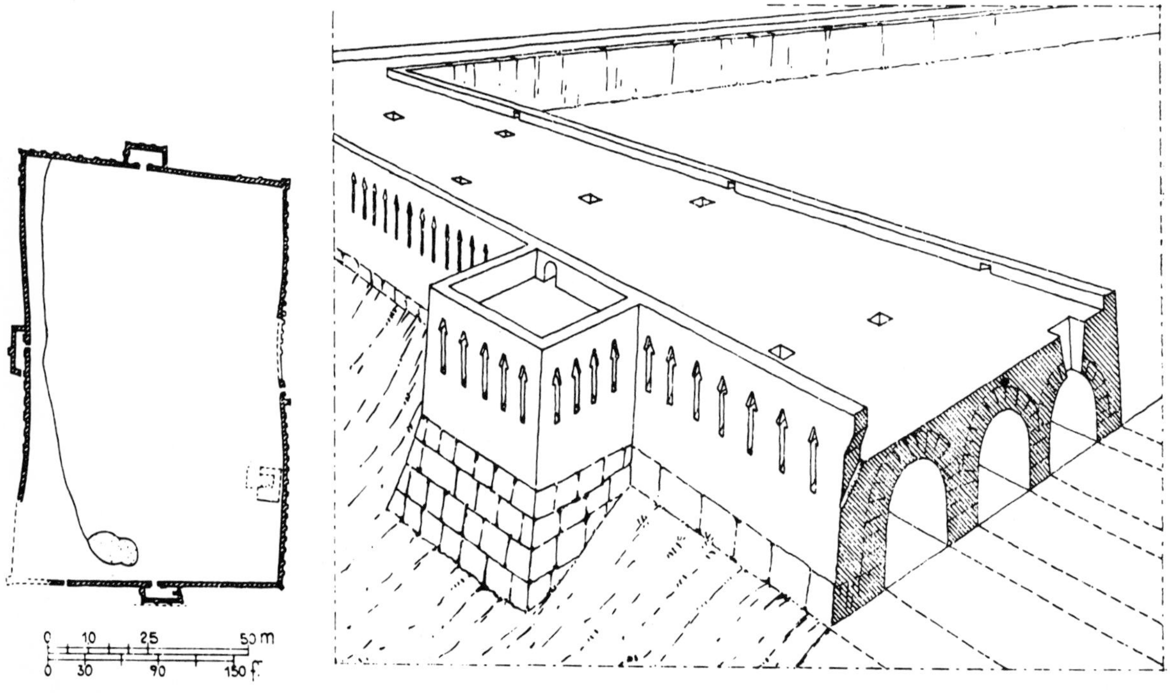

Fig. 60. Khwarizm settlement, late first millennium B.C. Dwellings were fitted into the town wall left and right of a central corridor, which was lighted by openings in a flat-roofed street.

tions as an astrolabic circle, surrounded by a chambered outer ring. The circle alone would not justify a conjectural connection between Khwarizm and the Baghdad plan because it was an international symbol that occurs in the inner circle of the Inca fortress of Sacsahuaman on the crest of the Andes (*Fig. 58*), in the inner sanctuary of the Tomb of Augustus in Rome (*Fig.*

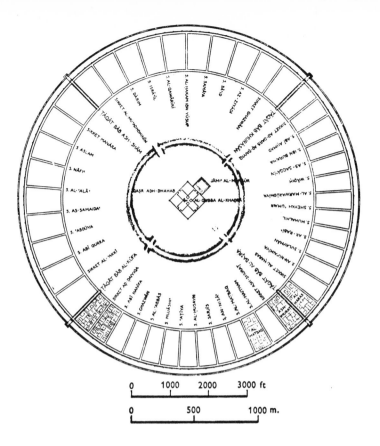

Fig. 61. Plan of Baghdad, founded in A.D. 762 by the Abbasid caliph al-Mansur, whose patronage of the sciences marks the transition from astrology to astronomy. The strictly geometric arrangement of the central palace and the adjoining mosque within a perfect circle with compass-oriented gates seems like an abstract diagram of the concentric-planning concept, which had reached its apex and its termination.

Fig. 62. A fasil, or wall street, in the second enclosure of the circular city of Baghdad, based upon Creswell's graphic reconstruction of the original plan. Although several aspects do not concur with his text, the fasils have been established and could have derived from Khwarizm prototypes.

125), and in many other places. It is the concentric superstructure of Koy-krylgan Kale as reconstructed by Tolstov (Fig. 59) that proves the influence on Baghdad (Fig. 61). As in the Khwarizm city (Fig. 60), the outer ring-wall of Baghdad rose 75 feet, while the inner ring around the palace had a height of 90 feet. This was not all Caliph al-Mansur learned from his Asiatic advisers. He combined the cosmic round with another unique feature of Khwarizm planning tradition. The earliest settled communities of Khwarizm, from the middle of the first millennium B.C. onward, had huge rectangular enclosures formed by continuous stone walls into which dwellings were fitted on either side of a central interior street.* In Baghdad, uniform houses were built contiguously against the circular walls, divided from each other by a street called a *fasil* (Fig. 62). Houses had interior courtyards, which must have been missing in Khwarizm, and their scant light came from windows facing

* S. P. Tolstov's work is in Russian, but D. Skvirsky, *Archaeology in the USSR* (Moscow, 1959), furnishes some references to Khwarizm.

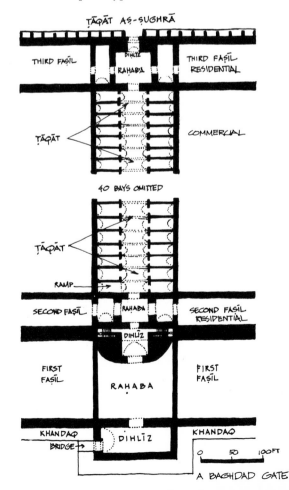

the *fasil* instead of from windholes in the flat continuous roof as in Asia, but it is only in such details that the overlapping of the ancient Oxus urbanization and the first Arabian attempt at city planning is not apparent.*

Like all circular cities, Baghdad did not survive in its original form. Following an ancient tradition, the merchants were excluded from living in the perfect astronomical order and had their own quarters along the river quay. Within 100 years after the founding, the population had burst through the walls and had started to settle in unplanned disorder on the embankment opposite the circular capital. Travelers reported that by the beginning of the twelfth century, al-Mansur's perfect cosmos had vanished.

But the longing for containment in the cosmic round re-

* K. A. C. Creswell, *A Short Account of Early Muslim Architecture* (Baltimore, 1958). There exists considerable disagreement among historians on the precise details of the Baghdad plan. Creswell's popular reconstruction does not conform to his verbal description because it omits a third, interior double wall shown on Fig. 61. There exists, however, a general agreement among archaeologists that the plan was astrolabic and compass-oriented.

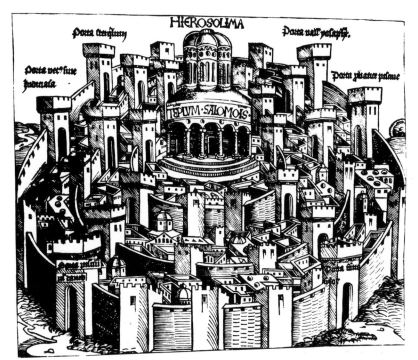

Fig. 63. Heavenly Jerusalem. *Although the medieval artist who made this woodcut never saw Jerusalem, his presentation of the spiritual capital of Judaism and Christianity has remarkable historical precision. From the Haram (city terrace) rises Solomon's Temple surmounted by the circular Dome of the Rock. Clearly seen are the three historic wall enclosures built successively by Herod, Simon Maccabaeus, and Agrippa, and the city gates surmounted by crenellated towers. The Tomb Church of the Holy Sepulcher is recognizable by its dome. The ideal City of Faith is here made visible as the realistic city of power.*

64

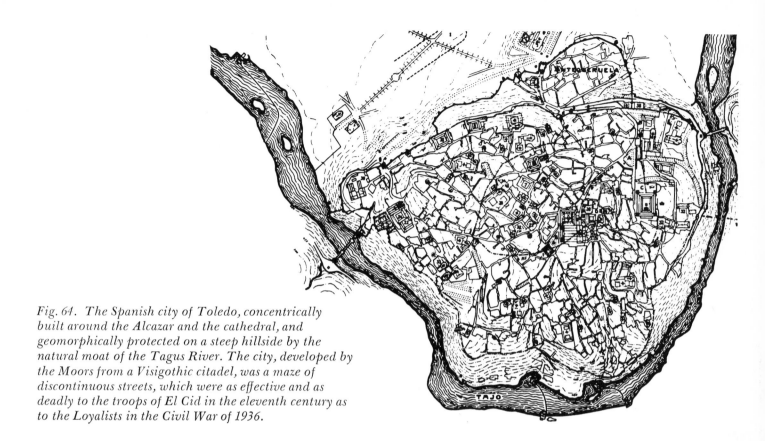

Fig. 64. The Spanish city of Toledo, concentrically built around the Alcazar and the cathedral, and geomorphically protected on a steep hillside by the natural moat of the Tagus River. The city, developed by the Moors from a Visigothic citadel, was a maze of discontinuous streets, which were as effective and as deadly to the troops of El Cid in the eleventh century as to the Loyalists in the Civil War of 1936.

mained impervious to practical failure. Throughout the history of cities, planners continued to turn in circles whenever the proposed community believed in a privileged cosmic or ideological position. In 472, appeared the treatise *De civitate Dei* by Bishop Augustine of Hippo in Africa. It was more than a coincidence that this was the same decade in which Roman world domination finally came to an end. The abstract ideal of a Christian republic, symbolized in the Biblical ideal of Jerusalem the Golden, gradually replaced the orthogonal urban order that had held the classical world together. Cruelty, chaos, extortion were to be endured in a "vale of tears," leading through death into the perfect circular containment of the City of God. Later, in the Middle Ages, uncounted illuminations, woodcuts, and broadsides offered Jerusalem to the citizens of the world as the tangible ideal of their dreams, which centered around the Temple of Solomon (*Fig. 63*). It was no small irony of history that the Crusades adopted at the close of the eleventh century the holy image of ultimate Judaic unity for their unholy conquest of Islamic Palestine.

The cities that emerged after the long amnesia of the great migrations that flooded Europe with steppe nomads between the fourth and the seventh century owed their concentric, single-focused plans to the dominant Christian tradition of the City of God and to defensive necessity. The network of Roman roads that had spanned the world was cut and destroyed, and even within the towns unconnected dead-end lanes (*Fig. 64*) offered greater security against marauding invaders than the arrow-straight Roman decumanus. Like their far-distant ancestors at the dawn of the Bronze Age, each town became again its own state with the cathedral as *axis mundi,* reaching from the dead center of the community toward salvation in the sky. An early medieval settlement like Hildesheim in Germany consisted of four townships each closed up in its own centricity and each fiercely hostile to the other (*Fig. 65*). Only with the foundation of an orthogonal merchant town in the late Middle Ages would this hermit crab syndrome gradually vanish. The French town of Brive is a telling cosmocentrical example with

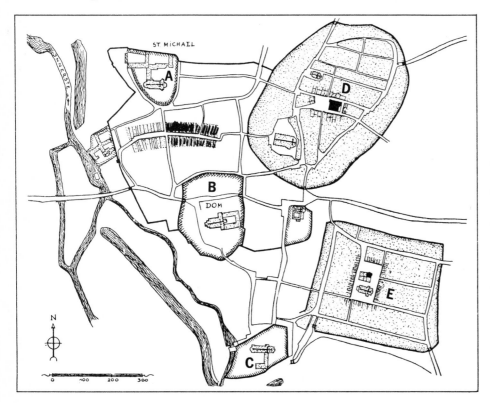

Fig. 65. The Carolingian bishopric of Hildesheim provides a northern version of the ancient tradition that each concentric settlement is its own cosmological center. No love was lost between the aristocratic Benedictines (A), the imperial cathedral (B), the poor mendicant monks (C), and the artisan city with town hall and market (D). Only the pragmatic merchants of the thirteenth century succeeded finally in uniting the antagonistic power symbols into a unified urban complex (E).

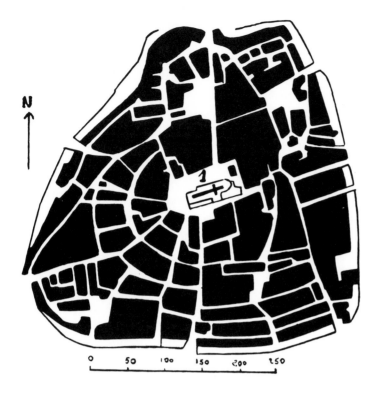

Fig. 66. The medieval city of Brive offers an instructive lesson in the contrast between Arabian astronomy, based on inductive observation, and mystical astrology, based on the most ancient numerological symbols. Gates, streets, and parishes are configurations of the number 7.

seven gates, seven concentric roads, seven streets radiating from the cathedral center, and seven parochial quarters (*Fig. 66*). Many concentric towns put a magic "blue stone" in the center of the market place to claim their very own world navel, or erected a seven- or nine-stepped miniature "world mountain" with a "column of justice"—a dim memory of the ziggurat as center of the world. (*Fig. 67*).

The triple dose of Oriental magic, Christian mythology, and barbarian superstition that had invested man-made environment of the early Middle Ages with psychic significance had found its visual expression in the core structure—the Romanesque church, whose columns and tympana crawled with supernatural and subnatural manifestations. The subsequent scholastic era of the High Gothic dispelled mysticism with Greek *logos*. A new type of man, educated in universities and used to travel, founded worldly merchant cities with orthogonal street systems and cathedrals of daring height and dazzling splendor, whose symbolic message lay somewhere between the Tower of

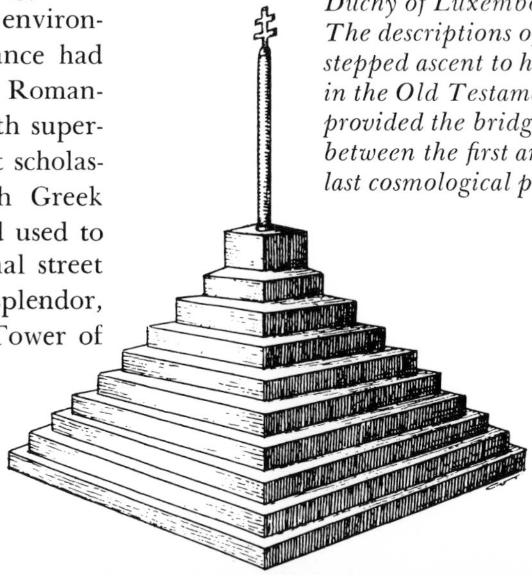

Fig. 67. A "world mountain" with a law column, in the dead center of a small town in the Duchy of Luxembourg. The descriptions of the stepped ascent to heaven in the Old Testament provided the bridge between the first and the last cosmological plans.

Babel and the Chase Manhattan Bank. Their planning concept will be described later. It might seem surprising that after this cool separation of the Scriptural City of God and the actual City of Man during the Gothic period, a new epidemic of cosmological urbanism erupted during the Renaissance and Baroque period, rated as golden ages of humanism. Creative harmony between architecture and art was firmly anchored in perspective, and lavishly financed by art-struck and power-obsessed princes of the market place and the church. If one looks at facts rather than art-historical theories, the sixteenth and seventeenth centuries must rate as one of the most upsetting periods in the history of Western civilization. The awakened critical intellect of individual man collided head on with the ancient powers of church and monarch, desperate to retain their authority. The Reformation, which to us today looks like the ultimate step toward liberation of the conscience, was to its contemporaries a return to blackest early Christian orthodoxy, producing in Luther and Calvin monsters of intolerance. By 1560, witch-burning was in full bloom; and by 1600, the Inquisition, revived by Ferdinand and Isabella in 1480, had executed more than 500,000 "witches, heretics, Jews, and Moslems." In 1547, the Index of the Catholic Church condemned many of the books and classical translations on which the European mind had matured in the brief intellectual dawn of the Quattrocento. Along with the 8 million ounces of gold from Peru that flowed into Europe between 1498 and 1600 came inflation, bankruptcy, and syphilis. The peasants revolted and were destroyed by the nobles (with the eager consent of Martin Luther); the guilds revolted in the cities against the monopoly of the great trade leagues and the banking houses that financed the spreading national power of monarchs. And the astronomers —Copernicus, Giordano Bruno, Galileo—paid with torture and death for having shaken the very foundation of man's pride in himself as the master of cosmic wisdom and power over nature. The dense medieval cities became unbearable for the urban masses, who were packed into airless and lightless quarters, while princes of the church, the crown, and the counting house built glorious urban islands paid for with oppressive taxes. Lamented John Donne, " 'tis all in pieces, all coherence gone."

In such an age, ridden by a great fear, the environment makers became environment dreamers, exactly as in the declining twentieth century. Consciously or subconsciously, the

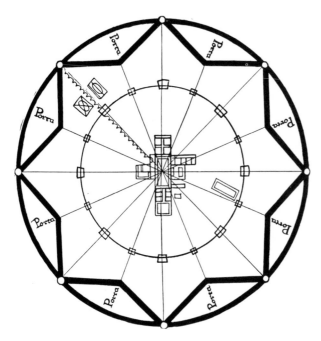

Fig. 68. Thomas Aquinas, the master of Scholasticism, had said in his Summa Theologica: *"The city is the perfect community . . . and building cities is the duty of kings." The Sforza of Milan commissioned the architect Filarete in 1457 to construct "an ideal city for a tyrant," seeing obviously no contradiction in terms. The two superimposed squares form an eight-cornered star, signifying planetary constellations. The palace stronghold has the plan of a gnomon, above which would have risen a stepped tower, a world mountain.*

new man on the moving star sought a new central place in a dislodged universe. A. N. Whitehead, who can be mined for supporting quotations as successfully as Shakespeare and Goethe, wrote, "In each age of the world, distinguished by high activity, there will be found some profound cosmological outlook implicitly accepted, impressing its own type upon current springs of action."*

CONCENTRIC ABSTRACTION

Whitehead's generalization describes the tragedy of post-medieval cities. Physical replanning for a changed social world was scant, confined, as we shall see, to attempted re-creations of Roman grandeur, and in the north of Europe only to a few replanned German and Dutch merchant cities. From Italy spread a fad that exhausted architectural planning by utopian schemes of planetary constellations. These symbolic diagrams are close-ups of a thoroughly dislodged society. Ideal capitals for tyrants abounded as if to promise a new security (*Fig. 68*). There were concentric diagrams, very close to the Indian *Silpa Sastra* schemes, that seemed to search for solace in the old cos-

* A. N. Whitehead, *Adventures of Ideas* (New York, 1933).

69

mologies (*Fig. 69*). Michelangelo, although working at the height of the revival of Roman paganism and archaeology, designed for the Campidoglio Plaza in Rome a twelve-pronged star pattern, weaving outward from a single center, that can be found on the nave wall of one of the oldest mosques of Islam, in Kairouan, North Africa, and goes back to an Indian meditation pattern of incalculable antiquity (*Figs. 70A, 70B, 70C*).

The fearful tensions of the Reformation and of the astronomical revolution were resolved only by a century of religious wars. When the smoke of battle cleared in 1648 at the conclusion of the Thirty Years' War, the Catholic Church had abdicated its role as a check on worldly power and had formed a firm alliance with anti-urban monarchic absolutism because it was antidemocratic. Inspired by the Sun King at Versailles, stellar plans achieved a different meaning: their focal points celebrated the divine monarch. Mannheim, refounded in 1720 (*Fig. 71*), combined this dynastic star image with Vauban's gigantic defense system, ridiculously out of scale compared to

Fig. 69. Two examples of "ideal cities": left, a plan by Andreae from 1619 in the shape of a labyrinth, an ancient chiffre, *or cryptogram, of man's endless search for salvation; right, a plan by Scamozzi from 1605 in the shape of a twelve-pronged star, its interior organization faultlessly geometric, including a thoroughly tamed river.*

A

Fig. 70. The influence of Eastern cosmology on sixteenth-century Renaissance concepts.

A) A Shri-Yantra meditation pattern from Buddhist ritual.

B) A cabalistic sign on the main nave wall of the mosque at Kairouan, Magreb, Africa.

C) Central design by Michelangelo for the Campidoglio, Rome (1567).

B

C

71

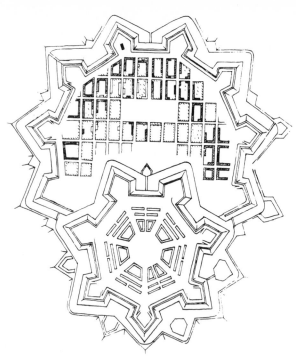

the scant row housing. Leblond's plan of Petersburg (*Fig. 72*), residence of Czar Peter, who wanted "to open a window to the west," is a curious combination of the Assyrian river city (the Czar was an avid shipbuilder) and the concentric star plan.

In an age of dynastic-ecclesiastic absolutes, salvation was promised to the faithful patriot as well as to the religious supplicant. In 1746, the concentric medieval plan of Paris, focusing on the Ile de la Cité and the Cathedral of Notre Dame, was enriched by nineteen *places royales,* each of which had a statue

Fig. 71. Plan of the ducal residence of Mannheim, Germany, started in 1720 and following le système *of Vauban (1633– 1707), the fortification specialist of Louis XIV. Vauban's combination of purely theoretical abstraction and concentric star patterns had a decisive influence on the theory of city planning. Like the scientific system planners of today, he compressed expanding populations into a uniform and rigid pattern, which had to be demolished within two generations.*

Fig. 72. Leblond's plan of 1710 for Czar Peter the Great's capital—to be named St. Petersburg—underwent many modifications in its final form, but the original plan illustrates clearer than most other absolutistic schemes the cosmic-dynastic grand illusion. There is again the Assyrian inclusion of the river as chief artery and, in its natural frame, the great palace, sending its rays of surveillance and benevolence into the four corners of a geometrically-disciplined urban universe.

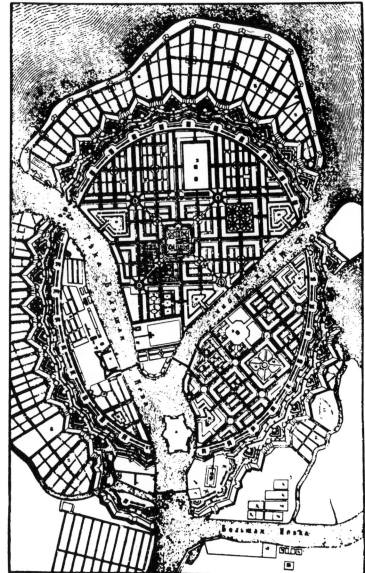

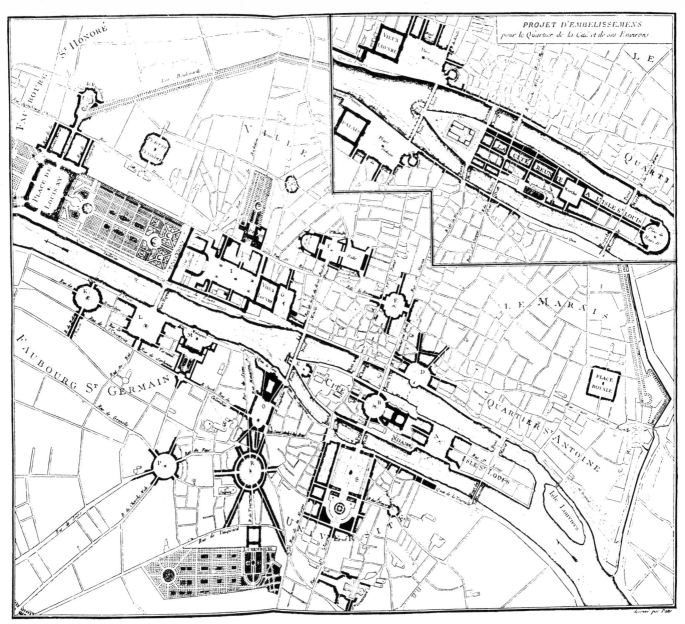

Fig. 73. *As successor to Louis XIV, Louis XV wrote out a competition for the embellishment of Paris to eclipse Versailles. M. Patte inscribed the winning designs in a plan of Paris, dated 1746. The picture shows a part of the star-spangled capital, each* place royale *a cosmos in itself, with a statue of the divine monarch in the center and access routes like rays fanning out, only to meet a sudden end where they abut on ordinary city streets.*

of the Divine Monarch Louis XV in the center (*Fig. 73*). The poor fellow had started his reign with a towering inferiority complex, induced by his predecessor and great-grandfather, Louis XIV, whose star-patterned Versailles saw the most famous planning achievement of the seventeenth and eighteenth centuries. By multiplying his image in the city of Paris, Louis XV followed the precedent of Pharaoh Rameses II, who also had to overcome the blemish of the epigone by serializing his royal presence.

Fig. 74. Robert Pemberton's Happy Colony proposed in 1854 for New Zealand. One hundred thousand families in ten villages were to support each other by voluntary labor in the fields, morally sustained by a model farm in a center core surrounded by planetary constellations and four curved college buildings in the latest Crystal Palace style of glass and iron.

It is comforting to believe that humanity will be forgiven its worst trespasses because in the path of exploitation and depravity always stood a reformer with a mandate from heaven. The French Revolution and the following industrial-commercial revolution of the nineteenth century swung the urban pendulum once more from concentric to orthogonal. But even this decisive change in man-made environment did not invalidate the primordial commitment of man to create an ideal community, centered around a divine image of himself. As the thunder of the approaching French Revolution grew louder, the visionary Neoclassical architect Claude-Nicolas Ledoux (1736–1809) attempted to avert the lightning by designing, among other ideal habitats, a perfect factory town around the Royal Salt Works at Chaux. Its oval center contained such educational facilities as a "House of Vice and Virtue," planned in the shape of a phallus, to strengthen young men's resistance to sin. Anticipating the *Communist Manifesto* by seventy years, he solicited public support for his Temple of Humanity at Chaux with the appeal: "Build temples to social virtue; support your ideals on the basis of a universal pact which challenges the qualities of the whole race to serve the well-being of all."*

* Emil Kaufmann, *Architecture in the Age of Reason* (Cambridge, England, 1955).

74

The universalism of the French rationalists kindled the imagination of reformers in England, where the rapid spread of factory towns and labor slums in the nineteenth century produced the worst environmental abuses. There were suggestions for "planetary" villages, such as Robert Pemberton's "Happy Colony" to be founded in New Zealand (*Fig. 74*). A social reformer and pupil of Jeremy Bentham, whose utilitarianism is anticipated in the American Declaration of Independence, Pemberton envisioned ten concentric villages around a community

Fig. 75. Concentric model town built since 1962 at Urubupunga, in the Brazilian interior. A model farm takes up the core, around which 10,000 construction workers are housed in a perfect circle. As in Pemberton's plan, the community is focused on the ideal of land settlement, while the spiral growth protects the agricultural areas from urban sprawl.

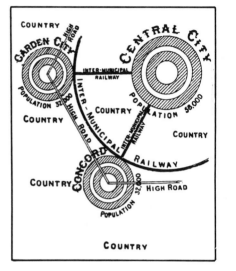

core with a model farm, surrounded by celestial spheres and four colleges built in iron and glass, like Paxton's Crystal Palace.* In the 1960's, the celestial spheres forgotten, a centrifugal model city was built for 10,000 construction workers and their families at Urubupunga on the Paraná River in the Brazilian interior (*Fig. 75*), in a renewed effort to turn the empty continent into a city-bearing region.

The concentric utopias of the nineteenth century ultimately produced the garden cities envisioned by the London court stenographer Ebenezer Howard in 1898. He shared with all other concentric utopians the extraordinary obsession that linear living breeds vice and concentric living promotes virtue. It would have been as impossible for Howard to present his "planetary town system" (*Figs. 76A, 76B*) in a linear-orthogonal shape as it would be, a century later, for Le Corbusier to associate curves with wholesome human environment.

* Robert Lang, "Robert Pemberton," *The Architectural Review* (August, 1952).

A   *B*

Fig. 76.
  A) Ebenezer Howard's ideal concentric city (1898) had a glass-covered Crystal Palace in the form of a circular shopping street and a hierarchical core of culture and good government. The inviolate greenbelt separating it from its smaller satellite duplicates was to be filled with sheep, grain, orchards, and insane asylums, instead of factories and cluster housing.
  B) The Capital Planning Commission of Washington, D.C., assumed that a hundred years later people would still believe in this lovely utopia, all evidence to the contrary, and surrender their real-estate holdings and speculation houses to the state or the center city for perpetual safekeeping of uncontaminated nature.

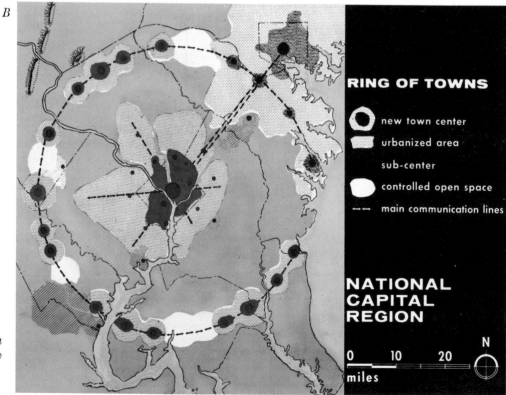

RING OF TOWNS

◉ new town center
⬭ urbanized area
  sub-center
⬬ controlled open space
--- main communication lines

NATIONAL CAPITAL REGION

0   10   20
miles

N

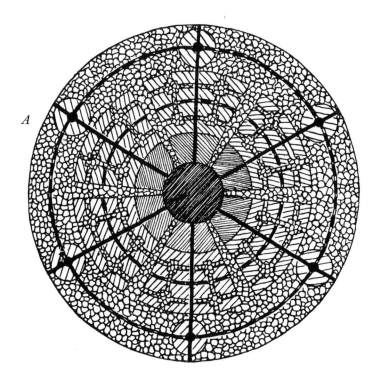

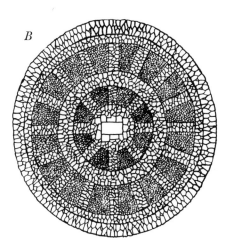

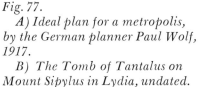

Fig. 77.
A) Ideal plan for a metropolis, by the German planner Paul Wolf, 1917.

B) The Tomb of Tantalus on Mount Sipylus in Lydia, undated.

In 1910, the German city planner Rudolf Eberstadt looked into his crystal ball and came up with the prediction: "The inherited city constellation has a centripetal plan. The new one will be centrifugal." To prove the point, his partner, Paul Wolf, designed a city of the future whose concentric plan was a very slight variation on the cosmic plan of the Tomb of Tantalus in Lydia (*Figs. 77A, 77B*). It is not that Eberstadt's crystal ball was any more clouded than that of other concentric planners. The blatant misconception in his prognosis is the eternal confusion of knowledge and truth. Knowledge enabled the Assyrians to liquidate the confines of the concentric centrifugal plan and to move on to orthogonal-linear ecumenism in the planning of cities. It did not affect the truth in man's heart that he lives as a mere spot within a rotating galaxy, and that there is something in this fearful realization that compels him to build round cities by which to recognize his place in the universe.

When the first kibbutzim in Israel were built in the 1920's, they were concentric and remained so where the ideological determination was strong enough, as in Nahalal (*Fig. 78*). The early settlements of a new Israel are a nostalgic echo, con-

Fig. 78. Nahalal, in Israel, planned in the 1920's by Richard Kaufmann. The official town core is separated from the centrifugally expanding residential belt by a concentric ring boulevard, reminiscent of Vienna's beloved Ringstrasse. *The mood conveyed by the plan is faith in a higher order, and self-containment of a pioneering community.*

sciously or subconsciously, of two unique East European planning prototypes. Vienna (*Fig. 79A*) had started on a Roman site as a concentric cathedral town, surrounded by a fortification ring. When the walls were razed in the nineteenth century, the city did not follow the example of other capitals, sprawling outward in endless ribbon developments, but ordered its new growth concentrically in clearly defined subcities (*Vorstädte*) forming a link between the commercial core and a uniquely beautiful surrounding landscape.

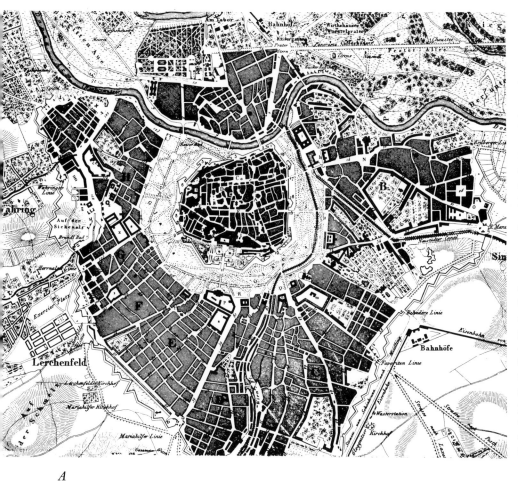

A

Fig. 79.

A) Plan of Vienna, after the fortifications had been eliminated (by 1860) and a landscaped park belt had been created around the old city core. Suburbs (C to H) were founded as a ring around this urban core, preventing for at least a century the destruction of a beautiful rural environment.

B) Plan of Böszörmöny, a typical Hungarian Alföld town. The Alföld plan developed from medieval campsites around the chieftain's stronghold. Under the democratic urban development preceding the conquest of Hungary by the Hapsburg monarchy, the guiding principle was equal land distribution, equal distance from the protective space in the city core, and radiating roads wide enough and straight enough to permit easy communication.

The Alföld towns of Hungary (*Fig. 79B*) might have furnished the other example for the concentric new towns of Israel, planned by East European immigrants. These Hungarian towns grew from campsites of the seminomadic Magyars, clustered around a central stronghold, but jealously aware of their independence. The result was a civic organism in which each group of citizens—from truck farmers to magistrates—were equidistant from the open assembly plaza in the core. Wide access roads allowed swift withdrawal to the core in times of peril and provided communication to the landholdings to which each citizen living in the city center was entitled.

If we should ever fulfill our latest craving for power over things, people, nature, and destiny, and establish a "strategic foothold" on the moon, the cosmic circle of the concentric city

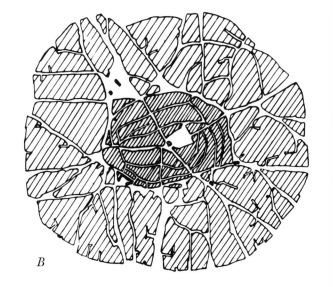

B

Fig. 80.

A) Moon City by Paul Maymont, 1965. The cosmic dream of a man's community as an image of the universe has finally been projected into outer space.

B) Four-thousand five-hundred-year-old ceramic patterns from the Indus Valley civilization, representing town or building plans in an ideal concentric symmetry that is eternally harmonious.

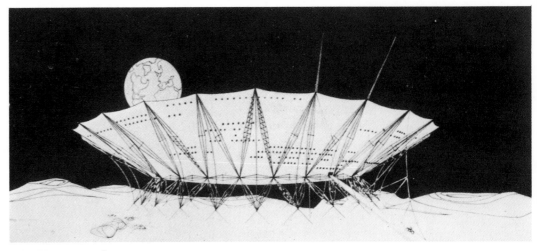

A

B

will have been closed. Indications are that moon cities will all be round, focused on Explorer 1001 in the dead center as the high priest of outer space scanning the unbreathing blackness for manifestations of cosmic law. He will have joined the ancient planners of the Indus Valley who left us like curses the imprints of their single-focused vision (*Figs. 80A, 80B*).

PROTO-ORTHOGONAL CONCEPTS

Medieval cities are works of art. We have to understand their pattern of growth like those of an individual palace, a statue, or a painting.*

This statement is characteristic of art-historical rhetoric, which is meaningless where the development of urban environment is concerned. Whatever "the pattern of growth" of a work of fine art may be (if, indeed, the terminology is not a contradiction in itself), it does not apply to the formation of spaces, volumes, and lines of communication which were responses to often contradictory regional, ethnic, economic, political, and religious developments. The ultimate "pattern" in the original meaning of "archetype" was never, as in a work of art, the revelation of a single creative individual, producing a singular, unrepeatable configuration; it was the predominance of one communal concept over other co-existing ones, and it repeated itself where similar conditions prevailed. The geomorphic community was superseded by concentric planning patterns when cosmic concepts became stronger than chthonian ones, and when diversification of knowledge and skills promised a better standard of living. But there is no clearly discernible break, and the two concepts—response to the form of the land and response to the single-power focus—are often intertwined (see *Figs. 31, 49*). They were arrested in their dynamic development when orthogonal planning became the dominant urban pattern. What Henri Bergson said about biological and zoological groups is just as valid for the history of urban origins: "The species cannot be defined by exclusive characteristics, but only by the tendency to emphasize them."

The third strain in the canon of urban history lacks the overt transcendental and aesthetic concepts of the concentric city. The first practitioners of the new planning concept were the

* Wolfgang Braunfels, *Mittelalterliche Stadtbaukunst in der Toscana* (1953).

81

last of the Mesopotamians and the first of the successful imperialists—the Assyrians. The change from cosmological to strategic city planning spread through the bad offices of the Assyrian-Babylonian-Chaldean power complex that dominated the Middle East between 900 and 600 B.C. Although they were perpetually hostile neighbors throughout their existence, Babylonians, Assyrians, and Chaldeans belonged to the same Semitic stock and had inherited the same Sumerian-Akkadian civilization. This explains the homogeneity of their city planning and justifies the omission of their separate social developments, which is the domain of the political historian. One important difference did, however, influence the origins of urban development. Babylonia remained a city-state despite repeated bids for world domination, while Assyria became the first successful empire, and Chaldea, or Neo-Babylonia, did translate the double legacy of city-state and empire into a capital image.

The Assyrians had been ubiquitous traders, rising from an obscure tribe in central Mesopotamia to become the barnacles on the flanks of Bronze Age cities. When they thought their chance for world conquest had come, they yielded their "connections" to the Phoenicians who, in turn, relinquished their accounts to the roaming Greeks before they perished in the attempt to conquer Rome. It is interesting to speculate who would have inherited the mail order business of antiquity if Pericles had succeeded in his imperialistic ambitions. The chief deity of the Assyrians was Marduk, who had been a minor offspring of the Sumerian water god Ea. In the middle of the second millennium B.C. the rising Babylonian dynasty ordered a drastic textbook revision to spiritualize the promises of imperialism. *Enuma elish,* the Babylonian Genesis, records how the eternally quarreling and carousing gods grew tired of supervising "action by authority." With abominable treachery they snared the two most powerful primordial deities, Tiamat, "The sweet waters dancing in the depth," and Apsu, the *ancien régime*'s fatherly authority. Then Ea, the all-powerful, willed Marduk to be reborn from the dying Apsu. The new junior partner was "surpassing all things in perfection—tall, strong, incomprehensible in his decisions, terrible to behold, with four eyes and four ears, fire blazing from his mouth when he spoke." Elated with the result, the gods transferred "power over all things" to Marduk, the Lance, as he was henceforth to be called, who started his career by killing Tiamat, fashioning from her halved body the round of the sky which he studded with new constellations of sun, moon, and stars "that changed destinies."

Fig. 81. Foley Square, New York City. The old County Court House with its Corinthian portico is the architectural incarnation of the nineteenth-century myth of historic nationalism. The new Federal Building with its modular curtain wall is the architectural incarnation of the twentieth-century myth of technology in the service of the state.

The toils of action were transferred to Lullu—"man be his name"—who had sprung from the blood of Tiamat's supporters, "to set the gods free."*

No historical analysis could explain more lucidly than this legend what brought about the second urban revolution. The primordial mother and the waters of the deep, representing Nature from which man had sprung, were eliminated. The many-faceted image of human ambition was streamlined into a hero-leader who personified power over people, nature, wealth, and destiny by brute force. By the eighth century B.C., Assyria ruled from the Mediterranean to the Persian Gulf and from Armenia to Egypt.

All planned cities are the interpreters of social myths. Nineteenth-century cities were called upon to visualize the myth of unlimited free enterprise, successful colonialism, and oligarchic

* As quoted in John Weir Perry, *Lord of the Four Quarters* (New York, 1966).

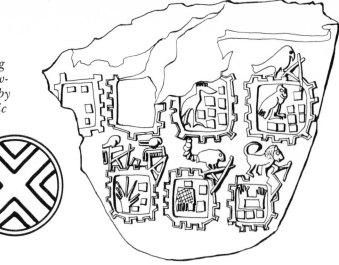

Fig. 82. Egyptian hieroglyph meaning "town" and prehistoric fragment showing the destruction of circular towns by early pharaohs, symbolized by heraldic animals.

government through eclectic architecture, intimating a political descent from the splendors of Imperial Rome (*Fig. 81*). The twentieth century is still in breathless pursuit of the technological city image, unaware that the mechanical age is already obsolete.

The designers for the sudden "urban explosion" in the ninth and eighth centuries B.C. had to find persuasive concepts to interpret the world domination myth. The self-sufficient city-states were wiped out by an imperium. To comprehend the conceptual diffusion that led from concentric regionalism to

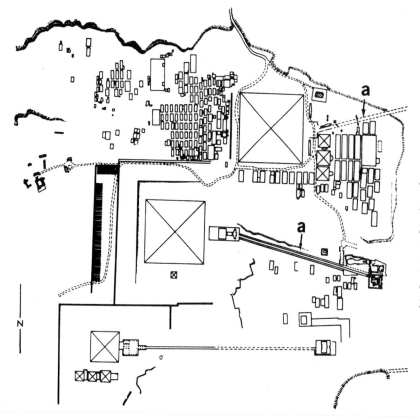

Fig. 83. The necropolis of Giza, Egypt. The layout is rectangular, in keeping with the sacred number 4. The approaches along the causeways (a) are linear, suggesting a continuation of the tomb-temple axes. In Cheops' and Chefren's causeways the oblique approach from the river emphasizes the prismatic mass of the pyramids.

84

ecumenical urbanism, it is important to realize that the vocabulary for the orthogonal empire-city was developed in the Egypt of the Old and Middle kingdoms, although the existence of cities as independent political-social organisms was totally alien to pharaonic rule.

Hieroglyphs and stele fragments prove that predynastic Nilotic towns resembled the concentric plans of Mesopotamia (*Fig. 82*). They differed from Sumer in favoring animistic rather than anthropomorphic deities, and lacked the topographical or architectural symbol of the world mountain. At the close of the fourth millennium B.C., a ruling class of unknown origin consolidated all land along the Nile under one centralized rule and reduced the city-states to *nomes,* or provinces. From the dynasty of Memphis (2900–2200 B.C.) onward, all Egyptian governments were theocratic. The chief executive, the pharaoh, was man-as-god and god-as-man, a concept of such serviceable ambiguity that it remained effective throughout all subsequent cultures where political and religious rule were unified. The principal line of extraterrestrial communication was the processional path of the man-god, oriented toward the Pole, or North Star. These ceremonial causeways were not ordinary roads with beginning and destination (*Fig. 83*); they were astronomical radius vectors joining the sun to the earth as the center of the universe. One might imagine that the focal point of the

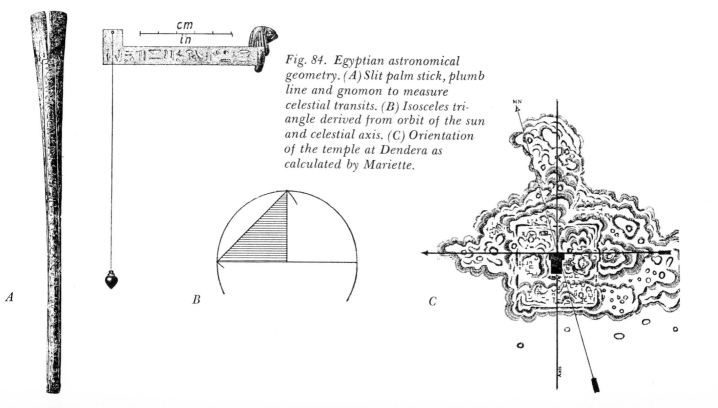

Fig. 84. Egyptian astronomical geometry. (A) Slit palm stick, plumb line and gnomon to measure celestial transits. (B) Isosceles triangle derived from orbit of the sun and celestial axis. (C) Orientation of the temple at Dendera as calculated by Mariette.

A

B

C

sun, the vertical shafts of the rays reaching the flat earth, and the ceremonial path of the sun god's representative, the pharaoh, suggested the triangle (*Figs. 84A, 84B, 84C*). From this, the most seminal figure in all geometry, arose the pyramid whose base is composed of two triangles. Its corners, oriented toward the compass points, made four the most sacred number of the Egyptians.

Some architectural concepts take many generations to achieve perfection. They filter slowly and fumblingly through average talents till they reach perfection and general application. The arch and vault are good examples of this long process. The invention of the orthogonal, movement-oriented environmental plan was achieved by an exceedingly rare stroke of genius. In about 2650 B.C., at the beginning of the Third Dynasty of the Old Kingdom, the Pharaoh Zoser commissioned his prime minister and physician, Imhotep, to start constructing a royal mastaba, or tomb chamber, which would serve his mummy as temporary home. In three successive stages, this mastaba became the first pyramid, stepped in five stages as were the ziggurats of Mesopotamia, but built in stone not in mud-brick—the first monumental stone construction known. The necropolis designed by Imhotep around this vertical symbol had no eggshells of Mesopotamian prototype clinging to it (*Fig. 85A*). It was an environmental achievement of inexplicable originality. The buildings and connecting open spaces are conceived centripetally, from the enclosing and delineating wall inward, and therefore pre-established as a coherent whole instead of growing by accretion. Casting around for a rational explanation, archaeologists and art historians have assumed that Sakkara was a re-creation of the capital of Memphis across the Nile, whose whitewashed city walls were famous. Considering that Egyptian cities, even capitals, were built of perishable material, without foundations or discernible plans—as were all secular structures —this is most unlikely. In the light of later history, Sakkara seems to be the first example of the "heavenly city" that persisted for 4,000 years until the time of West European Baroque. The otherworldly image was re-created as a sort of countercity on earth, a promise to mortal man.

The enclosure of Sakkara, 1,800 by 900 feet, constructed of exquisite stone-block buttresses rhythmically spaced, raised a barrier between the profane world and the vertical summit of the divine tomb. From the moment of entry through the single gate, the compulsion to move forward into its sacred precinct became inescapable. The entrance colonnade had no architectural termination. It was the first perspective axis leading to an open

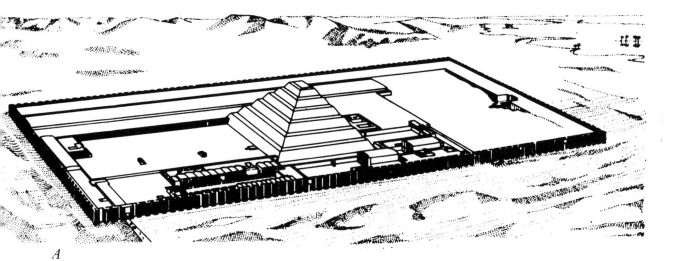

A

Fig. 85.

(A) The temple city of the pharaoh Zoser at Sakkara, Old Kingdom, 2650 B.C. Oldest known preplanned orthogonal building group representing a Town of the Dead.

(B) Perspective line-up of simulated chapel elevations without interior space along the Heb-Sed court, where the pharaoh had to run a ceremonial race at his jubilee to prove his continued fitness. The plan emphasizes linear motion.

B

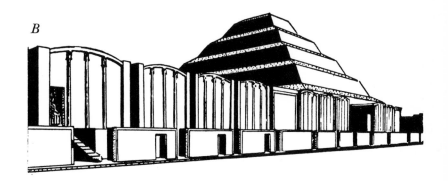

plaza, the empty Grand Court which, like all true plazas, offered alternatives of direction. Passages, turns, entries, and exits led into chapels and halls of unknown purposes; small and long courts, and, finally, the funeral temple on the far side of the pyramid impelled the visitor forward. The fact that the pyramid was not placed in direct line with the entrance indicates the deliberate incentive to forward motion. Some of the pre-Sargonic temples and some early palaces in Sumer had complex interior-exterior relationships. The uniqueness of Sakkara lies in the calculated variety of environment—a necropolis for the royal dead, whose presence was more real to the Egyptians than that of the anonymous living in the mud city of Memphis. Elevations vary, from the "row housing" of identical chapels whose dummy facades are backed with rubble to emphasize their purely visual aspect (Fig. 85B) to units of varying height, width, and decora-

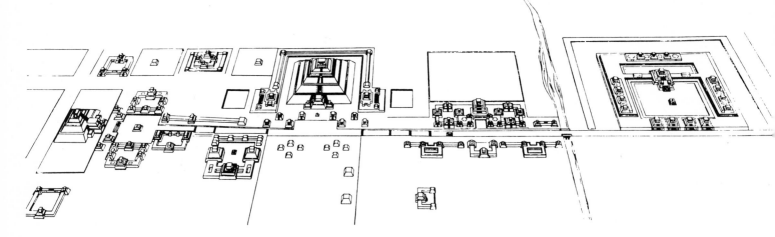

Fig. 86. Schematic presentation of the ceremonial center of Teotihuacán near Mexico City, built from ca. 200 B.C. onward. The affinity with the Egyptian necropolis at Giza (see Fig. 83) is conceptual. A central "road of the dead" serves as a ceremonial causeway, whose ritualistic use connects the main structures. The number 4, which had symbolized symmetry and order for the Egyptians, has been employed as dominant module for building groups and terraces. From George Kubler, The Art and Architecture of Ancient America *(1962).*

tive treatment—attached columns, long-stemmed lotus strips, and square pier buttressing. Entrances reveal nothing from the outside. The bent-axis approach demands entry and participation of the visitor who found the planar-angular emphasis of the exterior elevations continued in the angular space divisions of the interiors.

We do not know whether Imhotep's concept had any secular offspring. The cities of Egypt vanished without a trace, indicating a sharp separation between secular and sacred construction—the one unparalleled in corrosion, the other in durability. From the pitiful rubble heaps of Egyptian towns one can draw the confirmation of Ernst Curtius' statement, "Urban character and temple domination stand everywhere in opposition to each other."

The most fruitful ideas for the future Assyrian and Hellenistic orthogonal cities came from the burial grounds and temples of later pharaohs, inspired by Imhotep's linear-orthogonal prototype. The vast necropolis at Giza is a lesson in systematic orientation despite 400 years of continuous use (see *Fig. 83*). The three large pyramids stand in an angular relationship to each other which aligns but does not obscure. The flat mastabas of court officials and dependents form street blocks similar to the regulation housing of later Roman military camp towns. The causeways, from the valley temples on the Nile to the funeral temples in front of the pyramids, follow a calculated line of approach that is not yet bound by undeviating axiality, but keep a slightly oblique direction that brings the gleaming angles of the pyramids into full effect. Archaeologists see a mere coincidence in the close resemblance between the Giza necropolis layout and the ceremonial center of Teotihuacán (*Fig. 86*), built near Mexico City, probably by the Olmec people in the last centuries of the first millennium B.C. But the variation in size that distinguishes Chefren from his father Cheops is echoed in the two pyramids at Teotihuacán, only by later settlers identified with sun and moon. Whether they, too, were royal tombs, and whether the geometric structures and the stepped altars around them served a death cult, is really quite unimportant. What matters is a complete harmony of concept between the Egyptian and the Mexican site, based on linear motion.

Apart from the "housing development" of El-Lahun, the New Kingdom city of Amarna remains the only Egyptian urban design of which we have a record. It is characteristic of a basically anti-urban people that Ikhnaton's heretical capital Akhetaten was leveled to the ground after the death of the mad monarch in 1350 B.C. But during the great monotheistic revolution, the fame of this unprecedented new town, with its huge geometric palace and with temple enclosures open to the sky, must have spread throughout the Middle East. Amarna itself is a planless conglomeration of large and small houses unrelated to the royal road, the earliest known artery having a cross-axial intersection, complete with overpass (*Fig. 87*). It permitted the

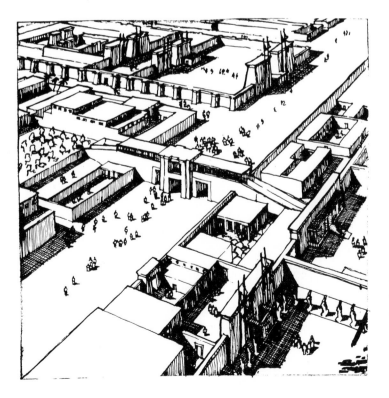

Fig. 87. Royal road in Amarna, Egypt, with overpass. New Kingdom, fourteenth century B.C.

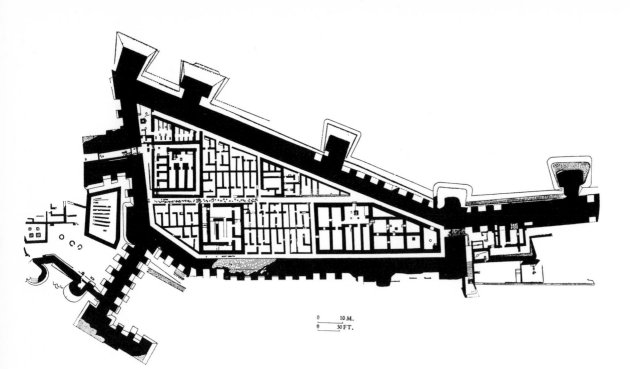

Fig. 88. The Egyptian fortress of Uronarti, Middle Kingdom, ca. 1900 B.C. It became the prototype of most fortresses built in Europe and Asia during the next 3,000 years.

king to cross on foot from his official to his domestic palace without descending to earth.

The construction of Amarna coincides with the first upsurge of Assyrian imperialistic ambitions under Ashuruballil and Kurigalzu (1365–1324 B.C.). The influence of the orthogonal-geometric message from Egypt expressed itself in the square-walled reconstruction of the concentric sacred areas that the Sumerians left behind. They adopted watchtowers, deep buttressing, and geometric interior spaces from the squared Egyptian fortresses of El-Kab and Uronarti of the militant Middle Kingdom (*Fig. 88*). The most important feature copied by the Assyrians was the concept of "the royal progress" through the city which thus became hallowed by the rulers.

Nineveh, capital of the second Assyrian Empire which came to power after 900 B.C., had probably the earliest fully developed *via triumphalis* (84 feet wide); it connected the palace of Assurbanipal with the Ishtar Temple where all rulers assumed kingship (*Fig. 89*). Twelve gates connected twelve interior streets with twelve exterior roads. The decisive difference between royal road and communication street is illustrated by a decree from Nineveh from the eighth century that whoever will encroach on the "path of kings" shall be impaled on the eave of his house.

Nineveh was wicked, "made of gold," with enormous angular

90

palaces, one of which housed Assurbanipal's library. Although the palace library of Gudea at Sumerian Lagash was 1,300 years older, the world owes to Assyria the library as a standard fixture of cities. There are no libraries in villages.

Sennacherib, who loved Nineveh, constructed the first aqueduct for its water supply. It is a brilliant engineering feat in ashlar masonry, which the Romans copied by raising the water channel on arches. The Assyrian aqueducts carried man's encroachment on the natural environment one step beyond the Ubaidian-Sumerian irrigation system, which after 2,000 years of alternate flooding and evaporation had started the fatal trend toward soil salination, destroying the agriculture and with it the cities of southern Mesopotamia.

If Nineveh was wicked, Borsippa was pious (*Fig. 90*). In the ancient Sumerian tradition, Ezida, its temple district in a walled

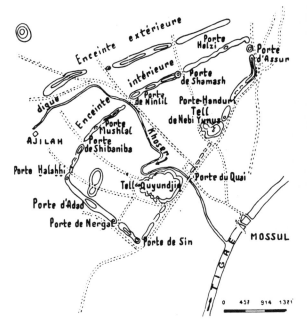

Fig. 89. Plan of Nineveh, capital of the Assyrians, rebuilt in the ninth century B.C. *The plan is most instructive as a transition from the inherited concentric concept to orthogonal-linear divisions. Twelve city gates (portes) pierced the interior city wall (enceinte interieure), and provided the termination points of wide streets that subdivided the city into superblocks.*

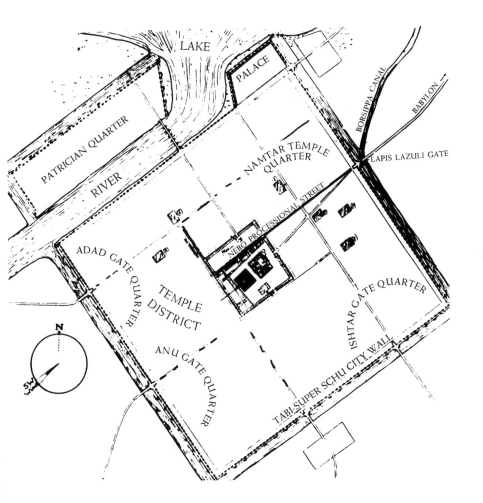

Fig. 90. Assyrian Borsippa in the seventh century B.C. *The perfect orthogonal plan has been achieved. If recent conclusions about the influence of Western cultures on the formation of Chinese city-states are correct, then the Borsippa plan is the link between the Egyptian temple temenos and the "forbidden city" enclosures of Peking and other Chinese cities of the first millennium* A.D.

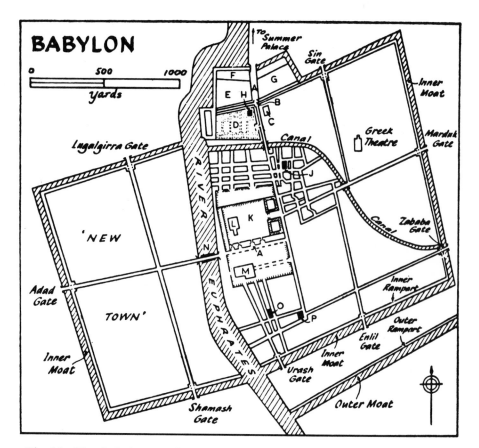

BABYLON

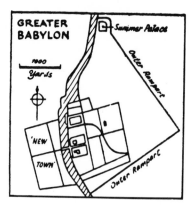

GREATER BABYLON

A. Processional Way
B. Ishtar Gate
C. Temple of Ninmah
D. Southern Citadel
E. Principal Citadel
F. Northern Citadel
G. Defensive structure
H. Hanging Gardens
J. Temple of Ishtar
K. Etemenanki
L. Ziggurat
M. Esagila
N. Bridge
O. Temple of Gula
P. Temple of Ninurta

Fig. 91. Neo-Babylon as rebuilt in 680 B.C. and completed by the Chaldeans in the sixth century. The orthogonal city has been perfected. The official buildings form a monumental center spine, flanked by the regulated river and the processional road connecting the Ishtar Gate and the palace with the temple of the city god (P). Again there are nine gates, but zoning and waterway distribution show highly practical concerns.

enclosure, was oriented toward the intercardinal points. The perfect square of the city area was protected by a water-filled moat and a city wall, pierced by six gates and six roads. The seventh, or Lapis Lazuli, gate was the terminus of the Nebo Road leading only to the sacred precinct. The interior of Nineveh was divided into nine superblocks formed by 3 times 3 urban quarters. The numerological significance of this plan was 3, 6, 9, which, added, gave again the cross-number 9 ($3 + 6 = 9 = 18$; $1 + 8 = 9$).

The identification of philosophy and religion with mathematics—expressed in the dictum of Pythagoras that all things are number—arose from the same search for transmissible order and power symbols that created cities. Numerology and planning are inextricably interwoven. Mathematics is an urban achievement. The specialized community of men needed an intellectual tender outside the hazards of semantic interpretation. This urban currency was the significance of numbers. Applied to city planning, numbers expressed the hierarchical importance of spaces and buildings. Sumerian-Babylonian numerology, the system adopted by subsequent Western civilizations, rested on 6. As an echo of prehistoric matriarchates, 6 was the perfect female number, the sum of its divisors that are less than itself. Therefore 6 quarters, 6 gates, and, later, 6 portico columns, their height 6 times the diameter of the base. Infinitely varied arrangements dealt with the antecedent 3, the triad, sacred to religions the world over. The counterpart of 6 was 7, which is male, indivisible, unattached to other figures. Seven is as finite as 5, yet superior to the primordial 5 of the planets by being a divisor of 28, the next highest perfect number after 6. While all of this sounds utterly ridiculous to contemporary ears, it should be considered in the light of the unabated obsession of architects with modules and numerical series—Mies van der Rohe's faith in the 24-foot module, Buckminster Fuller's "magic triangle," and Le Corbusier's Modulor.*

In 671 B.C., Essarhaddon finally realized the thousand-year-old Assyrian dream of conquering Egypt. He had himself anointed pharaoh and was carried in triumph along the famous royal road connecting the temple cities of Karnak and Luxor. In 680, he replanned the city of Babylon which his father, Sennacherib, had destroyed and turned into a swamp in one of the choleric rages that seem to be the occupational disease of dictators. Babylon came back to life as the first preplanned orthogonal city (*Fig. 91*). Its plan proceeded neither from the sacred center nor from the accumulation of dwellings but from a system of major and minor roads, coordinated with the gates and access to the river and the canal. The Euphrates was tamed to become part of this inner city communication network, regulated within stone embankments and a canal that prevented flooding. Spanning the river was a stone bridge with a removable wooden center section.

The main gate, dedicated to Ishtar, combined the decorative lavishness of an Egyptian temple pylon with the thick fortification of a Hittite mountain stronghold. The double walls and gigantic towers were so feared and admired that they became the eighth wonder of the world. Beside the cavernous citadel

* Le Corbusier, in *Modulor 2,* 1954, explains his inspiration from Hindu and pre-Socratic sources.

93

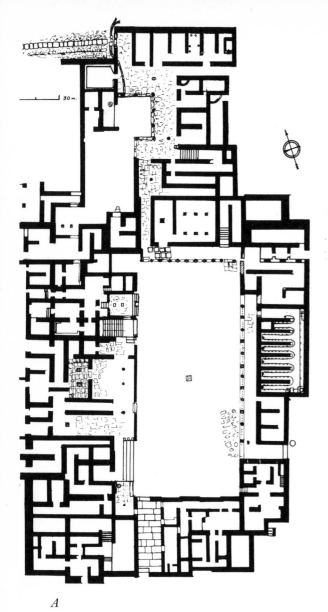

A

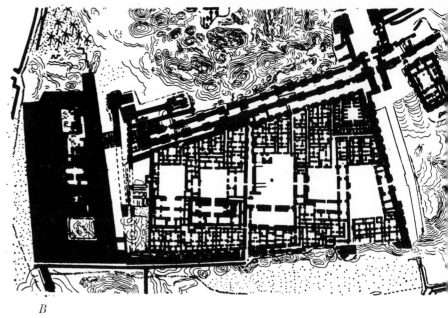

B

Fig. 92. *The Assyrians were thoroughly eclectic, choosing the components of their orthogonal plans from the expiring Bronze Age cities. The five palace units of Babylon were adaptations of Cretan palaces that combined a large refuge and assembly court with audience halls, residential quarters, and vast storage facilities.*

A) The Cretan Palace of Malia from the early second millennium.

B) The palaces of Babylon, flanked to the left by the impregnable walls of the citadel and protected against the open country by the famous double-wall system.

stretched the largest palace of the ancient world. It was composed of five individual palaces built around a central court, in the Minoan manner (*Figs. 92A, 92B*); these could be closed off from each other by blocking narrow connecting gates, or could form a crossaxial enfilade of spaces. In the center of the city rose Etemenank, the Tower of Babel. The preplanned concept of the city can be read from the residential and parochial quarters (*Fig. 93*). They are unrelated to the cumulative maze of Mesopotamian tradition (see *Fig. 43*). The street and the plaza have become urban regulators.

Although the city was completed by the short-lived Chaldean dynasty (626–539 B.C.), its conception is Assyrian. In one of those ironies of history, the same people who "made the earth tremble, made the world a wilderness, and destroyed the cities thereof," in their inexhaustible greed for other people's urban wealth, advanced beyond the concept of the regional city-state. They lifted the taboo against traders within city walls, remembering perhaps their own origin as peddlers of the Bronze Age. Babylon had a merchant quarter in the New Town. As a precaution, the wooden beams that formed the center section of the bridge over the canal that divided the new city from the palace city were removed at night; but in a further move toward the ecumenical character of a cosmopolitan city, one of the huge spaces outside the palace enclosure was designated the Square of the Foreign People.

The unique role of the Assyrians in the continuity of urban history lies in their conceptual distinction between tradition and innovation. The ancient sacred cities of the Sumerians and Akkadians—Nippur, Babylon, Sippar, Assur, Harran—were not spared destruction. But once subdued and rendered harmless, they became *kidinnutu*, free cities exempted from corvée work, taxes, seizure of cattle, and conscription. This system was one of the many bequests left to Rome and the medieval Holy Roman Empire, where tribute-free cities lost their privileges only after World War II.

The second conceptual crystallization of the Assyrians as city founders was the clear distinction between the hierarchical significance of urban areas—the "withinness" and "withoutness"

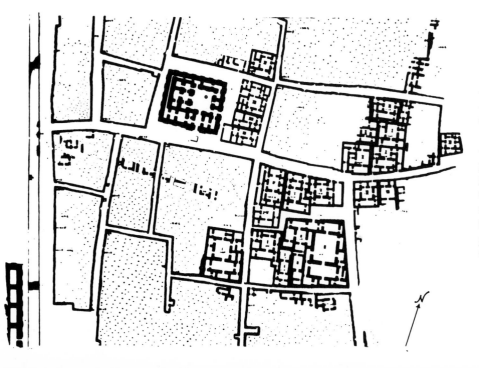

Fig. 93. A sector in the city of Babylon. A systematic layout of major and minor roads is clearly recognizable, based on orthogonal intersections. Buildings are fitted into the street pattern rather than street passages fitted between continuous buildings, as in the concentric cities. The interior court has remained the nucleus of each residential lot, as in previous plans, but a larger degree of uniformity in house plans is evident.

of areas under city domination. In the spontaneous urbanization of Sumer, no special significance was given to distance between city core and city limit, and no exceptional sanctity to the gates. The Assyrians who had adopted from their Egyptian idols a fanatical faith in bureaucratic organization as the highest guarantee of sustained power, codified territorial status. The forbidden city, or *kirhu,* was surrounded by the *libbi ali,* the center city for true citizens and functionaries. This again was surrounded by a wall whose gates were named according to the will of the god of gates and the protector of each outer city sector named after its particular gate. Beyond lay the suburbs and the harbor section with its special legislative status. The Assyrian city, then, was based less on faith in a street network than on faith in walls. To keep invaders out, Nebuchadnezzar built a wall from Babylon to Kish, in 600 B.C., 400 years before the celebrated Chinese wall and 2,500 years before the Berlin "solution."

The revolution brought about by the Assyrians, then, was based on a proto-orthogonal urban plan that moved from the defensive wall inward toward the urban center, on a hierarchic territoriality within the city that was no longer derived from material possession, as in Sumer, but from social and physical proximity or distance to the "forbidden palace" in the center of the world.

The ancient Hebrews, whose unfortunate habitat on the main highway between Syria and Egypt made them the prey of every conflict between north and south, did not conceal their delight at having both their archenemies liquidated. Of Egypt, Lamentations says: "And when I shall put thee out, I will cover the heavens, and make the stars thereof dark; I will cover the sun with a cloud, and the moon will give no light." The obituary notice for the Assyrians on the other hand is full of spite, of unconcealed *Schadenfreude:* "Behold the Assyrian was a cedar . . . the water made him great . . . . And strangers, the terrible of the nations, have cut him off and have left him. . . . And all the peoples of the earth are gone from his shadow."

The strangers who did the cutting down were the Persians. They had been recently weaned from a tribal existence, and were too busy emulating the Assyrians as world conquerors to have any constructive influence on the origins of urban environment. Like all Indo-European invaders they were seminomadic and anti-urban, and their main cities, Susa and Ecbatana, were of pre-Persian origin. Coming at the very end of the Bronze

Fig. 94. *Unless the Assyrians departed radically from the world-wide custom of rendering in clay models faithful replicas of existing house types, one must assume that their extraordinary structural skill succeeded in erecting ten-story-high buildings in mud brick with "curtain wall" façades. The load-bearing skeleton in the interior can only have been wood.*

Age, they played a role in history similar to scavengers in the animal world. By burning the cities of Asia Minor and Greece, the Persians cleared the ground for the second urban age of Western civilization—the rise of the orthogonal Hellenistic city.

A note on population figures and city sizes should be inserted here. There are no reliable records about either, and it seems futile to repeat the more-or-less educated guesses of various scholars. Ancient figures connoted symbolic bigness or smallness rather than quantitative units. This can be verified from the reports of Herodotus about the size of the cities he visited. As a good Greek skeptic he reports the figures he was told, adding frequently, "which I consider impossible." The Romans introduced census taking, but even these records are unreliable because each emperor was obsessed with the ambition to rule over a Rome larger than that of his predecessors.* Estimates of the size of Babylon under Chaldean rule vary from 200,000 to 1 million, and those of Chan-chan, capital of the Peruvian Chimús, from 60,000 to 500,000. Densities per square acre or mile are even harder to guess because we do not know how high domestic buildings were or how many children per family were average. Andrae has excavated clay models of houses in Assur which have set-backs, as in New York, and are up to ten stories high (*Fig. 94*). If they were really "apartment buildings," their construction in mud-brick and wood framing would have been an extraordinary achievement, and the population they accommodated immense. Since this book is concerned less with statistics than concepts, figures, necessarily unreliable, need not overly concern us.

* Jérôme Carcopino, *Daily Life in Ancient Rome* (New Haven, Conn., 1966).

The next wave of empire builders were the Macedonians. By ethnic origin they belonged to a mixture of Celtic tribes inhabiting the most northerly part of the Greek peninsula and Greeks at the most southerly boundary of the Balkans. The Macedonian chieftains who ruled the country at Pella were Illyrian-Thracian mountaineers. Their society was matriarchic, their bodies tattooed, and they worshiped Dionysus the goat in uncouth happenings. Remnants of the southward-migrating Hellenic people settled among them late in the second millennium B.C. The strongholds of the Hellenic people clustered around Mount Olympus whose indigenous mythology was updated according to Indo-European traditions. Philip of Macedon (359-336 B.C.), whose heart belonged to the Attic culture in the south, had larger territorial ambitions than the half-civilized fringe of the Greek world. He decided to tear Greece from the teeth of Persia, which had been actively engaged since the beginning of the fifth century B.C. in stamping out Hellenism. His son Alexander the Great (336-323 B.C.) inherited a superb military organization and the obsession to apply the Greek city-state ethics to an ecumenical empire. Demos and ecumene—nation and state—were abstractions of Greek philosophy, not tangible political realities. To give them place and function, Alexander relied on inspiration from the Assyro-Babylonian urban developments rather than on the territorial parochialism of the Hellenic polis. Yet it would be a mistake to discount his ideological awareness of the city nucleus as a generative force. Alexander's tutor was after all Aristotle, who arrived in the Macedonian citadel of Pella in 343 B.C. when his pupil was thirteen years old. He left seven years later after his employer, King Philip, had been murdered.

It has been asserted that Aristotle's influence on the young prince was vitiated by a fierce antagonism between father and son and by the black magic of Alexander's mother, who was a Thracian witch. But seven years of exposure to one of the most fertile intellects ever produced by mankind left its imprint.

99

Aristotle's modifications of the philosophy of Plato, with whom he had maintained a twenty-year partnership at the Athens Academy, must have occurred in Pella. Against the epiphenomenon of the soul, Aristotle postulated the concrete, experimental occupation with *bios*, life. Plato's changeless *stasis* was set in motion by Aristotle's *dynamis*, and the nature of created things viewed as potential rather than completed. The common grounds of Plato and Aristotle were the conception of virtue as knowledge and the will to act for the polis, the community of men, which was the frontier of the Greek social horizon. Plato and Aristotle sketched ideal communities differing only insofar as Plato's is qualitative, based on cosmological predestination derived from Mesopotamian and Hindu sources, while Aristotle's urbanism was legalistic, quantitatively controlled, and based on logical realism.

The community as the matrix of human action was established as an a priori concept in Alexander when he became king in 336 B.C. Entering Babylon in 332 B.C., he found a new city image that differed sharply from the Aristotelian urban philosophy. Its most conspicuous difference from the tribal concept was the shift from city as symbol of an ethnic nation to symbol of a political state. Etymologically, "nation" derives from the Latin *nasci*, "to be born," while state derives from *status*, "position." It is a distinction as fateful as that between kingdom and imperium. For all Bronze Age urbanists, the concept of "unity of place and action" had been binding. This ethnic-territorial

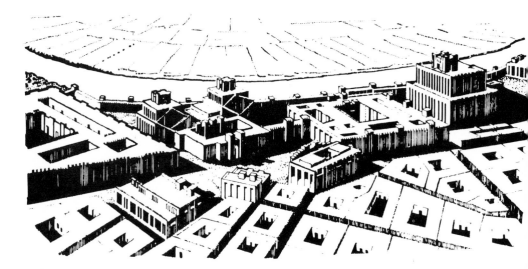

Fig. 95. Reconstruction of the main palace and temple area in Assur. The stepped ziggurat, with a tiny temple on top, and the gigantic Anu and Adad complex, with two ziggurat towers, face the Tigris Canal, the greatest engineering achievement of the trade-oriented Assyrians.

Fig. 96. The United Nations Secretariat, New York, which symbolizes its message to the world across the river rather than toward the city.

unity was broken by Assyrian-Chaldean imperialism. No longer did city make the ruler, but the ruler made the city. The cosmic or tribal justification or territorial possession gave way to the claim of "land won by the spear."

The effect on city planning was tremendous. According to excavations, the great palaces, temples, and public buildings of Assur faced the river embankment that had been regulated by a 4,900-foot-long sea wall and esplanade (*Fig. 95*). The *axis mundi*, the center, which prevailed in the ancient Mesopotamian cities rebuilt by their Assyrian conquerors, was now replaced by an extroverted display of power, facing the conquerable world. The change in concept from metaphysical to mundane power symbolism can still be read from the gilded cupolas and the dazzling marble lacework of the Basilica of St. Mark's and the

Palace of the Doges, signaling Venetian power to the sea, from London's Westminster Palace, turning its giddy Tudor-Renaissance broadside toward the Thames, and from the United Nations Secretariat in New York, proclaiming a fictitious unity of nations to the East River (*Fig. 96*).

The identification of the city with territorial conquest rather than with national tradition led to a proliferation of "royal cities" with special privileges and obligations. From the middle of the first millennium B.C., that is, from the beginning of the second urban age, there existed two kinds of capitals: strategic and ethnic. Political capitals were and are changed at will according to the political fortunes of the rulers—Constantine's move from Rome to Constantinople, Peter the Great's founding of St. Petersburg, Jocelyn Kubitchek's downgrading of Rio de Janeiro in favor of Brasília, to name a few examples. In strongly ethnic societies, the fortune of the entire nation was identified with the fate of the historic rather than the strategic capital. Its reduction in status was a special act of contempt by a conqueror. To the vanquished group the mother city remained forever valid. Catalans revere Barcelona and not Madrid, Ukrainians Kiev and not Moscow, Armenians Ani and not Ankara, and the image of Jerusalem has preserved Jewish identification through 2,000 years of diaspora.

The young Alexander, embarked on world conquest, found in the Assyro-Babylonian administrative and military organization the instruments to slough off the ethnic urban concepts of his teacher. Instead of the Aristotelian division of citizens into barbarians to be conquered by *despotes* ("masters") and Greeks to be ruled by *hegemones* ("leaders"), he introduced *homonoia* and *koinonia,* human accord within the fellowship of men, regardless of race or creed. His cooperative ideal was no longer the isolated, race-conscious, world-isolated polis. The new ideal was *cosmopolis,* the universal city. Instead of local idol worship, religion turned toward ethics, the mutual agreement of right conduct.

Elating as these concepts must sound to Western ears of the democratic twentieth century, their ultimately fatal flaw was that their revelationary truth was accessible only to the ruler. His own vision made Alexander into *kosmokrator,* crowned with the *corona* of Apollo and living in a tent whose dome rested on four golden poles and was covered with the sun, moon, and stars of the firmament.

Alexander's testament (323 B.C.) demanded mass emigrations

from Europe to Asia and Asia to Europe "for the purpose of bringing these two great continents into mutual accord (*homonoia*), for the establishment of cities by synoecism, the ancient Greek custom of the amalgamation of small communities with similar economic and religious interests; and the promotion of racially mixed marriages to further *oikeiosis*—domestic ties."* No mere dreamer, Alexander added provisions for the building of 1,000 men-of-war to subdue recalcitrant nations unwilling to be saved. His policy, "Redeem the world, and send in the Marines," should sound familiar to American ears.

Despite an understandable inclination to debunk the excesses of nineteenth-century Grecophile hero worship which conveniently overlooked the shady side of Macedonian imperialism, there was more to Alexander than the exploits of a power-drunk madman who had a Messiah complex, epileptic fits, and ambidextrous sexual habits. He changed the environment of man. His amalgamation of Aristotelian ethics with the needs and functions of secular society not yet conscious of its changing status was of shattering originality. Without Alexander's concept of the world as *oikumene* and of himself as "the reconciler of the world," the spread of Christianity would not have been possible.

It is customary to credit the philosopher Zeno, who founded the Stoic school, with having provided the ideological basis of urban Hellenism. But Zeno was born on Cyprus twelve years after the island had welcomed the Macedonian, in 332 B.C., as liberator from the brutal exploitation of the Persians. In 300 B.C., he reached Athens, twenty-three years after Alexander's death, and started teaching in the Painted Stoa from which his philosophy derived its name. As a Semitic Phoenician, conscious of the prejudices of Persians and Hellenic Greeks, he must have absorbed the ecumenical message of Alexander with his mother's milk. He paid him handsome tribute in many immortal epigrams. On an imaginary tombstone he wrote:

You who pass here: if thou art Syrian, say to me *salam;* if thou art a Phoenician, say *naidios;* if a Greek say *chaire*. They are all the same. . . . We all live in the same country, and that country is the world.

Another epigram denounced Semitic eye-for-an-eye justice: "Not: may I perish if I do not revenge myself on you, but may I perish if I do not make you my friend."

* Quoted from Diodorus Siculus in Ernest Barker, *From Alexander to Constantine* (New York, 1956).

And 300 years before Christ: "Love is a god, being a fellow worker about the salvation of the city."*

Stoicism became a philosophy that for the first time in the history of human thought did not draw on myth or nature, but based its conclusions on the relationship of man to man. Its completely urban character explains the spread and duration of stoic philosophy for the next 700 years through the period that saw the formation of Christian theology.

As his temporary capital Alexander had chosen Babylon. There he centered civil service, tax collection, and military planning which would become prototypical for Rome and the Western world; and there he learned to respect the image of the city which his native Pella had lacked. For his permanent capital he selected Egypt, where he could combine a highly advantageous strategic and economic position with the prestige of the oldest known civilization. Much of his spectacular success in subjugating what then was the world lay in a carefully emphasized respect for historical continuity. Wherever he conquered, he paid homage to the local deities. Even if he destroyed the government, he maintained native law, and permitted the troop levies to wear native dress. It is amazing how literally the Romans later copied the administrative details of Alexander without providing the image of the conquering hero.

On his arrival in Egypt, Alexander made the long, difficult voyage through the western desert to the oasis of Siwa and the Amon-Re sanctuary. He was anointed a pharaoh and given the secret advice—favorable, of course—of the resident oracle. Then he founded the first and foremost of many cities that would bear his name. The architect he entrusted with the conception of the new capital entered immortality in a manner that must be highly recommended to other ambitious young planners. In the Introduction to Book II of his *Ten Books on Architecture,* Vitruvius tells how Dinocrates, an unknown architect, had in vain hoped for recommendations to the great city founder. Getting no place, he decided to recommend himself with his "natural gifts." Stripped and pleasantly anointed, he appeared among the gray flannel togas of Alexander's planning commission, wearing no more than a chaplet of poplar leaves on his head, a lion skin over one shoulder, and a club of authority in his hand. Having caught the emperor's attention, he introduced himself as

* Ernest Barker, *op. cit.*

a Macedonian architect who brings thee ideas and designs worthy of renown. I have made a design for the shaping of Mount Athos into the statue of a man in whose left hand I represented a very spacious fortified city, and in his right a bowl to receive the water of all the streams which are in that mountain so that it may pour from the bowl into the sea.

A few thousand years later (1921) Bruno Taut landed the job as replanner of the German city of Magdeburg by arousing public attention with sensational proposals to convert the peaks of the Alps into a city of crystalline shapes (*Fig. 24*). In Dinocrates' plan, the brilliant monarch saw the clever combination of urbanism and aesthetics but had highly practical reservations about economics and location. Alexandria, the new capital, became a creative collaboration. It was built on the site of

Fig. 97. Plan of Alexandria by the Macedonian architect Dinocrates. The city was founded in 331 B.C. and perfected and completed by the Ptolomaic dynasty. The road system is the generator of the plan. Orthogonality is adjusted to the variations of the site. Even at their very best, Roman and Renaissance builders would never surpass this plan.

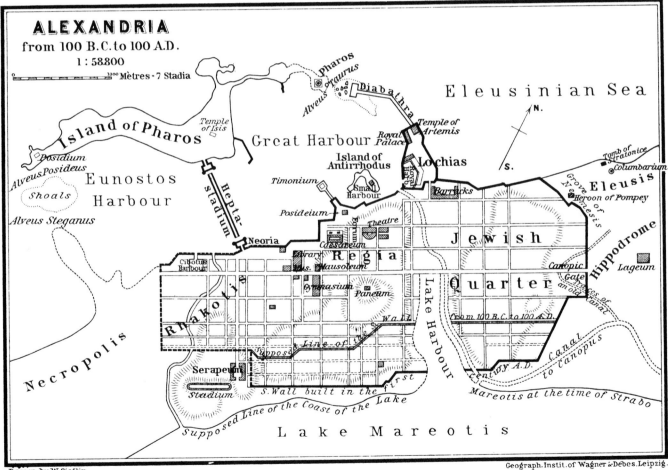

an ancient Egyptian settlement, Rhakotis, between two natural harbors and a large inland lake that joined the new harbor with the Canopic arm of the Nile and, therefore, with the African hinterland (*Fig. 97*). The elaborate founding ceremonies illustrated the two most decisive changes from concentric to orthogonal and from centrifugal to centripetal planning. The periphery of the new city was fixed by sacred cord bearers in the way Egyptian temple enclosures had been laid out, and the lines of future fortifications were indicated by millet. Cities were no longer centrifugal power centers, dispensing fate to their inhabitants; they were containers, maintained centripetally by the spoils of empire stored within their walls. All new imperial cities founded after the example of Alexandria were nodes in a vast network of interests and communications whose importance was extrinsic, no longer immanent.

The young emperor never saw his most lasting achievement completed. He died in Babylon after conquering northern India (323 B.C.) and returned to Egypt wrapped in a golden cloak and encased in a glass coffin. In a fine example of submission to the living and revenge on the dead, the priests of the Amon Temple refused him a place among the pharaohs and Alexander was buried at the crossroads of his own city, Alexandria. At the time of Julius Caesar's visit there in 48 B.C., the dynasty of the Ptolomies had realized their own bid for immortality by the completion of the capital. The orthogonal multifocused harbor city, the *portus*, surpassed the Babylonian prototype in the perfect interaction of the principles which would from the third century onward serve as measure of a true world metropolis: open society, overseas trade, conversion of goods, banking, monumentality, and cultural leadership.

The axes of Alexandria were two main avenues, 200 feet wide, lined with marble columns, and supplied with underground drainage canals. The east-west Canopic canal connected the sea at Eunostos Harbor with the canal to the Nile, while the north-south crossroad, called Soma after Alexander's burial enclosure, was the thoroughfare from the gigantic inland lake Mareotis (today a fraction of its original size) to the Great Harbor. Both axes served the Regia, a walled-in city within the city, that held palaces, administration buildings, and the Mouseion, the home of the muses of philology, science, mathematics, and geography, and of 100 invited scholars of all races and creeds who did not teach but "furthered knowledge." The only difference from the Institute for Advanced Studies in

Princeton was the patronage of the monarch who made the appointments, supplied the funds, and participated in some of the projects. Euclid, the mathematician, Eratosthenes, who measured the circumference of the earth, and Ptolomy, the astronomer, Philo, the Jewish philospher, Archimedes, the physicist, the translaters of the Septuagint—in short the Who's Who of Hellenistic culture worked for 500 years, from 300 B.C. to A.D. 200, in an ideal environment of laboratories, workshops, observatories, a dining hall, a zoo, a park, and the greatest library of antiquity. The chief librarian was the head of the Mouseion because his work was considered most vital to all the various endeavors. There were 500,000 scrolls in the stacks and a catalog of 100 more.

It is one of the characteristic frauds of Western history that the Moslems are blamed for a spectacular bonfire that destroyed this collection of ancient learning, when Amr captured Alexandria in 641. Most of the manuscripts had already been burned by Christian Copts who descended in wilder and wilder raids on the pagan city after the advent of Christianity and the founding of monasteries in the Wadi Natrum.* Their illiterate hatred was less spiritual than national, the revenge of the native Egyptians on the Greek usurpers. In 415, they lynched the Platonic woman philosopher and mathematician, Hypatia, on her way to the Mouseion, and started 1,000 years of anti-urbanism that undid what Alexander had planned. When the Caliph Amr conquered Egypt in 641, he was helped in his conquest of Alexandria by the anti-Greek monastic mob who sealed their own doom by replacing Greek comopolitanism with Islamic religious fanaticism.

The real antagonist of the Christian mobs was not the Mouseion, whose significance they could hardly grasp, but the cult of Serapis whose temple—the Serapeum—stood in the center of the old native quarters of Rhakotis. The urban significance of this synthetic deity, created by Ptolomy I Soter, is great because he illustrates the unabashed pragmatism of Hellenistic cosmopolitanism. Anthropomorphic in shape, Serapis combined Osiris, the most widely accepted and beloved god of light and resurrection, with Apis, the bull of strength and fertility, to whom were added various characteristics of Dionysus, the reveler and god of *joie de vivre,* and of Pluto, the god of wealth. There could have been no more felicitous reinterpretation of

* See E. M. Forster, *Alexandria: A History and a Guide* (Gloucester, Mass., 1961).

Fig. 98. *William Strickland's Second Bank of the United States, Philadelphia 1824. The identification of banking and temple architecture is based on Hellenistic precedent, established when private property for the first time attained that quasi-religious significance it still has in the United States.*

the fundamentals of civilization, which the cunning Sumerian goddess Inanni had wrested from the father god of Eridu 3,000 years earlier. Serapis became the most successful god of all Hellenistic cities. His enormous popularity, also as a Roman deity, might explain the destruction of all his statues by the Christians.

Hellenistic Alexandria was irretrievably lost under the continuously inhabited city. Its architecture was of the manneristic late-classical style. Inland, the Greek pharaohs continued the traditional Egyptian temple architecture, showing an excellent sense of political expediency by distinguishing between the native and the foreign populations. But not only the urban building style was new to the Egyptians of Alexandria; their economy underwent such a drastic change that the majority of the natives were unable to adjust to it. After millennia of pharaonic paternalism, which had regulated the entire supply, demand, surplus, and trade-exchange system, Alexander's heirs introduced a highly competitive, free economy in which temples acted as banks, taking 10 per cent interest on loans.

The currency system was Assyrian, based on gold for reserve, silver for foreign trade, and copper for local exchange—still today the basis of monetary standards. Alexandrian silver coin, backed by the temple treasuries, was the first international tender. The temple as bank was one of the few historical traditions fully understood by the founders of America. Pious Philadelphians were the first Americans to commission bank temples, similar to their Hellenistic churches, introducing religion to banking and banking to religion (*Fig. 98*).

The best testimony of the concentrated power of the first great portus of the world, reared in the spirit of Alexander's *oikumene*, is a papyrus from the first century, which states: "All cities are only cities in relationship to the territory they are in. In relationship to Alexandria they are but villages, for Alexandria is the city of the whole civilized world." Much later, O. Henry would echo this pride of port: "All cities say the same; New York says it first."

Alexandria had said it with 4,000 palaces and villas, 4,000 baths, 12,000 dealers in victuals, 40 theaters for entertainment and sports, and 40,000 tribute-paying Jews, forming in a city of an estimated 1.5 million inhabitants the world's largest Jewish community.

Alexandria had fittingly signaled its greatness across the sea with the most enduring and tangible symbol of urban power: the Pharos. A lighthouse well over 400 feet high, it made the list of the seven best-known wonders of the world. On a square base rose an octagonal central shaft and above it a cylindrical section, surmounted by a colossal statue of Ptolomy I Soter which reputedly shouted signals at approaching fleets and flailed its arms. The rotating lantern could not be reconstructed by the Arabs after they captured the city, but the shape of the Pharos became the prototype for the minarets of Western Islam and, through them, for the church towers of the Romanesque period.

Paraphrasing Churchill's verdict on World War II, it can be said that as Hellenism progressed it became less and less ideological in character. One of the reasons was prosperity, the accumulated loot of three successive empire drives. The Persians had plundered the Neo-Babylonian treasuries which had been heir to the inestimable hoard of the Assyrians. After the defeat of Darius at Gaugamala in 331 B.C., the Persian treasure was seized by the Macedonian army. One can estimate the total wealth from the share one of the Alexandrian successor states, Pergamon, received, which was 9,000 talents, close to $1 million. In the second century B.C., the golden age of cities, much was spent by the heir of this fortune, Eumenes II, to complete the

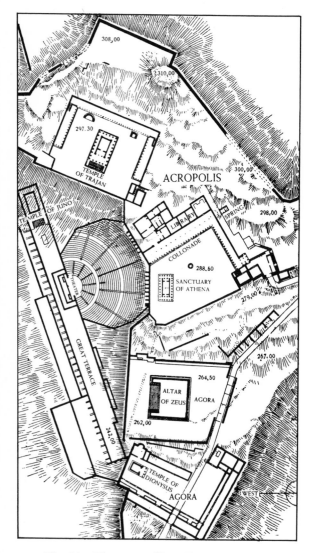

Fig. 99. The acropolis of Pergamon, built mainly during the second century B.C. It is a summary of 3,000 years of city planning: geomorphic in its site adjustment, concentric in the focal emphasis on the theatre—whose hemicycle connects the upper and lower city—and orthogonal-linear in the succession of squared temeni. Each has its own focal point but is connected with the whole plan through the mountain terrace and a principal road.

greatest urban composition ever carved from a mountainside (*Fig. 99*). Pergamon is important because it demonstrates the three stages of urban origins on a grandiose scale. The original setting follows the geomorphic concept of the Greek citadel: nature provides the form over which man's designs are molded. The theater, scooped from the slope, surpasses all earlier Greek theaters, because in addition to its topographical plan it is clearly conceived as a concentric focal point. The rhythm, of the hemicycles, natural above and man-made on middle ground, is held together by the great terrace, its linear precision emphasizing the centricity of the vast auditorium. The final development in the genesis of Pergamon was the establishment of orthogonal relationships between the urban elements: the precise meeting of walls, the crossing of streets, the geometry of stone architecture in temples and public buildings. Pergamon demonstrates this new phase of city building almost to exhaustion in the rectangular variations of the acropolis.*

There are two aspects of Pergamon which deserve additional attention. One is the site analysis by the planners in order to enhance the city. It is a pride modern city planners have lost. The cliffs of upper Manhattan, the bay front of San Francisco, the dramatic slopes of the valley of Caracas have been heedlessly disfigured, as though a city could afford to despoil the natural gifts that form its unique profile.

Even more superior—more "advanced"—than anything done in the nineteenth and twentieth centuries, was the respect shown by the Pergamene builders for a master plan. Pergamon wasn't built in a day, but over a period of 500 years; yet each subsequent generation entered into the original concept. So dedicated were the Attalid kings of Pergamon to their urban creation that their last ruler delivered the state as a gift to the Romans rather than see it conquered and destroyed by them (133 B.C.). And in handsome acknowledgment of this unique wisdom, the Romans enhanced and enlarged what the Hellenistic Greeks had planned.

The unifying concept of Hellenistic city planning can perhaps best be characterized by Le Corbusier's definition of architecture as "the foot that walks, the eye that sees, and the head that turns." It transformed the chaos of the Greek polis into the calculated experience of an environmental kaleidoscope. Louis Kahn's *bon mot* of "the street that wants to be a building" came

* Theodore Fyfe, *Hellenistic Architecture* (Cambridge, England, 1936).

110

Fig. 100. Pennsylvania Avenue, Washington, D.C. The lost art of creating memorable urban landscapes with which the citizen can identify his ambitions and affections. The zealots for social housing and Hudson Street rehabilitations will never understand that aesthetic deprivation can be as antisocial as the worst slum. Why should anyone respect and cherish a city when, in the words of Gertrude Stein, "there's nothing there there"?

true in the unified design of peripatetic spaces and public building elevations. The Roman writers Cicero and Quintillian developed a whole system of urban memory, called mnemonics, for the inhabitants of Hellenistic cities that established a relationship between personal thoughts and designed environment. The thinker selected perceptive features of the city that evoked his response to certain ideas and problems. He deposited, so to speak, what occupied his mind in the urban forms and spaces, a safekeeping of his inner life with the urban landscape which would return what he has deposited to his memory upon re-identification with the designed location. The reader is invited to try Circero's mnemonics in Manhattan, for instance, or along Pennsylvania Avenue, in Washington, a few blocks from the White House (*Fig. 100*).

Although Alexander's *oikumene* and *homonoia* were lost in the fratricidal competition between Hellenistic cities, they retained the polarity between materialism and intellect, between the greed and cruelty of exploiters and a profound respect and passionate concern for creativity and knowledge. The competition among the great city libraries for the works of the great

111

thinkers was so fierce and ruthless that Aristotle's heirs had to hide his famous collection of manuscripts in a cellar to escape revenge from defeated bidders. Ptolomy IV of Egypt forbade the export of papyrus when he heard that the library of Eumenes at Pergamon had 20,000 titles, which threatened serious competition for the Mouseion library of Alexandria. The chain reaction of this embargo was far-reaching. Pergamene scribes tanned pig skins to write on but found the manuscripts too thick to be rolled like papyrus scrolls and had to bind them between wooden plates. Thus, the book was born, written on "pergament," the parchment from Pergamon.

Alexandria, Antioch, and Pergamon did not have greater talents or wiser men than Egypt, Miletus, or Athens before them. The change in intellectual environment came from the systematic patronage of the ruler, whose ambition it was to balance his record as the conqueror of the world with an image as the teacher of men. Trajan emblazoned this ideal much later on his column as *ense et stylo*—"the shield and the pen." The medium that amalgamated both aggression and erudition

Fig. 101. The "bank window" of Palmyra, with column brackets where successful caravans advertised their return and the profits made.

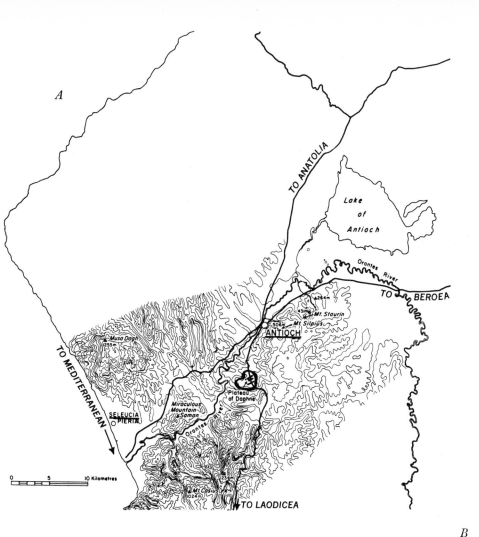

A

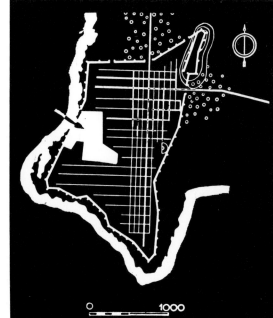

B

Fig. 102.

A) The Seleukis, a combination of four cities founded in 301 B.C. to secure all land and sea trade in the eastern Mediterranean to the Seleucid kings.

B) Laodicea-ad-Mare, the main port of the Seleukis. The plan has a strong resemblance to that of Manhattan drawn 2,112 years later, because the urban intentions were the same: maximum access routes with minimum detours to the waterfront and accommodations for a population whose interests were exclusively commercial (see Fig. 221). By a comparison with Antioch, the capital, the gifted flexibility of Hellenistic planning becomes obvious.

was urban wealth. The 3,500-feet-long main avenue of the caravan capital of the Middle East, Palmyra, had along its 69-feet-wide central roadway a continuous portico of 454 columns, 31 feet high. Each column carried on a marble bracket the insignia and dates of particularly successful caravans, together with the exact figures of their profit (*Fig. 101*).

City spirit was from its inception intolerant of pomp and dictatorship. Around A.D. 30 the citizens of Alexandria paid with a bloody massacre for taunting the Emperor Caligula (who had made his horse a senator). Three hundred years later the Emperor Julian retaliated in a more urbane manner for the scorn heaped by the people of Antioch on his efforts to restore the pagan approach to "the true citizenship of free men." Against the rising tide of Christianity and its unshaven monks, he wrote a satire, *Misopogon* ("The Beard Hater"), which was posted near his palace gate "at the Tetrapylon of the Elephants,"

113

permitting the assumption that most of the city population was not only literate but literary.

Antioch survives as the most successful member of the first regional planning project of antiquity. In 301 B.C., Seleucus the Conqueror, decided to found two matching pairs of port cities and inland cities in the border region between Anatolia and Syria.* The Seleukis was formed by Seleucia Piera and Antioch inland, and Laodicea-ad-Mare and Apamea on the coast (*Figs. 102A, 102B*). The urban chain would give double security, against sea raids and the endless incursions of mountain tribes. It would also link all trade of the Eastern Mediter-

* Glenville Downing, *Ancient Antioch* (Princeton, N.J., 1963).

Fig. 103. Fortuna Redux, *the Tyche of Antioch, presided over the birth of the worldly metropolis in the Hellenistic Age, just as the Venus of Willendorf—whose outline looms behind her—presided over the birth of the geomorphic village community. Despite the sheaf of grain she holds nonchalantly like a fan, Tyche was the mistress of man's urban fortune, wearing the mural crown of the* Portus *as later Tyches would wear diamond chokers.*

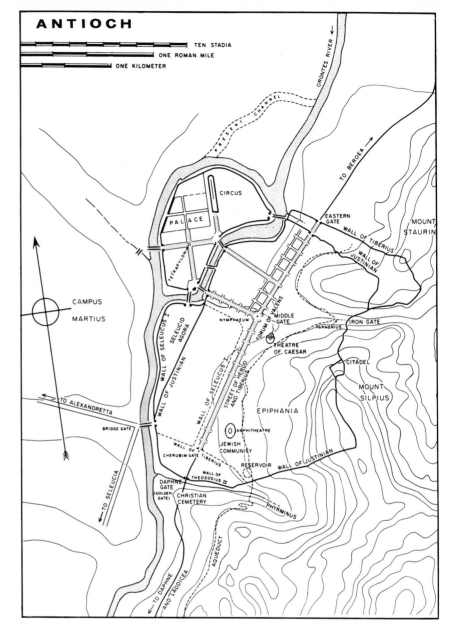

Fig. 104. Plan of Antioch in the second century A.D. The original city of the Seleucid rulers concentrated on a natural island formed by the Orontes River. It is a masterpiece of orthogonal planning within natural conditions. The palace, circus, and race course dominate the layout, because Antioch was a worldly, pleasure-loving metropolis whose carefully maintained control over the east-west flow of trade attracted a multiracial, liberal population. Columned main roads act as directives toward the river, the famous Nymphaeum—a roofed botanical garden—and the vast Seleucid agora, where traders from all over the world offered their wares. Surrounded by water and facing the magnificent slopes of Mount Silpius, Antioch offered the perfect synthesis of Hellenistic civilization and given natural advantages, of which none were left unused.

ranean to the point where the ancient caravan routes crossed from Central Asia to the West and from Byzantium on the Bosporus to Alexandria. The symbol of the Seleukis and of Antioch in particular was *Fortuna Redux,* the Tyche of Antioch, whose statue with the mural crown was carved by Eutychides in 296 B.C. (*Fig. 103*). Her significance for the Seleucid Empire was as great as that of Serapis for the Ptolomaic dynasty of Egypt. Tyche, "bitch goddess of success," guaranteed safe return

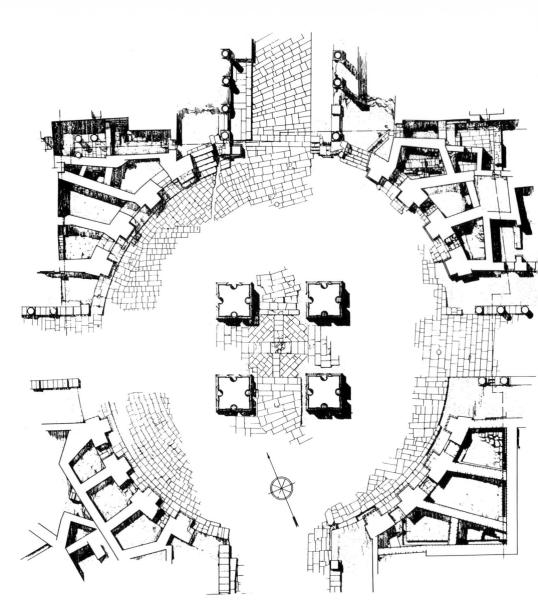

Fig. 105. The tetrapylon of Gerasa in Palestine gives a clear picture of the functional plan of Hellenistic street intersections. Similar in function to the English "circus" and the American "rotary," they forced traffic by man and vehicle along the two main city streets to change pace and direction. But the difference in aesthetic responsibility is enormous. In Gerasa the long perspective of the colonnaded streets terminated in a plaza whose monumental center columns contrasted pleasantly with deeply recessed, modular "store fronts," which housed the most prestigious shops, professional services, and offices of the city.

from foreign ventures, was sophisticated, city-bred, and a work of art; and she replaced once and for all Demeter, the earth mother, who had been worshiped by men before they learned to build walls against nature.

The Seleucid capital, Antioch, was a master solution of Hellenistic planning (*Fig. 104*). It exploited the advantages of the given site for an orthogonal, multifocused imperial city. The Orontes River and Mount Silpius furnished the perimeter; palaces and stadium (the Antiochians bet passionately on horse races) were placed on an island formed by a river loop. The

116

crossing of the two-columned roads of the palace island and the main intersection in the city were designed as tetrapylons, four cornered gates of which a fine plan has been excavated at Gerasa in Palestine (*Fig. 105*). In Antioch, the middle gate housed the city Nymphaeum, a combination greenhouse and shrine to the water nymphs, of which we have some idea from Sallust's famous example in Rome. The seven gates of Antioch were sacred to the inhabitants, being the points of entry into the capital and of exit into the empire. The reconstructed main cardo, in addition to which five other avenues existed, had a thirty-one-feet-wide center traffic lane, flanked on each side by thirty-two-feet-deep porticoes lined with shops.

Before seeing Hellenistic cities vanish in the orbit of Rome, the builders of Antioch must be credited with one achievement of civic wisdom that deserves to be remembered. Five miles from the city, on a pleasant plateau above the Orontes Valley, they founded Daphne as a "fun city." Daphne was not a suburb or an exurban cluster but a town with a famous temple and an agora, porticoed houses along its streets, and rich villas with beautiful gardens, as graphically described by Libanus, an Antiochian poet who lived under the Romans in the second century (*Fig. 106*). The special attraction of Daphne was its right of asylum, offering refuge to anyone who had been indicted under the strict civil laws of the capital. While this

Fig. 106. Only some fragments of a floor mosaic in a ruined villa of Daphne give an indication of what its townscape must have been like. From these, combined with the descriptions of travelers, emerges a city image much like the main street of the small town of Noale in the Roman Campagna. The two accents are variety in unity and a rhythmic alternative between linear progression and lateral open spaces, leading from public into private domain. The deadly monotony of Western cities and the persistent attraction of Mediterranean and Oriental towns becomes evident from this acknowledgment of the urban duality in Hellenistic planning.

Fig. 107. Reconstruction of the main road of Ephesus proving that indeed there was once "a street that wanted to be a building"—and succeeded. The memorial columns at the tetrapylon, soon to be appropriated by saints and emperors, lent by their height exceptional depth and perspective to the distant city gate and the mountains beyond the city.

Fig. 108. Restoration of the public assembly building (bouleuterion) in Miletus, Asia Minor, second century B.C. *The importance of the Hellenistic approach to planned cities was its integral character, which conceived of buildings as compositional groups rather than individual works of art. The colonnaded agora, the emphatic approach to the place of civic responsibility, the cloistered court with the symbolic altar, and the sober geometry of the senate house itself offer a progressive environmental experience that emphasizes the importance of the public domain against the anonymity of the merchant and residential city.*

earned for the beauty spot above Antioch the bad reputation of *Daphne mores* (Daphnean immorality), it saved wear and tear on police and magistrates of the metropolis and relieved public life of nonconformists who were free to enjoy each other's company in Daphne.

On his days off from Cleopatra's couch in Alexandria, Julius Caesar, last of the Hellenists and first of the Romans, absorbed the urban features that had carried orthogonal planning from

its ceremonial beginnings in the Old Kingdom of Egypt to its worldly perfection in the capitals of the Diodochae and Epigonae, the inheritors of Alexander's ecumenical dream. The basic concepts he tried to transplant into Rome, badly in need of directions for its role as world capital, were:

1. A hierarchy of street functions as structural system of the city: the central avenue, orienting perception in two directions, toward the given advantages of the site—sea, river, mountain, plain—accentuated by the gate as link between the town microcosm and the world, and, through colonnades, pedestrian walks, shops, etc., toward the city as the multispaced place that offers purpose, diversion, and sustenance to all (*Fig. 107*).

2. Designed building relationships, aiming at perceptional unity in the diversity of urban functions; the architectural definition of public spaces, the willed singularity of public monumentality (*Fig. 108*).

Fig. 109.

A) The sacred district on the acropolis of Lindos on the island of Rhodes. Though its development required hundreds of years, the designed movement within the confinement of the hilltop shows a superb rationality. The movement itself, the rising of body and spirit in the motion of ascending, becomes the religious experience. The two small temples (7 and 9) are merely terminal points of small importance compared to the progressive experience from approach (1), through propylaea (2), successive staircases, and colonnaded courts floating high above an unencumbered view of the Mediterranean.

B) The sacred district on the island of Cos is more grandiose but less sophisticated than the smaller example of Rhodes. The famous healing resort, rededicated by the Egyptian Ptolomies to Asclepius, the father of medical wisdom, was clearly shaped after the necropolis of Queen Hatshepsut in Deir el-Bahri, more than a thousand years older. Its uniquely Hellenistic character shows in the designed emphasis of approach and movement, of the rising ground and the freedom of space transversed which take precedence over the irrelevant enclosed spaces.

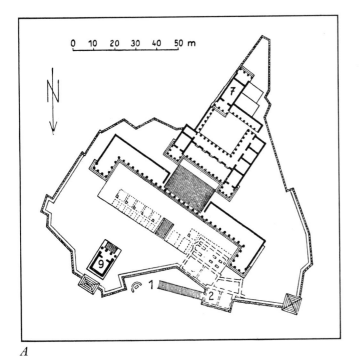

A

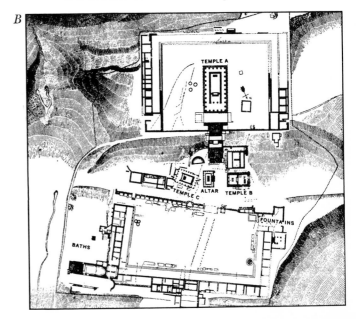

B

3. Change in grade and scale through steps, ramps, terraces, raised and lowered focal points of art, fountains, planting; perceptive discovery as neutralization of orthogonal linearity (*Figs. 109A, 109B*).

With Caesar starts the modification of Hellenism within the orbit of Rome.

History books record the end of Hellenism at the Battle of Actium in 31 B.C., which is as debatable as insisting that the Gothic period starts with Philip Augustus, and that the Renaissance ends with the death of Michelangelo. The canon of cities and buildings is a continuous composition. The Hellenistic plan survived long after the supposed termination of Hellenism. The temple compound at Baalbek from the second and third centuries, the replanning of Constantinople by Constantine and Justinian from the fourth to the sixth centuries (*Fig. 110*), and

Fig. 110. The plan of Constantinople, refounded as capital of the Eastern Roman Empire by Constantine in A.D. 330, is the link between Hellenism and the emerging concept of the Christian ecumenical capital. Orthogonal communication and natural site are adjusted to each other, recalling Antioch. The Palace and Santa Sophia—Emperor Justinian's gigantic monument to himself—serve as terminations of the main roads and as signals across the sea, placed as only Greek builders could place their temples.

Fig. 111. Colonnaded main street in Pichucalco, Mexico, shows the dignity of tradition and the elegance of the Hellenistic module.

a colonnaded main street in a remote Mexican hill town (*Fig. 111*) prove the tenacity of the Hellenistic concept. It is, however, true that the famous defeat of Mark Antony by Octavian had a decisive influence on urban environment. It liquidated Egypt, which for 3,000 years had been the inexhaustible quarry from which all young civilizations had taken their conceptual building stones. The role of Egypt as paradigm of Greek and Hellenistic design was usurped by Rome, which replaced the multiplication of competing capitals and their multiformed plans with the claim to be the city above other cities, the primordial urban matrix upon which all civilization had to shape itself.

Rome succeeded despite an embarrassing lack of cultural qualifications. She had no capital tradition and had to shop for national symbols wherever she could get odds and ends. Down to the sixth century B.C., the shepherds of the Seven Hills had lived in thatched huts, worshiped she-wolves and hollow oaks, stolen each other's wives, and carried their architectural ambitions no farther than the construction of turf altars. They were spoken of with contempt by their masters, the Etruscans, who had been lured from no one knows where by the old greed for metal to the center of the Italian peninsula. The Roman dilemma as heirs of the urban millennium was an embarrassment of riches. They awoke in their rough manger surrounded by the archaeological museum of Egypt, the militaristic bureaucracy of the Assyro-Babylonian Empire, the sybaritic charm of Greek living in the colonies of Southern Italy, the conspicuous materialism and worldly wisdom of Hellenistic Ionia, and the hocus pocus of Etruscan tribal magic.

From their neighbors, the Romans acquired the skills of aesthetic cribbing and keeping the population awed and compliant by priestly ritual. The Assyrians were mined for civil service tradition, army organization, weaponry, aqueducts. Greece and Asia Minor exported artists, scribes, teachers, banking, planning, and monumental architecture. The only thing that did not spring over was the Greek spark of inspiration. In the Hellenistic world the creed of the individual had been excellence, *arete*. In Rome it was and remained duty, *officium*. What Bismarck was to say of the Germans, that they lacked a shot of champagne in their veins, was true of the Romans.

Nevertheless, they were conscientious students of history. They shook off the pompous Etruscans after having copied their governmental system; they drove the frivolous Greeks from Magna Grecia, and liquidated one by one the city-states and empires established by Alexander the Great. It was unfortunate that subsequent Western history was based on the example of the Romans, who had intelligence without wisdom, energy without creativeness, and vitality without sensitivity. Like all colonizing countries after them, they imported form without content, and could imitate but not initiate. Their main contribution to designed environment was mannerism. The systematic Hellenization of the jumbled settlements on the flanks of

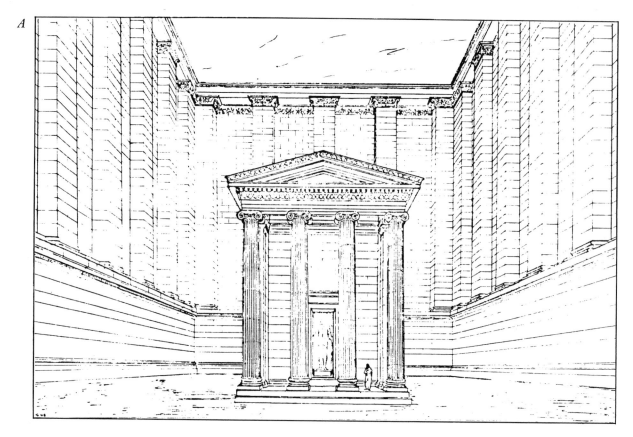

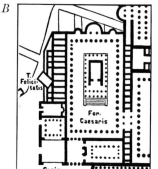

Fig. 112. The Hellenistic sanctuary of Didyma (A), near Miletus in Ionia, reminiscent of the boat shrines in Egyptian temple enclosures. It inspired Caesar to build the first of the Roman imperial forums (B) after its plan.

the Tiber Valley started with Caesar's Forum, a minitemple in a vast columned enclosure (*Fig. 112*). The plan was a replica of the Ionian sanctuary of Didyma, near Miletus, on which Julius Caesar had bestowed special privileges. The *Lex Julia Municipalis,* of 46 B.C., was the first planning ordinance intended to furnish guidelines for standardization of building heights, street widths, paving, maintenance, repairs, public works, fines, and city limits. To relieve the traffic jams of Rome, Caesar banned delivery vehicles in daytime and curtailed the display of merchandise in the narrow streets. But all the planning laws of

Caesar and his successors were powerless against a population explosion that swelled the capital from some 400,000 at the accession of Augustus to a reputed 1,200,000 under Trajan 100 years later. Two hundred sixty-five *vici*, or precincts, had wiped out Caesar's careful distinction between Urbs Roma, the city, and Ager Romanus, the surrounding country region. A new city had sprung up, in which lived a recorded 6,700 families on public welfare (*annona*).* In addition to the *plebs*, there were 12,000 soldiers acting as a police force, 400,000 slaves, an average of 38,000 visitors (*peregrini*), compared with a mere 150,000 independent self-sustaining citizens in Rome. The citizen oligarchy determined the life of the city and kept the emperor in office, although he was more often than not elected by the army. The *honestiores*, or honorable gentlemen, constituted a fluid hierarchy of titles, descent, and wealth. They lived in 1,797 houses or villas on the Pincio or the Ludovisi Estate, while the rest of the population occupied 46,602 speculation apartment buildings called *insulae*. Several city ordinances in the reign of Augustus tried to limit the height of these blocks to seventy feet, to sixty feet under Trajan, and to twice the width of the street or plaza under Nero. Despite zoning, one *insula* acquired world fame by being over 100 feet high. For the sake of space and economy, walls were restricted to a thickness of one-and-one-half feet, resulting in incessant collapses and the shoring up of sagging walls with thick beams, which obstructed the narrow streets. Juvenal, in the third book of his *Satires,* has described the nightly conflagrations of the wooden floors, caused by open oil lamps and charcoal braziers, the only heating equipment. The rightly famous aqueducts brought an estimated 222,237,000 gallons of water daily into the city, but it remained on street level. Public latrines were frequently pay toilets (*Fig. 113*), originating under the Emperor Vespasian, who observed wisely that "money does not smell." Man, woman, and child sat socially cheek by cheek among carved dolphins and gurgling streams connected with the main sewer, the Etruscan-designed Cloaca Maxima, whose ancient orifice still opens into the Tiber. *Tabernae* (shops), regularly spaced windows, and balconies for the second floor of the apartment buildings must have broken the monotony of the introverted houses built around courts, but the stench, noise, and dark narrowness of the streets make

Fig. 113. A public latrine in Imperial Rome.

* See Carcopino, *op. cit.* For architecture and planning, see Axel Boethius, *The Golden House of Nero* (Ann Arbor, Mich., 1960).

125

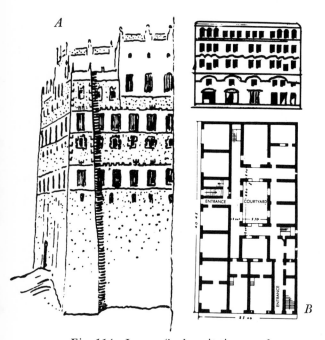

A

B

Fig. 114. Juvenal's descriptions and the vain attempts of authorities to restrict the height of Rome's speculative apartment towers make it more likely that they looked like the "skyscrapers" H. Hellfritz sketched in Arabia (A) rather than like the neat reconstructions of Ghismondi (B).

the neat reconstructions of art historians very unlikely (*Figs. 114A, 114B*).

The academic bias in favor of the Greek origin of Western civilization has obscured the decisive Assyrian-Babylonian influence on Rome. Urban provincial administration, economics, fortification, ballistics, and palace architecture had no prototypes in Greece proper, and the high-rise building was an Assyrian concept (see *Fig. 94*).

The *humiliores* (humble folk) of Rome were predominantly peasants, displaced by the ruling class for the assemblage of huge estates—a process that would be repeated in the seventeenth and eighteenth centuries in France and England. There were refugees from cities burned by the Roman army and dependents of soldiers killed in war. Their economic insecurity, but also their collective power, is reflected in the steadily climbing number of welfare recipients, in their eagerly sought and bought votes for political elections, and in the efforts of the last emperors to forestall riots and mass uprisings of this first urban proletariat by building huge baths (*Fig. 115*) and public forums.

The wealth of the Roman upper class has never been equaled in history. Fortunes running in the millions of dinarii were acquired by speculation on the stock exchange, usury, or based on latifundia, huge estates, granted by or bought from the emperor, producing income from conquered provinces. In the

Fig. 115. The baths built by the Emperor Diocletian in A.D. 302 surpassed all earlier thermae in size, accommodating 3,000 bathers. The plan provided a total recreational environment. In addition to the traditional hot and cold baths and private baths and gymnasiums, it offered shopping arcades, two libraries with Greek and Latin manuscripts, and a theater. Entrance was free to everyone. The patron of this munificent public playground was the same emperor who destroyed the last vestiges of democracy in Rome and, in a desperate attempt to save the imperium, imposed crushing taxation and total military control on the people. From Bannister Fletcher, History of Architecture (1961).

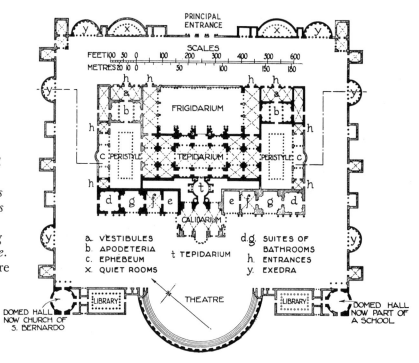

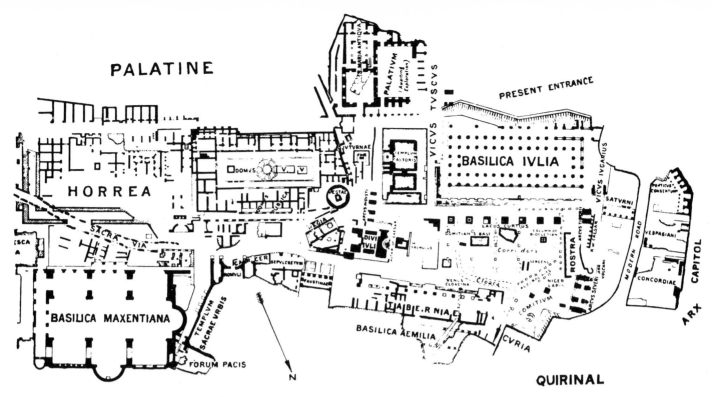

Fig. 116. The Forum Romanum, oldest and most revered of public spaces in Rome. Because of its symbolic significance for the formation of the state, buildings and monuments were crammed for eight centuries into its narrow space. As in pre-Hellenistic Greece, there was no planning and no building orientation.

Fig. 117. The highly manneristic convolutions of the Laocoön group, dating from the second century B.C., offer a sculptural analogy to the Roman delight in convoluted, purely formalistic space compositions. Photo: Bettmann Archive.

first and second centuries revenues from the rich African provinces were collected by six families. Egypt, more accustomed to imperial exploitation than to the free-wheeling rule of the Ptolomies, had to sweat out the entire revenue for the imperial household.

Pax Romana, a well camouflaged show advertised as a perpetual unconditional peace offer, lasted officially from A.D. 14 to 192. It offered protection from barbarian incursions and provincial backwardness in exchange for a contribution to the great society of Rome. Between 106 and 116, Trajan enforced the Roman Peace by conquering Dacia, the Transylvanian gold and silver mines, and parts of Arabia, and the Parthian Empire, where the wealth of the Orient was concentrated. He had, nevertheless, to make ends meet, and auctioned off 50,000 Dacian prisoners, the total able-bodied population of the land, to pay for the 115-feet-high marble column that portrayed his exploits in a sculptured cartoon strip 800 feet long, thus putting to shame all Egyptian and Greek friezes.

The formal virtuosity of Roman architects in designing building groups far outstripped the talent of their Hellenistic mentors. Under the Republic, building had been set beside building and temple aligned with temple without any attempt at grouping (*Fig. 116*). Perhaps it was the irregular ground that made orthogonal planning impossible and inspired Roman architects during the first two centuries A.D. to invent form-space combinations that had their analogy in the convolutions of Roman sculpture (*Fig. 117*). Building complexes were strewn over the Campus Martius like jeweler's pieces on a counter (*Fig. 118*). Although some are artfully harmonious in themselves, all are without either relationship to each other or to public spaces or to the continuity of the streets. Even the most grandiose spatial conception, the imperial forums, does not play a compositional part in the over-all city plan: The forums

Fig. 118. Even if one grants a certain artistic license, the eighteenth-century engraving by Piranesi of the Campus Martius at the height of the Roman Empire gives a clear indication of the curious reversal of the Hellenistic urban ideal. Piranesi was a serious student of antiquity, and much of his engraving appears in the fragments of the forma urbis, *a plan of the imperial city engraved on marble slabs. It shows that official Rome was a collection of stupendous exercises in conspicuous wealth and whimsical individuality. Public spaces—even the basic amenities of broad thoroughfares and interconnecting streets—were totally ignored.*

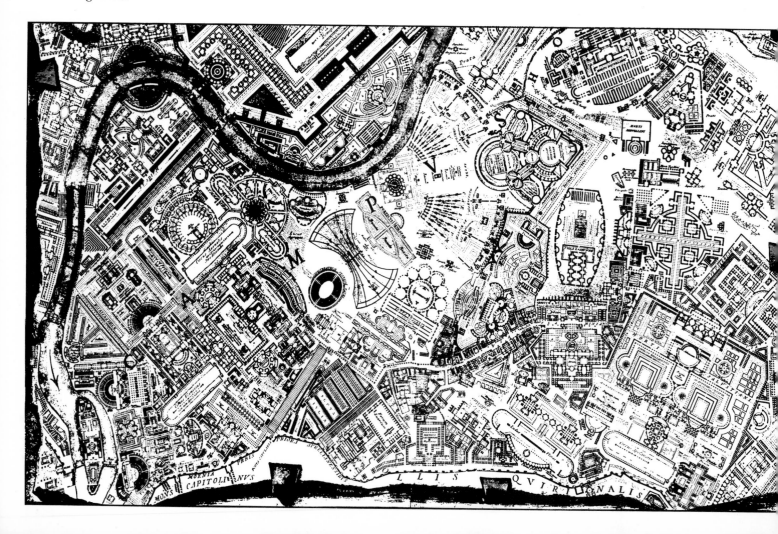

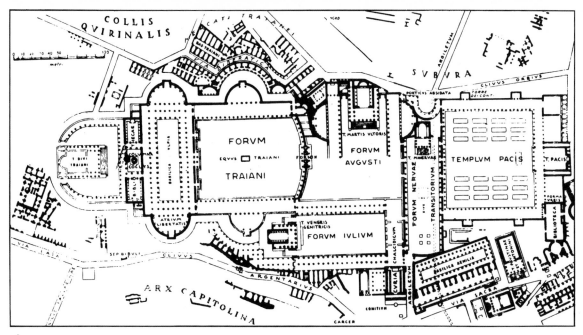

A

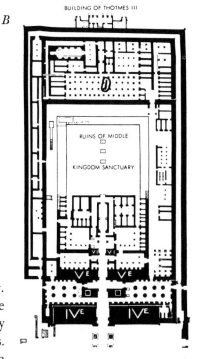

BUILDING OF THOTMES III

B

Fig. 119.

*A) The imperial forums of Rome. Each elected emperor
had to demolish an entire city sector to gain space for his
public monument. The relatively modest spaces of Caesar
(Forum Julium) and Augustus (Forum Augusti) became
mere anterooms to Trajan's superforum. Its planner and
architect was Apollodorus of Damascus, who started in
A.D. 107 on the gigantic undertaking.*

*B) Apollodorus' inspiration was clearly Egyptian, as a
juxtaposition with the center section of the sanctuary at
Karnak shows. Like the Egyptian temple enclosure, no
environmental context was established between the city
and the "roofless palaces" of the emperors.*

jostle each other like angry wrestlers grasping for a hold (*Figs.
119A, 119B*). Their sequence is an interesting reflection on the
gradual amplification of imperial theocracy which originally
had been totally alien to the dour shepherds of the Seven Hills.
Caesar had started with a modest temenos court, the Forum
Julium (see *Fig. 112*); Trajan concluded the development in
107 with nothing smaller than the main temple axis of Karnak.
His architect, Apollodorus of Damascus, came from the Syrian
heartland, full of early Egyptian and more recent Hellenistic
influences. Certainly the most brilliant of all Roman architects,
he re-created the spatial rhythm of the Egyptian temenos lead-

A

Fig. 120.

A) *Interior of the* mercato, *the shopping center Apollodorus laid like a necklace around one of the apses of Trajan's Forum. The interior of Trajan's market was a functional space accentuated by its brilliant structural achievement of groined concrete vaults and modular bays. From William L. Macdonald,* The Architecture of the Roman Empire *(1966).*

B) *Interior of a Milwaukee shopping center (Victor Gruen Associates, architects) built in 1961, which is different in materials but identical in concept and function with its Roman predecessor.*

B

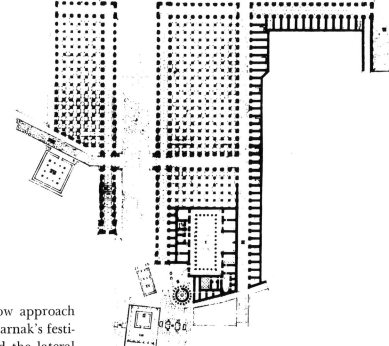

Fig. 121. The Neronian portico, which stood within the vast grounds of Nero's palace, symbolized the discontinuity of the Roman urbs *or capital city. It connected nothing, and by its excessive depth tried to create the mysterious half-light of the Egyptian hypostyle hall.*

ing from the columned forecourt through a narrow approach into the vastness of a porticoed square. He turned Karnak's festival hall (*Fig. 119A*) into a basilica (*Fig. 119B*) and the lateral Egyptian storage spaces into a Latin and a Greek library. Trajan's column, so clearly an adaptation of the pharaonic obelisk, defines the approach to the one-cella Temple of Trajan, whose plan, as that of all Roman temples, is unrelated to Greek counterparts but close to Egyptian-Etruscan prototypes.

As the first structural innovator since the invention of the arch by the Sumerians, Apollodorus knew where to use concrete vaulting and where to maintain traditional materials and forms. The great showplace he built for the worship of his Roman pharaoh was all columns, marble cornices, and Greek decoration. Trajan's Market (*Figs. 120A, 120B*), the first shopping center in history, rose on five levels in massive poured concrete, its groined vaults still intact. Here the crowds of Rome could bargain and splurge to their greed's desire while looking down on the statues, fountains, mosaic pavements, and public assemblies of their royal benefactor. Trajan's Forum was the urban grace of Rome. Other public buildings, basilicas, temples, nymphaeums, and the colossal enclosures of public baths, had no communication links between them. Porticoes had lost their contact with street elevations and stood around like buildings in search of streets (*Fig. 121*). The only two main avenues, the Via Sacra and the Via Nuova, were a mere 16 feet wide and surprisingly insignificant.

There were no visual focal points either as beginning or termination. Arched gates, which had played such a decisive role in the Assyro-Babylonian and Hellenistic street pattern, had lost their context. As arches of triumph, they were erected in or near the forums as monuments to the imperial epiphany rather than as communication links. To pass under the arch was the consecration of victory. Yet, no other Roman feature has been so profusely copied—from Paris to Brooklyn (*Fig. 122*)—and it is one more testimony to the tenacity of urban symbolism that the only grandiose public monument recently built in the United States is Eero Saarinen's Gateway to the West arch in St. Louis (*Fig. 123*).

With the destruction or subjugation of Hellenistic cities by the Roman steamroller, the perceptual function of the columned road was forgotten. In the major Hellenistic cities, their course had been directed in such a way that the eye focused upon a middle, an urban, distance. Subtle deviations in the straight line of the very long principal thoroughfares prevented the my-

Fig. 122. Grand Army Plaza, Brooklyn, improves upon other triumphantly arched plazas. Beside a creditable imitation of the Arch of Titus in Rome stands a gigantic Doric column with four solid bundles of Roman fasces *and four German eagles, whose symbolism should have caused embarrassment in the 1930's and 1940's, but didn't. Eclectic monuments are like Vespasian's public facilities: they are taken for granted. No one sees any meaning in them.*

Fig. 123. "Gateway to the West" (1960). Memorial arch in St. Louis, Missouri, to the settlers of the American frontier. Designed by Eero Saarinen.

Fig. 124. The Roman city gate of Siena, Italy, showing strength and functionalism so conspicuously absent in the fanciful triumphal arches of the Empire and their innumerable imitations.

opic confinement of the eye. No such art was wasted on the streets of Rome. The only roads that counted were the highways leading outward into empire—the vias Appia, Latina, Ostiensis, Labicana, and others. On them, the capital lavished the same engineering skill and landscaping care reserved today for turnpikes and elevated highways. Here the gates of entrance and return were of simple monumentality (*Fig. 124*), like modern toll gates inviting the motorist to rev up the motor and conquer the world that once had belonged to Rome.

The mission Rome had inherited from Hellenism—to urbanize the world and construct a bridge between Mediterranean civilization and Europe—failed through a curious cultural lag in her environmental concept. Rome conquered the world for the glorification and immortality of a single city. The historical implications of this contradiction between linear expansion and concentric, single-focused city-state are hard to grasp. As in cancer, one cell among the many urban cells that made up the civilized society of the Hellenistic age grew to fantastic proportions, devouring the strength and independence of the other cells. For over 300 years, from Caesar's subjugation of Western Europe, in about 50 B.C., to the founding of Constantinople as the new capital of the empire, in A.D. 330, the whole conquerable world was made a suburb of Rome, the *urbs,* the orbit of creation.

With the congenital denseness of soldiers and bureaucrats, the Roman republicans took the symbolic, nongeographic meaning of the cosmic world centers of Mesopotamia and India literally. In the Forum Romanum, they planted a black stone—the Lapis Niger—which henceforth was to be milestone zero from which all roads had their origin.

When Augustus decided to build himself a mausoleum after the example of the Egyptian pharaohs, he expressed his one-city-to-the-world message in a *meru,* the ancient Sumerian world mountain (*Fig. 125*). The Tomb of Augustus is a traditional five-staged ziggurat, 290 feet in diameter and covered by a tumulus planted with trees, like Etruscan funeral mounds. Compared to the 335-feet-high Dome of St. Peter that was to signify the center of God's realm on earth 1,500 years later, the height of 145 feet was modest. In a city with a maximum building height of approximately 100 feet, it provided the vertical symbol of power that has signified great cities from the round tower of Jericho to the Eiffel Tower of Paris.

More telling than the external form is the plan of the Tomb of Augustus, which was repeated by Hadrian 150 years later.

Fig. 125. Section and plan of the Tomb of Augustus in Rome, started in 25 B.C. It is a five-stepped ziggurat structure with an Indian stupa plan, covered with an earth tumulus as were the tombs of Etruscan kings and nobility.

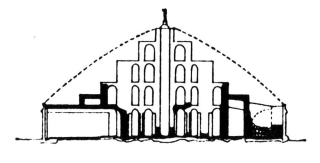

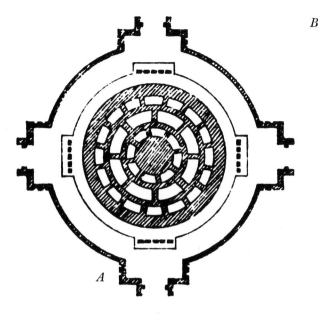

Fig. 126.

A) Plan of the ancient Buddhist stupa at Nagarjunakonda, India, showing the same configuration as the center of Augustus' tomb.

B) A Hindu-Buddhist mandala, an ancient Indian diagram of man's place on a square earth in the center of a sheltering dome of heaven, which is surrounded by the cosmos and populated by deities.

The core of this plan has strong affinities with the great stupas (*Fig. 126A*) built by the Emperor Asoka in the third century B.C. to hold relics of Buddha. It also is a mandala (*Fig. 126B*), a sacred diagram visualizing man's place under the sheltering round of heaven, in the square order of the physical world, and in the global envelope of the cosmic ocean. Four niches indicate the four world ages and the four eternal roads to the cardinal points. It is most likely that the twelve compartments forming the core of the Tomb of Augustus signify the twelve Etruscan *lucumones*, kings of the twelve cities of the Etruscan federation, surrounded by the symbolic presence of twelve counselors, without whom the Etruscan confederation could not be governed.* The wooden mast, surmounted by the umbrellas of the Enlightened One, which pierces Indian stupas and sikkharas, was replaced in Rome by a vertical cylindrical shaft, crowned with a gilded statue of the dead inhabitant as Jupiter Optimus Maximus.

The evidence of close contact between Rome and India is not only visual but also documentary. Early in his reign, Augustus received an embassy from the Indian emperor Pandya, whose fabulous gifts included a guru, who accompanied Augustus to Greece where he became engrossed in Greek mythology. Instead of returning with his patron to Rome, he anointed his body and jumped into a bonfire on the agora of Athens, declaring that he had learned all a man could learn in this life.† In the second century, Heliodorus, a Roman poet, assumed the title of bhagavata (Hindu saint). In the following century St. Hippolytus wrote a treatise, *Refutation of all Heresies,* which was directed mainly against the spreading influence of the Hindu holy books, the Upanishads.‡

Outside the *urbs* ruled the military legions with their telling emblem of the fasces, an ax blade in a bundle of rods. Neither their presence nor Rome's attempts to explain her Manifest Destiny with borrowed cosmology kindled any allegiance in the beneficiaries of the Roman peace. The growing influence of Christianity and a rising tide of barbarian incursions shattered the Roman power image and the empire. Only Rome herself became "eternal." The reasons for this imperishability, despite chaos, vice, and iniquity, are sociological and psychological rather than aesthetic and architectural.

Among city-of-God urbanists and grid-system planners, Rome is not a popular subject. This is unfortunate because she furnishes an answer to a question which has long eluded them: Why do anonymous people—the poor, the unprivileged, the unconnected—frequently prefer life under miserable conditions in tenements to the healthy order and tranquility of small towns or the sanitary subdivisions of semirural developments? The imperial planners and architects knew the answer, which is as valid today as it was 2,000 years ago. Big cities were created as power images of a competitive society, conscious of its achieve-

---

* See O. W. von Vacano, *The Etruscans and the Ancient World* (New York, 1960), and Perry, *op. cit.*

† Renaud, *Relations Politiques et Commerciales de l'Empire Romain avec l'Asie Orientale* (1863).

‡ Luce Boulnois, *The Silk Route* (New York, 1966).

ment potential. Those who came to live in them did so in order to participate and compete on any attainable level. Their aim was a share in public life, and they were willing to pay for this share with personal discomfort. "Bread and games" was a cry for opportunity and entertainment still ranking foremost among urban objectives. The Romans knew that the masses want to live in big cities because they offer competition, pride of collective ownership, and a sense of participation. They took advantage of this knowledge by erecting monumental public buildings and exciting, freely accessible gathering places: baths, circuses, stadiums, theaters, forums, basilicas, temple courts, botanical gardens, all studded with ornaments that met the taste of the ruler and the ruled. And never mind the motivation. The costs were not camouflaged as charity or gestures of social equality. They were the invested self-interest of the city powers who knew—as our contemporary democratic city powers do not —that urban prosperity depends on the good will and work load of the masses. Anyone who has watched public life around the ancient fountains of Rome, or the market places and mosques of Cairo, Damascus, and Istanbul, the evening crowds on the Zocalo of Mexico City, and the Plaza de Armas in Cuzco, knows what makes cities desirable to the poor. If, as the wailing brotherhood of social planners insist, Western cities are dying, it is not from too many automobiles or too few housing projects, but because of too little urbanity and too little opportunity for participation.

The architectural-aesthetic "heritage of Rome" is much better known than the sociological one because it has been classified by Renaissance scholarship. The considerable irony of the sixteenth-century renascence of Roman planning and architecture lies in the fact that it wasn't Roman at all. It was taken verbatim from Vitruvius' ten books on architecture. The suggestions for planning and design were nostalgic attempts to keep alive the Hellenistic tradition as described by Hermogenes who lived in the third century B.C. before Rome was urbanized. The only value of Vitruvius' writings for the origins of urban environment is the realization that his influence on the Renaissance perpetuated the concepts of Hellenism.* The orthogonal street pattern and the coordination of building elevations with linear perspective and the two-dimensional pictorial plane developed during the fifteenth century as a Hellenistic renascence.

* Axel Boethius, *Vitruvius and the Roman Architecture* (1939).

Fig. 127. Renaissance row houses in Florence. The remarkable achievement is a unified street elevation, despite individual façade treatment, and a combination of flat plane with perspective depth.

A group of row houses, built during the expansion of Florence to the left bank of the Arno (*Fig. 127*) shows a fine understanding of the classical concept without reverting to classical style elements.

The actual realization of Renaissance urban projects according to Hellenistic principles falls far short of theoretical plans. The dense old quarters of medieval cities blocked the way, and the devastating wars of the sixteenth century frustrated many revolutionary planning schemes which originated in the century before. Every architect knows Michelangelo's Campidoglio as a prime example of arrested space-form composition, but

138

Fig. 128. *Porta Pia and avenue by Michelangelo, ca. 1560. The sweep of the avenue, the elevated termination at the Dioscuri on the one end and the high gate with the landscape perspective beyond, are pure Hellenism. The Roman heritage shows complete indifference to the harmonious design of the house elevations along the great avenue.*

few know the Porta Pia design with its sweepingly Hellenistic movement from the Dioscuri group on the Lateran along a broad avenue toward the monumental gate and the landscape beyond (*Fig. 128*). More seminal for the perpetuation of orthogonal monumentality in the orbit of Rome was Donato Bramante, born in 1444 and thirty-one years older than Michel-

Fig. 129. *Sketch for an "ideal city" by Donato Bramante, ca. 1505. The Hellenistic ideal of the city as a continuous, designed entity is fully realized, enhanced by the conscious application of linear perspective and foreground and background lighting. The clearly Roman features are two: the very un-Hellenistic absence of any reference to given environment; and the dense energy of balanced masses on clearly visible structural systems.*

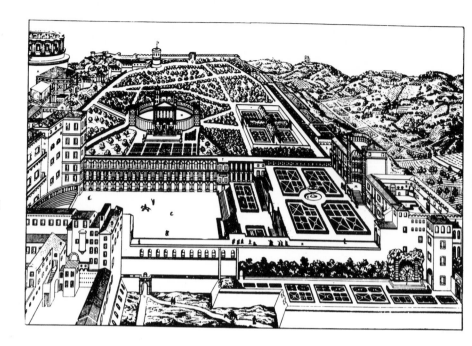

Fig. 130. Court of the Belvedere in the Vatican, by Bramante. Engraving by Cartaro (1574). This is what the grandiose concept was like before it was mutilated. The engraving reveals Bramante's command of architectural and urban requirements. The contrast between the physical size of the papal realm (0.17 square mile) and its spiritual significance was overcome by the creation of a public space so vast, so monumental, so diversified that anything outside it was insignificant. Every space-expanding device is employed: frontal and lateral staircases, their steep grades giving the palace an illusionary verticality; the hollowing out of the façade on one end, and an amphitheatrical termination on the other. The modular unity of the court elevations relies on the ancient device of a seemingly endless forward motion urged on by the rhythm of solid and void. The urban monumentality of the elevations is scaled down as one approaches the main terrace before the papal palace where intimations of the palace grounds and their isolation from profane eyes are given.

angelo. As a young man he had solved the problem of a church in need of an apse by painting on the rear wall of San Satiro in Milan an illusionistic choir approached through a long aisle. He arrived in Rome simultaneously with the French Army, which plundered and destroyed much that remained of the ancient city. A sketch for a stage design from about 1505 is perhaps the purest realization of Vitruvian theory and Renaissance space projection (*Fig. 129*). The architectural elements are inextricably related to the street and the plaza. As in Alexandria or Antioch, the city is again conceived as an orthogonal palace whose variety of space and form experiences rests on linear forward motion. The commission by Pope Julius II to construct a papal residence in the Belvedere of the Vatican, and focus it on successive courts, found Bramante well prepared (*Fig. 130*). The entire Hellenistic vocabulary of modular elevations, terraces and stairs as dynamic kinetic experiences, and artistic emphasis on entrance and termination achieves an ultimate apotheosis in Bramante's Vatican scheme.

Vasari's perspective exercise of the Uffizi, in Florence, and Palladio's urban stage set of the Teatro Olimpico, in Vicenza, adopted Bramante's concept that the essence of the linear street is its elevation, and the essence of the public plaza is its space.

In the fifteenth and sixteenth centuries, this space of the plaza was an attribute of the buildings for which it was created (*Fig. 131*). In the Baroque period of the seventeenth and eighteenth centuries, the interrelationship of building and plaza was reversed. By then it was the space that determined the form that bordered it (*Fig. 132*). Urban space which for more than 2,000 years had been an attribute of architecture was bidding for independence. The adornment of the public square was more important than the adornment of the buildings bordering it (*Fig. 133*).

The historical motivations behind this conceptual change in planning were the Counter Reformation and political absolutism. The intangible but fearfully real historical mood, the *Zeitgeist*, shaped a new environment. The universal church had never forgotten that in organization and world mission it had been styled after the Roman Imperium. At the height of the Gothic period, the bull *Unam Sanctum*, issued by Boniface VIII, stated, *Ego sum Caesar, ego sum Imperator!* Julius II had hoped to re-create in Bramante's new Vatican City the Hippodrome and Septizonium of the Palatine palaces.* As papal power recovered from the shock of the Reformation, it appropriated the ancient tradition of royal processions and advent, when "the king's appearance at the gate of the city was compared with, or was, the epiphany of a god."†

Fig. 131. Plan and plaza of the Palazzo Farnese, Rome, by Sangallo, started in 1530. Public plaza, interior cortile, and rear garden form an integrated successive space pattern in which the unroofed spaces are as much part of the architectural plan as the indifferently treated interior rooms. The Farnese plan is a climax and a termination of the palace as the microcosm of the city.

* James S. Ackerman, *The Cortile del Belvedere* (Vatican City, 1954).
† E. Kantorowicz, "The King's Advent," *The Art Bulletin*, Vol. XXVI (1944).

Fig. 132. Blondel's plazas, cut into the medieval city of Strasbourg in 1768. The sculptured space volumes are their own justification, and the building elevations mere delineations.

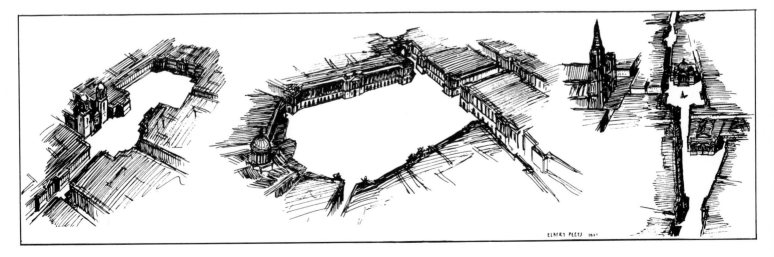

Fig. 133. Baroque fountain in Salzburg, Austria, emphasizes the importance of the public plaza against the anonymous building elevations.

Fig. 134. Colonnade of St. Peter's Square, Rome, completed in 1667. Few, if any, of the pilgrims moving in heightened anticipation toward the cathedral, will be aware that not the vastness of the piazza but the embracing curve and the rhythmic shadow play of Bernini's columns define their religious experience. Drawing: Steen Eiler Rasmussen.

The Reformation and the subsequent struggle of the papacy to retain religious leadership among Christians brought an intensification of the drive toward visualization of the papal epiphany. The most successful combination of the interior-exterior processional axis was the construction of St. Peter's Square by Bernini, finished in 1667. It guides the procession of pilgrims across an unconscionably vast plaza measured only by the light-dark intervals of lateral colonnades (*Fig. 134*). The rising steps of the portico continue into a 600-feet-long nave that terminates in the golden apparition of the baldachino and the floating Chair of St. Peter beyond.

It would have been bad management if the rulers of the

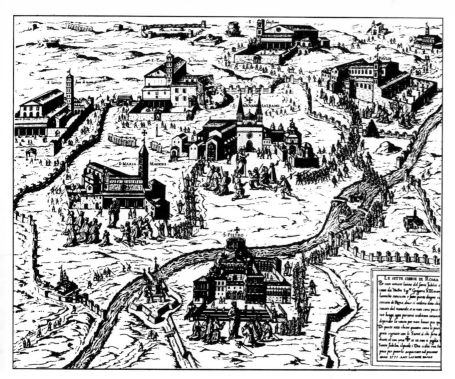

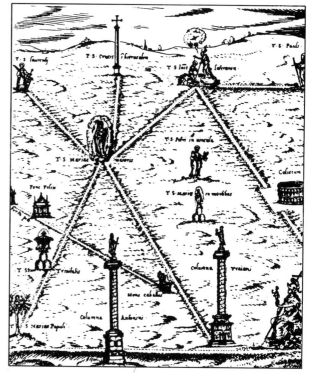

Fig. 135. Engraving (A) shows the seven principal pilgrimage churches of Rome; (B) shows the arrow-straight connecting roads which Pope Sixtus V constructed in his brief tenure of five years (1585–90). His roads, which cut through the most neglected section of the city, were not, as has been asserted, far-sighted experiments in urban renewal, but were part of a vast machinery to re-establish the Universal Church as sole caretaker of humanity. If the ancient shrines had been standing in a line, the road system of Sixtus would have been orthogonal. As it was, their interconnection produced a diagonal nodal layout which fused with the Star patterns of ideal cosmological plans (see Figs. 68–71).

Vatican had confined the pilgrim throngs to their own basilica. As part of the reconstitution of the universal church after the Council of Trent (1545–63), Pope Sixtus V decided to construct connecting avenues between the seven most famous pilgrimage churches of Rome (*Figs. 135A, 135B*). Sixtus V is the patron saint of American city planners who credit him with the first urban renewal miracle.* It is doubtful whether any saint has ever been canonized for less valid reasons. There is no evidence that Sixtus intended to change Rome from a maze of medieval slums into a planned orthogonal city by opening up linear

* Edmund N. Bacon, *Design of Cities* (New York, 1966).

143

communications and designing effective "reciprocal vistas." From the available documents, it is abundantly clear that he hated the worldly Romans, who were disenchanted by the stern strictures of the Counter Reformation, and that his nine processional routes through the sparsely built-up eastern section of town were designed for a blatantly anti-urban processional ritual of piety and penitence.

Sixtus' recoining of the Roman royal triumph in terms of Christian self-mortification had—as happens so often in history—the greatest influence on those for whom it was not intended. The absolutist monarchs and their planners who dominated the architectural activities of the seventeenth and eighteenth centuries were greatly impressed by the pope's brutal highroads to self-glorification, cutting insensitively through the natural topography of Rome. Venaria Reale, near Torino, designed in 1672 by Castellamonte for the duke of Savoy, Le Vau's Versailles, and Nymphenburg, near Munich, are famous examples of the straight-line, diagonal star pattern. It was left to the pragmatic British to apply this stencil of absolute authority, Roman in both the pagan and the Christian tradition, to a merchant city. Christopher Wren's plan for the rebuilding of London after the Great Fire of 1666 (*Fig. 136*) is a very popular textbook item, praised for its "logical configuration of the city." The thirty-four-year-old astronomy professor submitted the plan to his monarch immediately after the terrible disaster that destroyed two-thirds of London. He came from an ardently royalist family that had suffered much under Cromwell's Com-

Fig. 136. Christopher Wren's plan for London after the Great Fire of 1666. While the pope's intentions for Rome had been clearly pragmatic, Wren's intentions for London owed much to his training in astronomy and his Neoplatonist convictions. His star-shaped plazas adhere to abstract symmetry and his superblocks to a uniformity which Plato recommends in the Timaeus. *More important than these theories is the total separation of the plan from any three-dimensional architectural realization. A living metropolis had been reduced to an ideal utopia. Although the Royal Stock Exchange here occupies the pivotal point formerly assumed by the cathedral or the castle, the idea of a city had for the first time become more important than the city itself. This would have strong implications for the future of man-made environment, particularly in the traditionless New World.*

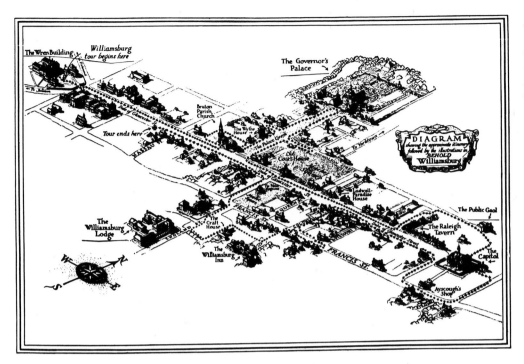

Fig. 137. Plan of Williamsburg, Virginia, laid out in 1699. There was a clear intention to emulate the European concept of a royal road in the 99-feet-wide Duke of Gloucester Street and the cross-axial Palace Green, terminating in the palace and an Elizabethan park. The handful of houses and shops were totally unrelated to the focal relationships between the Capitol, the college, and the nodal point of the Governor's Palace.

monwealth. In addition, he was a member of that fabulous generation of rationalist philosophers that included Locke, Spinoza, Newton, and Leibnitz. Although Wren was trained in the new sciences of astronomy, mathematics, and physics, he was an ardent Neoplatonist, believing in the pre-established harmony of the spheres and in God as "the unmoved mover," whose supreme laws are expressed in man's highest achievements.* His London plan is a symbolic configuration of intercommunicating 10-, 8-, 6-, and 4-rayed star-shaped plazas, the largest of which has the Royal Stock Exchange in the black eye of destiny.

There were two attempts to impose city plans on the virgin soil of America that reflected the tradition of the royal progress. The first one was the 1699 plan of Williamsburg, Virginia (*Fig 137*), drawn in the same year that Wren's plan for the College of William and Mary arrived in the colony, which surely cannot be mere coincidence. The authorship of the final layout is disputed, but it is evident that the 99-feet

* Eduard F. Sekler, *Wren and His Place in European Architecture* (New York, 1956).

145

width of the one-mile-long central axis, Duke of Gloucester Street, has no expedient purpose. With Wren's building on the west end and the state capitol on the east, that same reciprocity was attempted which Wren had designed for exchange, palace, and cathedral in London. Planned crossaxes of palace green and town hall were not realized because Williamsburg paid for its royalist origin by losing its status as capital in 1779.

The influence of Wren, the Neoplatonist planner and chief architect of the English Restoration under Charles II, can be seen in Major Charles L'Enfant and the second attempt to start Americans on the royal road. The choice of an architect for the new capital of the United States is as farcical as had been the presence of French royalists in the Revolutionary Army, engaged in throwing off the yoke of royalism. After his discharge from Washington's army, L'Enfant had built up an architectural practice in New York. When he offered his services to President Washington, in 1789, he made his hopes quite clear. He wanted, he wrote, to "lay the foundations of a city which is to become the capital of this vast empire."

Fig. 138. A juxtaposition of the main axis of Washington, D.C., with that of Versailles clearly indicates L'Enfant's source of inspiration. While there is absolutely nothing wrong with a successful adaptation, Washington's spatial monumentality is incongruous to American urbanism. The heritage of the Roman via triumphalis *demanded either great monumental architecture or great landscaping—and both are outside the ability of American city builders.*

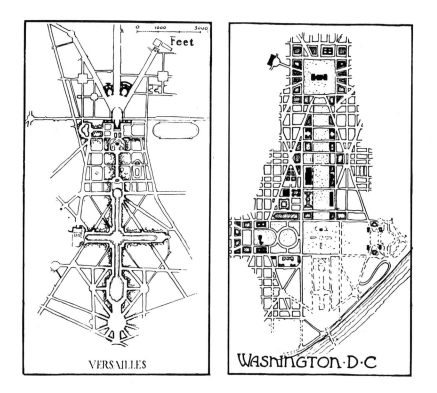

146

THE ELLICOTT PLAN

Fig. 139. *The final plan of Washington, D.C., drawn by L'Enfant's assistant, Ellicott. In the upper left is George Town, offering an interesting comparison between an eighteenth-century colonial grid plan and the star-struck vision of the capital's frustrated royalist planner. Faithful to Wren's example, the abstract constellation is unconcerned with the three-dimensional reality of a city. All buildings, so L'Enfant hoped, would be set back "beyond green slopes to avoid unsightly intrusions."*

L'Enfant was an educated man. He remembered the park axis of Versailles where his father had copied motifs for the Royal Tapestry Works in Gobelin (*Fig. 138*). He was acquainted with Wren's proposals for London, Patte's star-shaped *places royales* in Paris (see *Fig. 73*), and the make-believe residence Louis XV had planned at Nancy for his deposed father-in-law, the ex-king Stanislaw of Poland. L'Enfant came up with a plan (*Fig. 139*) of such unabashed eclecticism that it must have won him the immediate admiration of Jefferson, who dreamed of

147

Fig. 140. Cartoonist Laurie Olin's vision of the Washington Mall had L'Enfant's layout and Jefferson's architecture been realized.

housing the young republic in a museum of classical antiques. Following Wren's example, Washington became a plan without a city. Converging 160-feet-wide avenues lost themselves in the wilderness, separated from each other by "constellations of luxuriant growth . . . with palatial views of classical reminders of man's glorious past" on the horizon *(Fig. 140)*. Messengers with powdered wigs were to speed on black stallions along the vast mall between legislature and executive mansion, and foreign embassies were to be escorted in stately procession along green parterres bordered by statuary in front of primeval woods. "No message to nor from the President is to be made without a decorum which will doubtless point out the propriety of committee waiting on him in carriage should even his palace be placed contiguous to Congress."*

As in the whole textbook of urban origins, changing con-

* H. P. Caemmerer, *The Life of Pierre Charles L' Enfant* (1950).

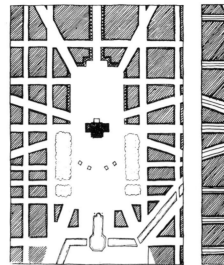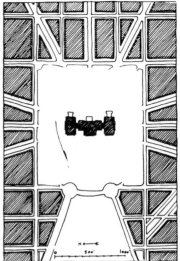

Fig. 141. On the left, L'Enfant's modest House of Representatives, a mere concession in the vast scheme of his empire capital. At right, the Capitol Plaza today, disassociated from the city below and unrelated in scale to any other building, including the White House.

cepts were stronger than static reality. The diagonal grid of superblocks, "at the disposal of the ruling gentry," was sliced into the same dismal speculation lots that had destroyed the Philadelphia dream of Thomas Holme, William Penn's surveyor general. The Capitol and not the White House, as planned, assumed the dimensions of Versailles (*Fig. 141*), ruining L'Enfant's scale. The odd-shaped little parks and circles

Fig. 142. One of Washington's circles today. The oddly shaped islands, resulting from L'Enfant's exercise in diagonal-orthogonal contradiction, are in a constant state of neglect. Washington is living proof that cities not only mirror but magnify the basic characteristics of their society. Whatever has been positive in American urbanism has come from private enterprise.

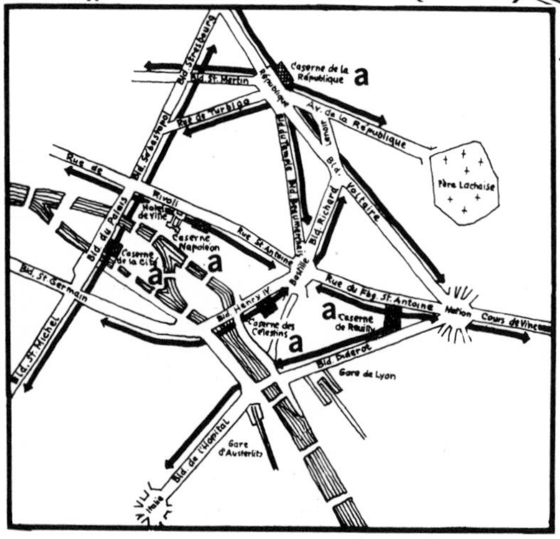

Fig. 143. *The concentric plan of Paris and the linear boulevards cut through the ancient fabric by Baron Haussmann. His intentions and those of Napoleon III were neither social nor communal. His "cannon-shot boulevards" were designed to prevent the building of barricades and to facilitate the deployment of troops during the periodic uprisings of the Paris proletariat. The insert shows five military barracks (a) built on the main city approaches. Haussmann's second purpose was commercial—furnishing a rising middle class with dwellings and places of business whose revenue would benefit the royal purse. His gigantic lifework—whose most important aspects were not boulevards but progressive sanitation and water-supply facilities and the erection of multistoried, multi-income speculation housing—terminated in 1871, in the bloodiest civil uprising recorded in modern history. It swept away the monarchy he had tried to secure.*

presented an upkeep problem a democratic government was unwilling to solve (*Fig. 142*), and the monumental emptiness of the ceremonial axis restricted the available space for government buildings so drastically that barracks started to cover what for L'Enfant must have been holy ground.

L'Enfant's attempt to create an ideal capital was not lost on Baron Haussmann when he was commissioned by Napoleon III in 1853 to redesign Paris with the dual purpose of enhancing its real estate value by constructing modern boulevards and suppressing riots by cutting through the medieval maze of a city whose population was known for republicanism and violence (*Fig. 143*). We are so used to look at city plans as linear drawings that it has become customary to see in Haussmann's concept an expression of nineteenth-century commercialism and

Fig. 144. A perspective survey of central Paris clearly indicates the "Roman" intentions of Haussmann's replanning. Despite later additions of two exhibition halls (the Grand Palais and the Petit Palais), the cross-axial monumentality of the Louvre and the Jardin des Tuileries on the right bank of the Seine, and the Esplanade and Dome des Invalides on the left bank echo the great axes of Versailles and Washington. The bird's-eye view also shows the discontinuity of Haussmann's great boulevards, behind whose imposing façades remained the chaos of narrow side streets. Paris, in contrast to London but in conformity with Rome, remains memorable through the quality of its architecture rather than through its planned spaces.

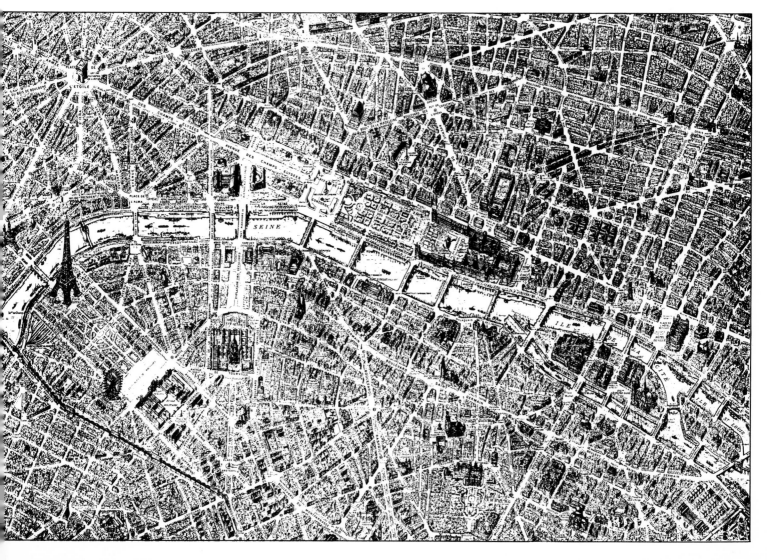

A

Fig. 145. New Delhi, India. It is
reliably reported that Sir Edwin
Lutyens and Sir Herbert Baker,
who were responsible for the plan
and official architecture of New
Delhi (A, B), were not on speaking
terms with each other throughout
the construction period, 1911–31.
This lack of communication
shows in the yawning emptiness
of the Roman triumphal axis.
Government House on "the Hill"
and the Empire Arch more than a
mile apart are not even in
shouting distance of each other.
The government buildings,
"combining Hindu, Moslem and
Classical features," are of a
monumental ugliness that cannot
be matched. In the boiling Indian
summer, each end of Kingsway
becomes a mirage—an empire in
the clouds.

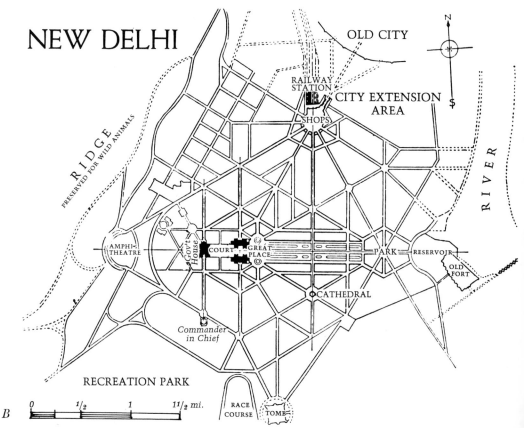

B

democracy. On a perspective plan (*Fig. 144*) it becomes quite clear that here is a continuation of the royal palace axes (see *Fig. 138*). The monumental main progression from the Palais du Louvre to the Place de la Concorde meets a minor axis in the Rue Royale and the Madeleine Church built by Napoleon I. The same spatial progression is repeated on the Left Bank with the Esplanade des Invalides leading to the Hotel des Invalides and the Champs du Mars terminating in the École Militaire. The whole concept is so derivative of L'Enfant's Washington axis that one should suspect a direct influence. Although the twentieth-century exhibition palaces have marred the continuity, the obelisque of Luxor on the Place de la Concorde still reads as a pivot whose American counterpart is the Washington Monument. Haussmann's imperial constellation has one climax in the dome of the Invalides and another in the Louvre, on which all the dynasties since the Renaissance had left their imprint. The Louvre is clearly the focus of Haussmann's intentions because his major boulevards are related to the great approach while his breakthroughs in other parts of the city peter out in dead ends. As an orthogonal-linear plan of a merchant city, Haussmann's achievement was only partially successful because it neglected the connective tissue of the minor streets and completely ignored any major road connections with the banlieu and the country beyond, which still plagues Paris today. As a hierarchical arrangement making an existing core of patriotic significance visible, it is a fine piece of planning, although it cost 300 million francs and bankrupted the City of Paris.*

The last royal progress routes originating from the orbit of Rome were constructed not in Europe but in "the colonies." Sir Edwin Lutyens' New Delhi plan of 1911 (*Figs. 145A, 145B*) is famed for the yawning emptiness of its monumental main axis, which during the hot months is unusable. There is, nevertheless, something satisfactory in the implementation of a dream of world empire by means of a super-Roman plan. Even though the *Pax Romana* had been recoined by Britain as Balance of Power, the Jubilee procession of George V as Emperor of India established a tangible continuity with the triumphant Hadrian striding through the conqueror's arch at Leptis Magna.

This rather simple-minded identification with the oldest suc-

* Brian Chapman, "Baron Haussmann and the Planning of Paris," in *Town Planning Review*, Vol. XXIV, No. 3 (1953–54).

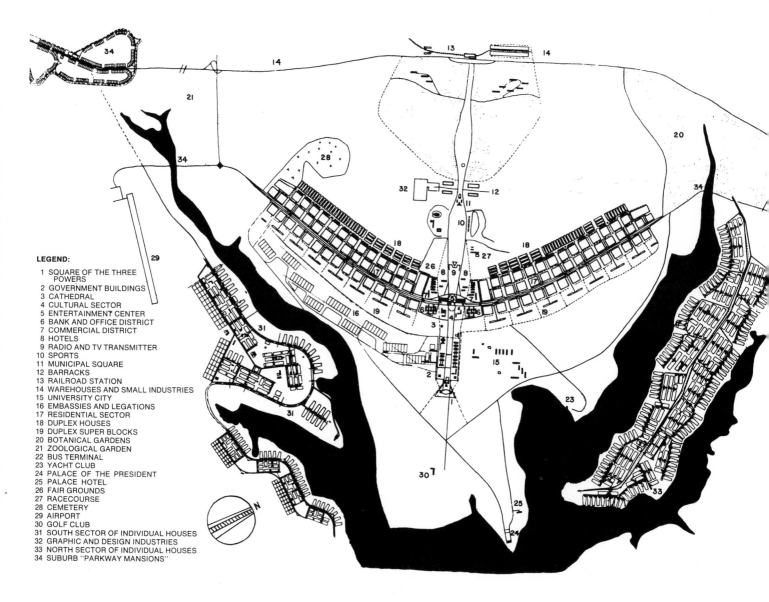

Fig. 146. Plan of Brasília, new capital of Brazil by planner Lucio Costa and architect Oscar Niemeyer. The modular housing (17 and 18) belongs to the grid concept of urban origins. The monumental axis (10) is totally unconnected with the urban body. The 1,200-feet-wide axis has been checked at one end (according to Costa's original plan) by the airport—the capital's only feasible link with Rio de Janeiro and the outside world—and on the other by the Plaza of the Three Powers. Not even hotel (25) or Governor's Palace (26) are permitted any contact with this aloof symbol.

cessful imperium acquired somewhat schizoid connotations when Lucio Costa and Oscar Niemeyer planned and built Brasília, the new Brazilian capital (*Fig. 146*). Like runners, unable to change their course, they raced down their 1,200-feet-wide avenue of triumph, shouting with winded voices that what they were after was the triumph of the people and not of the rulers. On a high platform they planted sculptured symbols of the Three Powers of government over the people, just as palace, fortress, cathedral and court house had symbolized the power of one class over another since the beginning of urban history (*Fig. 147*).

Le Corbusier's plan for Chandigarh, the capital of the Punjab (*Fig. 148*) attempted an interesting and sophisticated compromise between Roman heritage and twentieth-century de-

Fig. 147. The last of Rome! The royal adventus axis of Brasília.

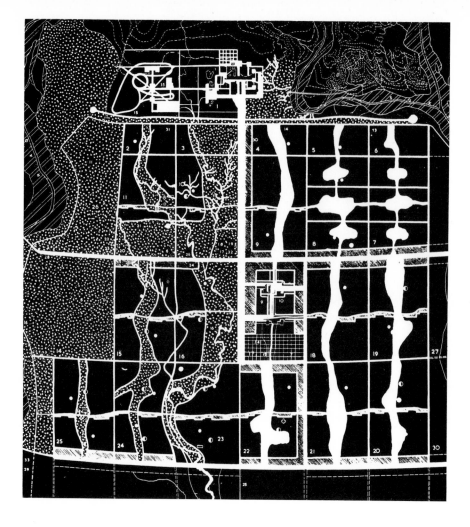

*Fig. 148. Original plan of Chandigarh,
new capital of the Punjab as developed
by Albert Meyer, Le Corbusier, and
Pierre Jeanneret during the 1950's.
Each numbered city sector constitutes
a subcity of its own, loosely related to
an administrative and commercial
center block. The acropolis (1) rises
both physically and architecturally high
above the town, acknowledging only
the proximity of the university (35).*

*Fig. 149. Secretariat and assembly
building on the acropolis of Chandigarh,
designed by Le Corbusier in the 1950's.
Despite the formal perfection
of these buildings and their relationship
to the sky and the Himalaya mountains,
there is an air of abandonment and
lack of recognition here. Le Corbusier's
crowning achievement as an architect
has a key place in the genesis of
man-made environment, because it
demonstrates the age-old challenge
of building as an art against building
as anonymous service. The tragedy
is the distance that separates these
buildings from the European-
Mediterranean sources that inspired
them. Outside the orbit of Rome, the
Chandigarh acropolis is a lost cause.*

Fig. 150. Wallace Harrison, Monumental Mall, Albany, New York, perspective and plan (1960's).

mocracy. His power structures—senate, supreme court and administration—are totally separated from the city by earth mounds that keep the monumental buildings from sight. They only relate to the Himalaya mountains on the horizon (*Fig. 149*). Le Corbusier's confession from 1929, "Today I am called a rebel, but I have had only one teacher: the past," is curiously borne out by his distinction between the ancient and irreplacable seats of coercive discipline, and the anonymous regimentation of the predetermined grid plan.

Has twentieth-century man really cut loose from the orbit of Rome? Albany, the capital of the State of New York, was thrown into chaos by the construction of a monumental central mall—part Timgad and part Taj Mahal—connecting in a reciprocal vista the revered architectural aberrations of America's Victorian past (*Fig. 150*). It is likely that even the Romans would have been embarrassed by so blatant a historical misunderstanding, which mixes architectural continuity as the leading force of the official avenue with the random shapes and scattered placement of business buildings.

157

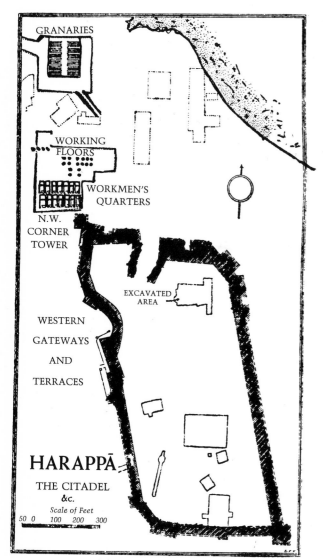

Fig. 151. The citadel of the Indus Valley city of Harappa in the middle of the third millennium B.C. In the upper left, the granaries that were the backbone of Harappan economy. Below, the standardized units of the workmen's quarters.

Labels within figure: GRANARIES, WORKING FLOORS, WORKMEN'S QUARTERS, N.W. CORNER TOWER, EXCAVATED AREA, WESTERN GATEWAYS AND TERRACES, HARAPPĀ, THE CITADEL &c., Scale of Feet 50 0 100 200 300

THE MODULAR GRID PLAN

To sum up the basic concepts of human settlement presented so far: the geomorphic approach is organic, characterized by interrelated growth between landscape and building; the concentric approach is ideological, deriving from a commitment to a supramundane ideal; the orthogonal concept is pragmatic (in the Greek meaning of *pragma,* "the thing done," i.e., business completed), adjusting the city to constantly changing requirements of communication and expansion. The geomorphic and the concentric concepts are static, because they are predicated on assumed absolutes—nature and faith. The orthogonal concept, based on man-made reality and change, is fluid, permitting a great variety of approaches. Within the pragmatic orthogonal pattern the modular grid as the basis for a designed settlement represents a peculiar compromise between a static imposed order and a flexible evolved order.

In contrast to the other types of urban foundations, the modular grid plan is not generated from within the community but is predetermined from without. To the genesis of urban intentions from rural to cosmological to ecumenical, the modular grid adds a coercive concept, whether political or religiously motivated, imposing on plan, building, and inhabitant the same predetermined dimensions. A module is a standard unit, whose measurements regulate the size and proportions of a composition. A brick is the module of a masonry wall, a 4- by 8-feet steel frame the module of a curtain wall, the 8- by 10-feet room the space module of a housing project. In the layout of communities, the module of the building lot or street block has a similar reciprocal relationship to the over-all plan.

The first geometrically precise alignment of modular units, creating a very specific kind of environment, is a one-and-a-half-mile-long row of cubicles, each 9 by 6 by 7 feet, which housed 4,000 workers on the plateau of Cheops Pyramid at Giza (*ca.* 2650 B.C.) (see *Fig. 83*). The centers of the third millennium B.C. Indus Valley cities Mohenjo-Daro and Harappa (*Fig. 151*), show compounds of uniform housing modules next to the granaries, which were the economic center of the Harappa civilization. Their uniformity stands in strong contrast to the individually subdivided city blocks (*Fig. 152*).* This telling contrast between selected and imposed environment is even more evident in the so-called workers' town of El Kahun, or El Lahun,

* J. H. Marshall, *Mohenjo-Daro and the Indus Civilization* (1927).

Fig. 152. *Excavated residential section of Mohenjo-Daro in the Indus Valley, which flourished in the third millennium* B.C. *The free arrangement of rooms and lanes is in strongest contrast to the modular workers' dwellings beside the granaries.*

some 500 years later than either Giza or Harappa (*Fig. 153*). Associated with the construction of the pyramid at El Lahun during the Middle Kingdom of Egypt by the Pharaoh Sesostris I (1970 B.C.), this settlement is a good example of socially stratified environment. It is the only example of Egyptian town planning still intact aside from the short-lived royal capital at Tell

Fig. 153. *Plan of the Egyptian town of El Kahun or El Lahun from the Middle Kingdom (2134–1786* B.C.*). A highly caste-conscious society is here expressed in three different house types: large mansions (a), serving most probably court officials; medium attached houses of varying sizes (b) for the next echelon, perhaps priests or scribes; and workmen's tenements (c), separated from the other two by a solid wall and conforming to a standardized minimum module. From Alexander Badawy,* Ancient Egyptian Architectural Design, *Middle Eastern Studies 4 (1965).*

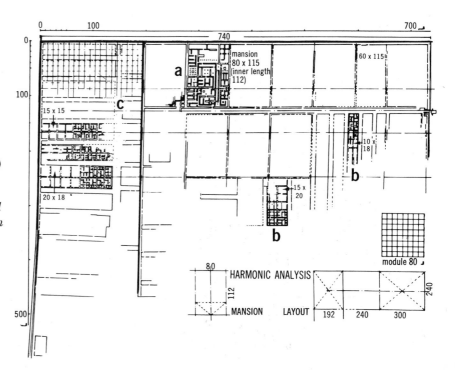

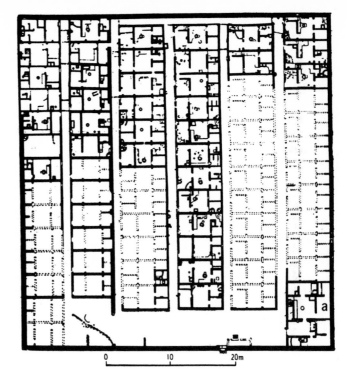

Fig. 154. The walled modular workers' compound at Amarna from the New Kingdom (1570–1085 B.C.), showing the contrast to individual planning in the house of the overseer (a).

el Amarna of a later time. Town officials or, rather, royal administrators, seem to have lived in sumptuous mansions of a bewildering variety of rooms and galleries, with interior garden courts still showing pits and irrigation channels for palm trees. The next social echelon, perhaps the priests or scribes, had

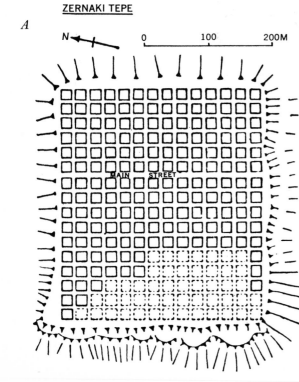

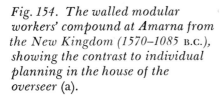

Fig. 155. Modular grid plan (A), excavated at an Urartian site in Anatolia. The characteristic settlement plan of the Urartians, as that of all Indo-Germanic people, was geomorphic, as seen in (B). The sudden and isolated appearance of a modular community points to the conquest and destruction of Urartu by the Assyrians, and to the establishment of a detention and administration unit by the new overlords. From C. A. Burney, "Urartian Fortresses," in Anatolian Studies, VII (1957).

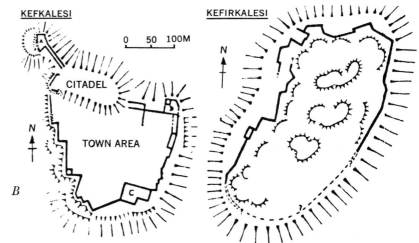

smaller attached houses varying in shape and size, situated on the same main blocks as the mansions. Separated from this "free town" by a wall were tight rows of "minimum housing," uniform in size and with little or no variation in interior partitions.

Another 600 years went by and Ikhnaton, the iconoclast, built his city to the sun god which we call today Tell el Amarna (see *Fig. 87*). It has an almost totally unplanned looseness of building distribution, except for a rigidly squared compound (*Fig. 154*) under the burning cliffs far away from the river. There lived the workers who achieved the backbreaking miracle of building the sprawling capital in less than a decade.

Only one site exists that seems to prove that the Assyrians adopted the modular-coercive planning pattern of Egypt. It must be assumed that the oppressive garrisons that the first successful imperialists imposed on conquered territories were modular grids. The fact that there are almost no remnants seems to prove their conceptual basis. They were wiped off the land as soon as the oppressors left. The Kingdom of Urartu in the Lake Van region of Anatolia was destroyed by Shalmanassur with particular cruelty and thoroughness, as indicated by the already quoted Sultan Tepe tablets and the bas reliefs of Nineveh. The Indo-European Urartians lived around geomorphically sited citadels similar to those of the Greeks. Among their devastated locations is one site, Zernaki Tepe, which shows the remnants or the beginning of a perfect gridiron plan (*Figs. 155A, 155B*). Each block measures 59 feet square; streets are 17 feet wide, with one main street 23 feet wide. All walls were 4 feet thick.* The conclusion seems inevitable that this must have been an Assyrian military-administrative camp serving as prototype for the garrisons founded by Alexander the Great in his march of world conquest (*Fig. 156*). None of these garrisons have survived, but numerous descriptions and archaeological finds permit a clear picture of these standardized Macedonian towns for veterans and deportees. Their existence is the dark side of Alexander's urban *oikumene*. Twelve of the grid-plan centers bore the name Alexandria, a custom which was later perpetuated by the emperor's successors. There were twelve Antiochs in addition to the capital of the Seleucids on the Orontes, and six Seleucias in addition to the original city. In the crucial borderland between Central Asia and India, in Bactria southeast of the Caspian Sea, these garrisons were part

* C. A. Burney, "Urartian Fortresses," in *Anatolian Studies*, Vol. VII, 1957).

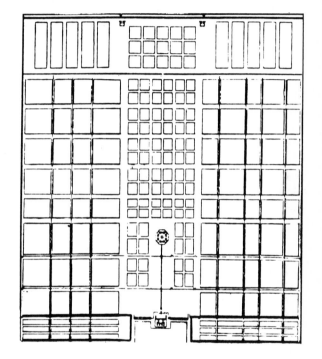

Fig. 156. Farahabad, a Persian military stronghold rebuilt in the seventeenth century over the remains of several successive garrison towns, resembles the katoika *of Alexander the Great. The* katoika *was a combination of garrison, concentration camp, and refugee city not unknown in modern times. Though many detailed literary descriptions of them exist, these communities have left no physical remains. However, the Farahabad plan conforms so closely to historical descriptions of the* katoika, *it seems justified to see in it the prototype of Roman and all later garrison sites. Drawn by E. E. Beaudouin.*

Fig. 157. Two Chinese military tschengs (refuge and administration centers) of the second century B.C., measuring 1,625 and 2,843 feet square. They were surrounded by a moat. Seven modules of enclosed ground were reserved for food production and raising fowl. After Ernst Egli.

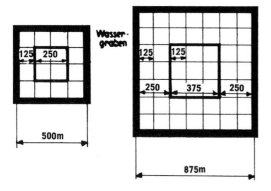

of a settlement and defense system consisting of towns, native villages, and the Alexander Wall stretched as a fortified spine across the Gurgan Plain to keep out the unconquerable nomadic hordes of the steppes.

Alexander's standardized garrison towns had as far-reaching an influence as the orthogonal-connective plan of Alexandria (*Fig. 97*). The obvious expediency of a single, precalculated, endlessly repetitive administrative and military settlement was so apparent that it spread East and West—to the Asiatic khans and emperors and to the Romans and their European successors.

Ch'in, the first emperor of a unified China and a fierce military dictator, copied the Alexander Wall in the Great Wall of China (started in 221 B.C.) as did Hadrian on the border of Britain and the Pictish highlands to the north, and Khrushchev 1,800 years later in Berlin, this time to keep in the fugitives. In his newly annexed territories to the west, Ch'in founded *tschengs,* military, administrative, and protective towns, laid out in identical modular grids (*Fig. 157*). Their basic pattern

Fig. 158. Plan of the Japanese royal city of Kyoto, founded in A.D. 792, supposedly after the prototype of the Chinese royal city of Ch'ang-an. The fascination of the twentieth-century functionalist doctrine with the Japanese preference for minimum everything is extended to this oppressive prison-camp layout.

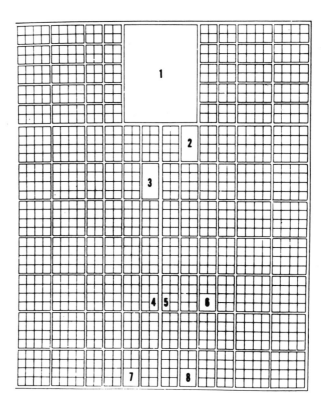

162

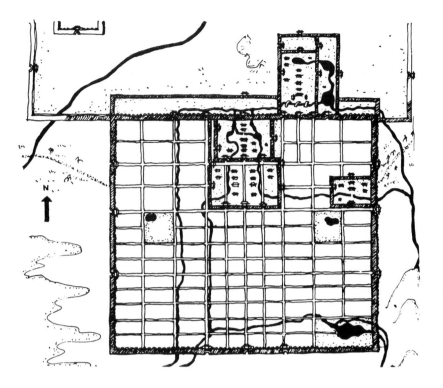

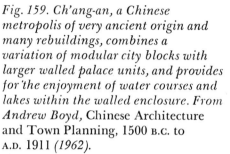

Fig. 159. Ch'ang-an, a Chinese metropolis of very ancient origin and many rebuildings, combines a variation of modular city blocks with larger walled palace units, and provides for the enjoyment of water courses and lakes within the walled enclosure. From Andrew Boyd, Chinese Architecture and Town Planning, 1500 B.C. to A.D. 1911 *(1962).*

was retained by later dynasties and appealed particularly to the Japanese. As a nation, conceived and reared on a tatami mat module (3 by 6 feet), they learned early to base their entire environment from toilet seat to kimono, from house to city plan, on a modular unit (*Fig. 158*). This in turn stirred twentieth-century functionalists to the grateful recognition that the ritualistic significance of the Japanese minimum module was actually the direct forerunner of the Bauhaus principle.*

The Chinese, under the fabulously creative Han Dynasty (206 B.C.–A.D. 200) broke through the rigid uniformity of the modular grid and devised a combination plan of orthogonal and modular interaction. As in the Assyrian cities of the first millennium B.C., a walled central enclosure was off limits; it was a government center, a "forbidden city" (*Fig. 159*). The city itself consisted of walled squares, occupied by tradesmen and professionals whose walled households made up the specific sector. These intersquared or nested units were contained in the rectangular circumvallation of the whole city. This is why in Chinese the same word is used for wall and town.

* Walter Gropius and Kenzo Tange, *Katsura: Tradition and Creation in Japanese Architecture,* (New Haven, Conn., 1960).

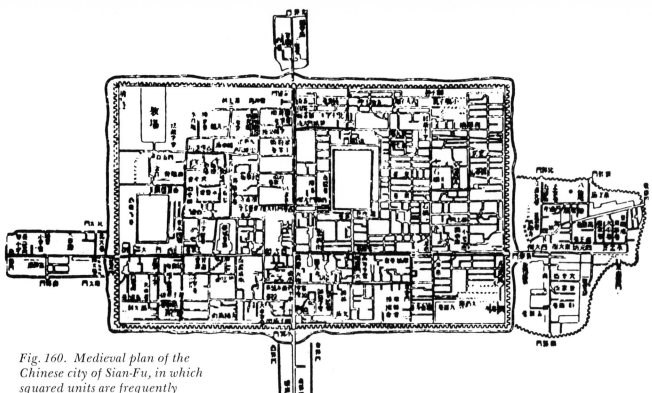

Fig. 160. Medieval plan of the
Chinese city of Sian-Fu, in which
squared units are frequently
divided from each other by canals.
They have the triple function of
delineation, transportation, and
sanitation. The clusters outside
the city wall are temple districts.

The virtuosity of the Han Dynasty and their successors in transforming grid and module into a living, interacting, visually varied city, despite adherence to an undeviating orthogonal-grid pattern, expressed itself in four major planning features: First, the size of grid divisions and neighborhood compounds

Fig. 161. Presentation of a city gate on a
rubbing from the first century A.D.
(Han Dynasty), with the symbolic crane
(bird of destiny) on the roof.

varied (*Fig. 160*); frequently, a canal or a regulated river fixed the boundary. Next, the variation in height of the wall enclosures and the flare and color of the tile roofs overhanging the walls furnished perceptive interest. Then, there was the designed experience of passage through many gates with an inexhaustible variety of openings, each shape carrying a poetic or transcendental message. Projected outside the dwelling, this concern with the aesthetics of movement extended to bridges in bamboo, stone, wood, and ceramic tile, to architectural accents of linear perspective and the gigantic stone gates of the city (*Fig. 161*). Finally, axial vistas were never terminated. They continued through walls, buildings, and parks, as if to maintain a continuous awareness that the connective dynamism of the city is without end.*

The most sophisticated element in the orthogonal cityscape of China was the rhythm of horizontality and verticality. No one has been able to explain why the Chinese alone among all civilized nations piled house upon house, complete with roof structures, instead of expanding horizontally with the acquisition of wealth and social standing. A noble of special rank was permitted up to seven stories in the Han period, but this was not sufficient as status symbol; beside many residences rose pleasure towers, *t'ais*, sometimes of wood and sometimes of masonry, ten or fifteen stories higher than the roofs of the dwellings (*Fig. 162*). Their purpose seems similar to the medieval towers of Bologna, Siena, and San Gimignano—to express power and wealth and a keen sense of local competition.†

When Buddhism invaded China in the third century, the secular splendor of the Sons of Han was destroyed. The frivolous gazebos became pagodas outside the walled cities and lost their function of vertical contrast.

Chan-chan, the capital of the Chimú Empire of Peru (thirteenth to fifteenth centuries) is so totally different from the urban centers in Mexico that a powerful foreign element must have determined its planning concept (*Fig. 163*). There are no pyramids, no causeways, no acropolis, and no large religious art objects. Chan-chan lies in the desert area of the Peruvian coast. Inside a square adobe enclosure, the two-and-a-half-

Fig. 162. Pottery model of a Han tower from the second century B.C. *(British Museum). It might be assumed that these pleasure towers—also used as watch towers— which rose to great heights, had much the same function as those of the Lombard cities in the Middle Ages. They were exclamation marks of pride, competition, and the exuberance of success.*

* Andrew Boyd, *Chinese Architecture and Town Planning, 1500* B.C. *to* A.D. *1911* (Chicago, 1962), and Osvald Siren, *The Walls and the Gates of Peking* (1924).

† H. H. Dubs (trans.), from Pan Ku, *The History of the Former Han Dynasty* (New York, 1938–55).

Fig. 163. Chan-chan, on the Peruvian coast, capital of the Chimú empire from the twelfth to the early fifteenth centuries A.D. It shows a close resemblance to the traditional Chinese intersquared city plan.

square-mile city is divided into walled *ciudadelas,* or neighborhoods, named today after their excavators—Bandelier, Uhle, etc. (*Fig. 164*). It contained cultivated tree-planted enclosures which relied on what Uhle called "the most extensive and sophisticated irrigation system invented by men." Since the whole city was built in adobe, not many buildings can be reconstructed. But those whose foundations survive show squared spaces around interior courts, and a preference for partitioning off multiple space units with walls in the Chinese tradition.

166

The estimates of the number of inhabitants of Chan-chan vary greatly, the average calculation being about 60,000 people.

The Incas who destroyed the Chimú in the middle of the fifteenth century, less than a hundred years before being destroyed by the Spaniards, were a nonurbanized mountain people who exterminated the urban culture of the coastal region. Then they proceeded in the age-old logic of war to build new cities in the image of what they had destroyed. Their capital, Cuzco, received an intersquared plan which is based on the prototype of Chan-chan, except for an elongated rather than a square area because of the given mountain plateau (*Figs. 165A, 165B*). Cuzcoquiti means Region of Cuzco, because the royal capital stretched close to fifty miles up the valley to the fortress of Sacsahuaman (see *Fig. 58*). The name of the city was pre-Inca, implying "the stone that marks possession" and referring to a sacred *omphalos* or navel stone, kept in the center of the canchas —walled palace compounds inhabited by living as well as mum-

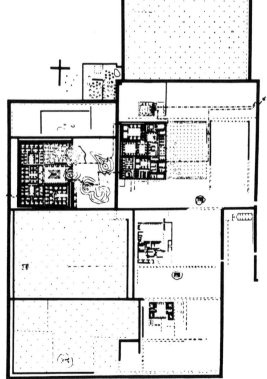

Fig. 164. Chan-chan, capital of the Chimú empire: the quarter called by the excavators "cuidadela Uhle." It shows densely built-up walled squared quarters and walled irrigated parkland, with the planting holes still visible.

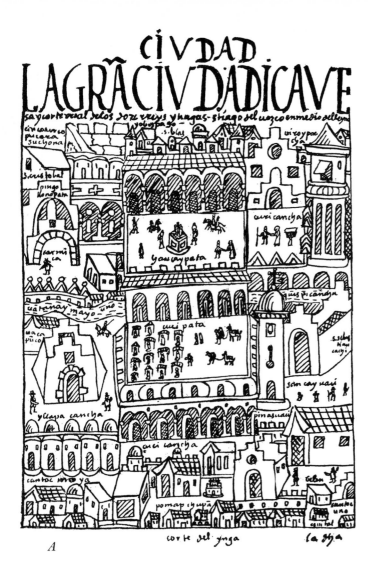

A

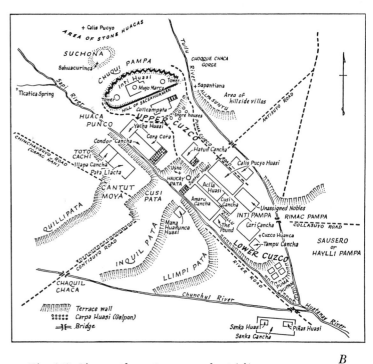

B

Fig. 165. *Sixteenth-century woodcut (A)
of the royal region of Cuzco, as recorded
by Pizarro's staff; and a reconstructed
plan (B) showing the intersquared
compounds and the empire road system.
From Burr Cartwright Brundage,*
Lords of Cuzco *(1967). Courtesy of
University of Oklahoma Press.*

mified Inca rulers, their families, and retainers. Other canchas
were assigned to lords of noble birth whose lineage decided
their place in the state organization. Outside the inner city
wall were the walled compounds of the *Micmacs,* meaning
conquered lords of high lineage, also called "unassigned nobles,"
serving as vassals. Only "the worthless people," the equivalent
of India's "untouchables," lived on open land. Each cancha was
a miniature city in itself, subdivided by rectangular interior
walls and governed by hierarchical laws that had to be obeyed
at peril of execution. Since there existed a Chimú compound
for nobles, it is obvious that the Inca had copied their feudal-

istic bureaucracy and its intersquared compound plan from earlier Americans.* Later Inca foundations show the intersquared plan even more clearly. Viracochapampa, for example, has a perfectly intersquared layout (*Fig. 166*) with a double wall providing a corral for the all-important llama herds. The most characteristic feature here and in other Inca foundations such as Cajamarquilla and Incahuasi remains the totality of the city as a walled compound whose character is centripetal, preplanned toward the lines of communication of the empire.

The Aryan cattle breeders who in the midde of the second millennium B.C. poured across the Himalyan passes into India belonged to the Indo-European race which has, throughout a long history, excelled in exterminating the cultures it has encountered. This was the fate of the native Dravidians, as it would later be of the Aegean Pelasgians, the English Britons, the American Indians, and the Australian aborigines. The old-

* Brundage, *op. cit.*

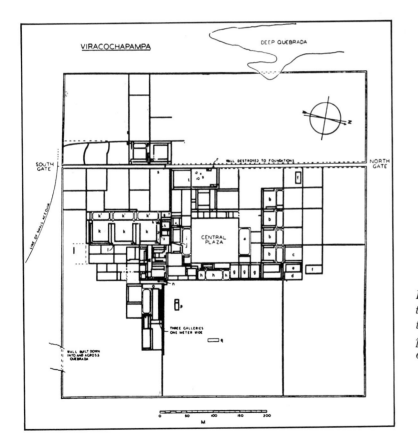

Fig. 166. The Inca mountain town of Viracochapampa, thirteenth century A.D., with a perfect intersquared orthogonal plan.

169

est collection of sacred lore known as the *Rig-Veda* has left an unabashed record of the aggressive fury of the Aryan god Indra, who was equivalent to the Indo-European deities Wodan and Zeus; he carried two spears and two thunderbolts and inspired his people to believe in Aryan supremacy, the inferiority of dark-skinned races, and the destruction of cities. The last song of the *Rig-Veda* establishes the caste system of "the four colors": Brahmans, warriors, artisans, and the untouchable laborers.* It is one of the highly satisfactory ironies of history that this feudal society in India, reared on the broken backs of the natives, succumbed in due course to the necromantic, mystical, fatalistic climate of the country. Toward the close of the last millennium B.C., some major cities were built as residences by a number of feudal kings. Nothing is known of their plans, but it might be assumed that they were based on the city system of the Indus Valley civilization (see *Figs. 151, 152*), which the Aryans had destroyed.

It is clear from their numerous treatises and compilations of sacred instructions that the Aryans considered the fortified place —not distinguished as either village or town—as the only valid

* E. B. Havell, *History of the Aryan Rule in India* (New York, 1918).

Fig. 167. *The basic modular grid of Hindu city planning as laid down in the* Manasara. *It is a perfect compromise between pre-established, inflexible units imposed by external authority, and a hierarchical system of intersquared units. It places Brahma in the "forbidden city" of nine squares, surrounded by eight chief deities, which form a link to thirty-six squared minor celestials. The coercive module has been made acceptable as divine law.*

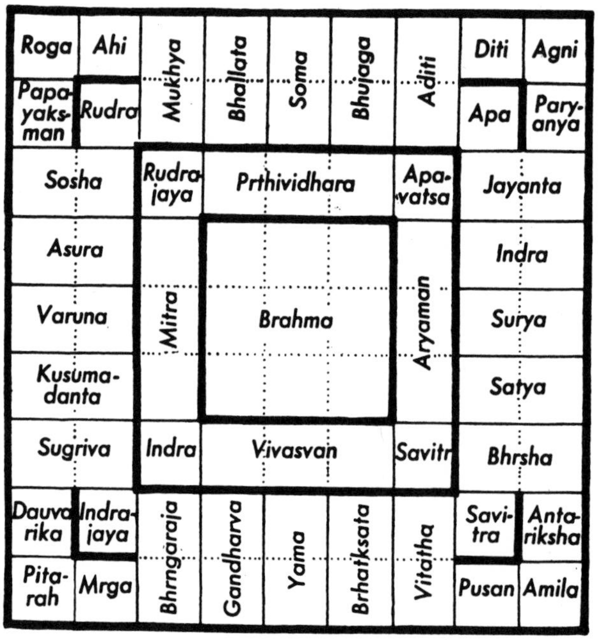

170

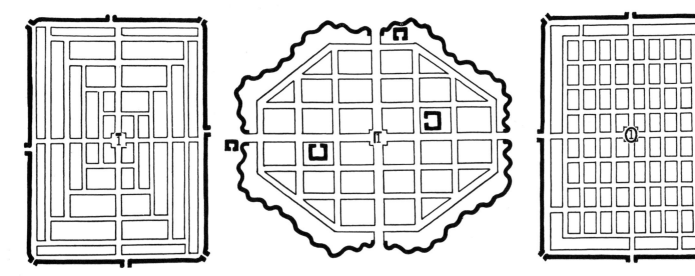

type of settlement. The orthogonal grid, imported from China, underwent considerable transformations to combine aggression with piety. It was systematized early in the first millennium A.D. in the *Manasara*, a handbook for city planners which forms one section of the *Silpa Sastra*, a vast compendium of Hindu arts and crafts. The urban syndicalism of the Chinese town, with its coordinated mosaic of social units, was here adjusted to the Indian caste system. In the basic grid, the *Paramasayika (Fig. 167)*, Brahma occupies the nine central squares of the forbidden city; his eight tutelary deities live in the neighboring compounds, surrounded by a strictly hierarchical order of thirty-six minor deities called *Paravatas.** There exist more than thirty variations of this cosmological order of the ideal Indo-Aryan settlement *(Fig. 168)*, ranging according to status and tradition from swastika plans for royal residences to circles for places of pilgrimage. Their common feature was a *mundus plate* in the center of the town, where the snake of creation (similar in concept to the feathered serpent of the ancient American cultures) had been transfixed by a wooden spike.

No actual towns from Vedic times or later that have been excavated conform to the sacred grid, although most Hindu and Buddhist monasteries contain elements of the *Silpa Sastra* plan. Its inclusion in a history of urban origins is justified by two city

Fig. 168. Schematic city plans from the Manasara *manual, each indicating a different subdivision resulting from the Hindu caste system. Their common core is the* mundus plate (1) *anchoring the city to the universe. These plans, dating from the beginning of the first millennium A.D., are similar to the "ideal plans" of the Renaissance (see Fig. 69).*

Where did the influence come from? When the Portuguese landed in 1502 in Cochin on the west coast of India, they found flourishing communities of Nestorian Christians, who had been converted by St. Thomas some 1,500 years before and whose sacred literature was still in Syriac. Through these Malabar Christians, the Portuguese were able to establish a lasting foothold in India and to enter into lucrative trade relations with Hindu and Moslem rulers. As in the time of the Roman Empire, Asian influence flowed to Europe across the Arabian Sea and the Persian Gulf.

* B. B. Dutt, *Town Planning in Ancient India* (1925).

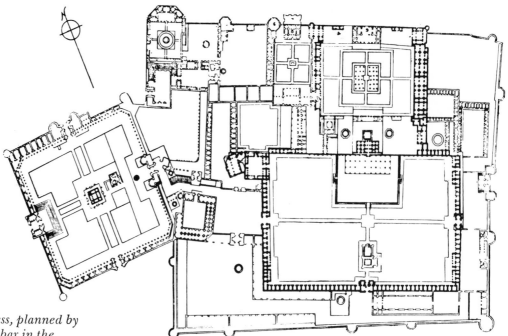

Fig. 169. Lahore Fortress, planned by the Mogul emperor Akbar in the middle of the sixteenth century. His plan emphasizes the intersquared compound concept, alien to the concentric city plans of Islam, so that the result is a curiously hybrid layout—a combination of Angkor Wat and the Great Mosque of Damascus.

plans that revived the *Manasara* cosmology at a much later date. Eighteen hundred years after Asoka, Akbar, the most remarkable of Indian rulers, conquered northern India, which he consolidated into the Mogul Empire. Although a faithful Moslem, he revived the Hindu religion, appointed Rajput Hindus as his administrators, and founded an eclectic faith, Din-i-Ilahi, based on extreme tolerance. In 1550, Akbar began building the Lahore Fortress (*Fig. 169*), whose plan is as syncretic as his religious ideals. It is intersquared orthogonal, with the modular rooms and geometric centrality of the sacred Hindu planning diagrams. The city of Jaipur (*Fig. 170*), rebuilt in the early eighteenth century over very ancient foundations, is a highly metaphysical interpretation by Jai Singh II, a ruler whose exclusive interest was astronomy. This might explain his *Manasara* city plan.

The modular gridiron city, then, had two ancestors—a realistic one and a spiritual one. The former saw the collective habitat as a coercive container, the latter as a geometric allegory of cosmic predestination. Both shared the conviction that the anonymous masses were not entitled to a free environmental choice but were to be molded by a module that was determined by an intelligence higher than their own. It is important

172

to keep this in mind when looking at modern gridiron developments. Visionary planners of millennial towns—from Plato's Atlantis and More's Utopia to Le Corbusier's City of Three Million People and Tange's Megacity in Tokyo Bay—have always appropriated to themselves a suprahuman power as matrix-makers for the common man.

The same dual influence of totalitarian and divine order has been ignored by historians as the logical explanation of the first appearance of the modular grid plan in Western civilization, the so-called Hippodamian plan. With the brainless monotony of Tibetan prayer-wheel spinners, text after text repeats the manifest falsehood that Hippodamus of Miletus was "the first city planner," that he "invented" the modular grid plan, and that he either personally designed the orthogonal cities of the Hellenistic age or was conceptually responsible for them. The lazy lumping together of Roman castrums, medieval bastides, Renaissance "ideal cities," and American grid plans as "Hippodamian" has no justification in historical or plain visual evidence. We have only a single plan which, on the authority of Aristotle, was executed by Hippodamus (*ca.* 470 B.C.), that of his home city, Miletus, in Ionia (*Fig. 171A*), after it had been destroyed in the Persian War. In addition, there is Aristotle's offhand remark that Hippodamus "cut up the Piraeus," the port of Athens. It is most unlikely on historical grounds that the labor-camp modules of Egypt and Assyria played any part in the planning concept of Miletus. She was the greatest, most

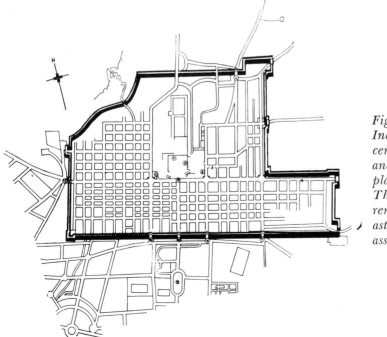

Fig. 170. The old walled city of Jaipur, India, refounded in the eighteenth century over a much older Indian site, and coming close to a classical Manasara *plan in its orthogonal subdivisions. The center of the city still holds the remnants of the largest collection of astronomical observatories and instruments assembled in pre-scientific times.*

Fig. 171.

A) The plan of Miletus in Ionia of ca. 470 B.C., as reconstructed by A. von Gerkan. Urban historians have conceived a violent affection for this exercise in modular coercion which —if it had ever been executed—would have looked like a nightmare to anyone who could think three-dimensionally. It would have been a rat's maze of blank walls, since all Greek houses were walled, bare of any compass orientation or ornamental identification features, and indifferent to a spectacularly beautiful location. View and access to the sea cliffs were barred by a wall that followed the cliffs' contours, as if to be certain that the inhabitants of a divinely inspired theorem were not distracted by the irregularities of nature.

B) A Pythagorean theorem demonstrating that in a right-angled triangle the square of the long side, the hypotenuse, is equal to the sum of the squares of the two shorter sides. Babylonian mathematicians knew this 1,000 years before the Greeks.

A

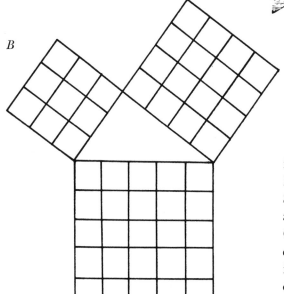

B

famous, and most independent city of the Greek world; she had planted more than sixty colonies from Egypt to the Black Sea; and she produced more famous men in philosophy, science, and the arts than Athens. After the brutal defeat suffered by the Greeks in the Battle of Lade and occupation by the semi-civilized Persians, emphasis on transcendental values, apparent in their numerical equivalents, is evident in the sacred geometry of Greek temples and in the spread of the cosmological "systems" of Pythagoras and Heraclitus. Hippodamus, the planner

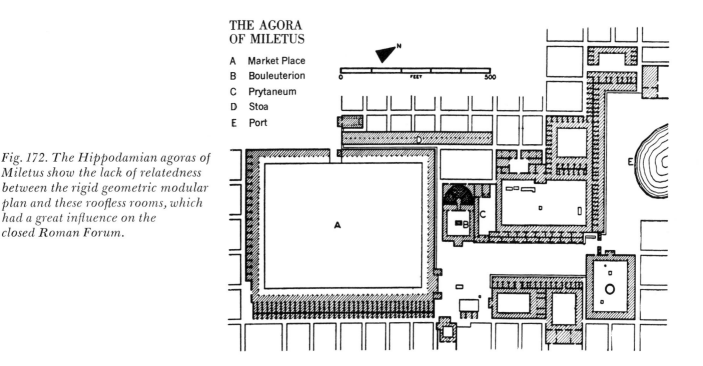

THE AGORA
OF MILETUS

A Market Place
B Bouleuterion
C Prytaneum
D Stoa
E Port

Fig. 172. The Hippodamian agoras of Miletus show the lack of relatedness between the rigid geometric modular plan and these roofless rooms, which had a great influence on the closed Roman Forum.

of Miletus, was a devout Pythagorean who wrote on atmospheric and geomantic influences. According to Aristotle's description in *Politics,* he was

a strange man whose excessive fondness for distinction led him into general eccentricity of life which made one think him affected . . . the first person not a statesman who advised on the best form of government.

In addition to creating an enduring professional prototype, he initiated the unfortunate practice of the mathematical "plat," based not on a topographical reality but on numerical configurations, whether cosmological or demographic. The Miletus plan is a Pythagorean theorem, based on ideal Pythagorean proportions of geometric relationships: $a:b = b:c$ (*Fig. 171B*). The grouping of the identical blocks abounds in "female" (even) and "male" (uneven) numerological constellations, such as 2×3, 2×5, 3×6, etc. The gnomon numbers 1, 4, and 7 (whose sum is 12) explained in Pythagorean writings occur in major constellations, with such "signs" as 28 and the triple-potential of 9. The agoras, which according to Lavedan are the only architectural contribution of Hippodamus (*Fig. 172*), are

Fig. 173. Pythagorean presentation of equation $(x + y)^2 = x^2 + 2xy + y^2$

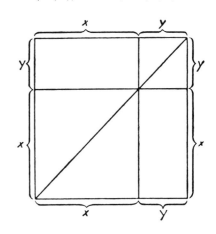

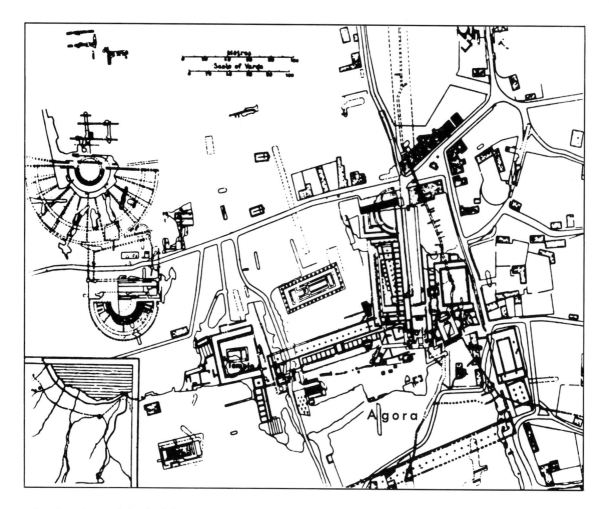

Fig. 174. Central Corinth in Hellenistic times, ca. *200* B.C. *It is easy enough to stand today on the vast agora of Corinth, which has been swept clean by time, and forget about the heap of structures and the gaudily painted temples that made up the city center in its heyday. The greatness of Greek genius, its still almost inconceivable contribution to the development of human self-awareness, did not express itself in city planning, because planning is a collective concern and submerges the nonconforming individual.*

closed units, roofless rooms, without any relationship to the city, or without any lines of communication connecting public and residential areas. On the total city plan, only two slightly widened crossaxial streets in the large-block sector break the uniformity of the cleavages between blocks. But it is doubtful that this was an attempt to improve urban circulation. The relationship of the two emphasized lines to the hypotenuse quadrant corresponds to the Pythagorean presentation of the incommensurable equation $(x + y)^2 = x^2 + 2xy + y^2$ (*Fig. 173*).

The identification of the ubiquitous Miletus plan with Pythagorean numerology and geometry is both circumstantial and visual, based on the fact that its creator was a confirmed

Pythagorean and that the Greeks had no previous city plans. A look at any pre-Platonic, pre-Hippodamian city shows that the Greeks, basically anti-urban, made a considerable mess of their polis centers (*Fig. 174*), not to mention the totally vanished residential quarters. No trace of a street arrangement has survived anywhere, because none existed. Despite the Miletus experiment in translating Pythagoras into reality, the old cities of the Greek mainland remained unplanned accumulations, and only those, completely rebuilt in Hellenistic times, acquired orthogonal plans..

In Diodorus' description of vanished Thurii there is literary evidence of one more authentically Hippodamian plan, that of the first "ideal city" founded by Pericles in Sicily in 443 B.C. "to get away from it all." A tetraktic relationship of four longitudinal and three lateral subdivisions added up to the potent number of twelve for the city area, of which ten blocks were turned over to the Decad of the Hellenic tribes.* In his comedy *The Birds,* written in 415 B.C., Aristophanes makes fun of Meton, an astronomer, planner, Pythagorean, and follower of Hippodamus. In the play, Meton's mission in the new city of Cloud-cuckoo-land is "a geodetic survey of the atmosphere of Cloud-cuckoo-land and the immediate allocation of all this aerial area into cubic acres . . . ." He indulges in geometric double-talk about "axial hub . . . global spokes . . . astral radii" till he is booted off the stage.

The archaeological report on the extent to which the Hippodamian plan of Miletus was actually followed is very vague. In the pick-and-shovel age, it would have been an almost inconceivable feat to build this network of absolutely uniform squares, disregarding obstacles presented by the rough plateau. In any age, the physical reality of such a plan would have been an almost inconceivable nightmare of blank walls and blind corners. The closed agoras would have offered no visual relief, for there were no golden-tiled curved roofs and multicolored, multistaged towers, as there were in Peking.

The Piraeus might have been "cut up" by Hippodamus, as Aristotle says, but it was put together again by someone else (*Figs. 175A, 175B*). The double harbor serving Athens shows strong Neo-Babylonian influences, in the use of a street network as primary factor of organization, and in the developed concept of a zoned merchant city. Inscriptions on boundary stones as-

* Only source: Diodorus Sicolus, Greek historian, first century B.C.

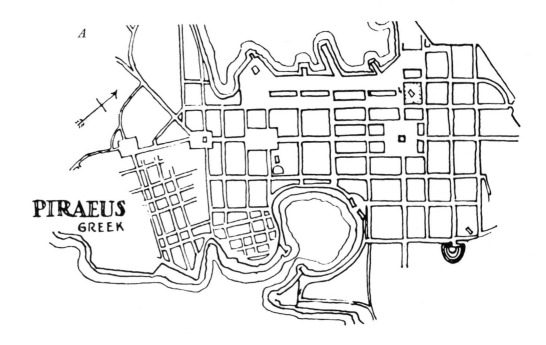

PIRAEUS
GREEK

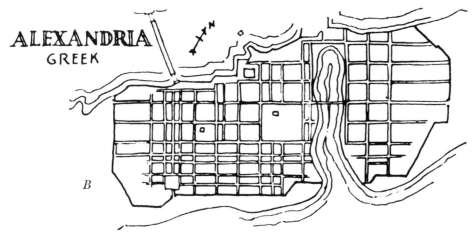

ALEXANDRIA
GREEK

A

B

Fig. 175. The Piraeus (A), described as Hippodamian, is not a modular grid plan like Miletus, but follows the orthogonal principles that came to fruition in the plan of Alexandria (B). The similarity between the two plans, which were created in the second half of the fourth century B.C., *is so great that one might suspect the same planner was responsible for both.*

signed so many blocks to the market, to the warehouse and dock areas, to mooring places for native and for foreign ships, and so on. The relationship to the somewhat later plan of Alexandria is so evident that the Piraeus looks like a finger exercise by the same planner for a community that no longer believed in Pythagorean numerology.

The published plans of Priene, the other Ionian city ascribed to Hippodamus, vary greatly. The reconstruction of the city belongs to Hellenistic times, more than a century after its destruction by the Persians. An eclectic mixture of concepts is clearly evident (*Fig. 176*). The longitudinal adjustment to the terminating cliff, the quadratic but by no means uniform block pattern of the residential areas, and the careful variation in street widths and public places are geomorphic and orthogonal-linear, archaic Greek and Hellenistic. The wide distribution of squares and agoras gives the center a unique openness, despite its geometric precision; there is nothing similar until one encounters the central plazas of the Andean cultures. A sizable "Sanctuary of the Egyptian Gods" is unlabeled in English-language plans because it might lead to unclean thoughts about Greek originality.

Alexander the Great and his planner Dinocrates were both formed by Greek culture. Their cities were therefore variations on the Pythagorean plan and its conceptual origin. The modu-

Fig. 176. The plan of Priene according to A. Zippelius. This is a typically Hellenistic orthogonal city, whose superblock modules are so freely subdivided and whose street pattern is so varied in width that it would be highly inappropriate to call this a Hippodamian plan. The existence of a Sanctuary of the Egyptian Gods (A) emphasizes the decisive influence of Egyptian art, architecture, and religion on Greek culture.

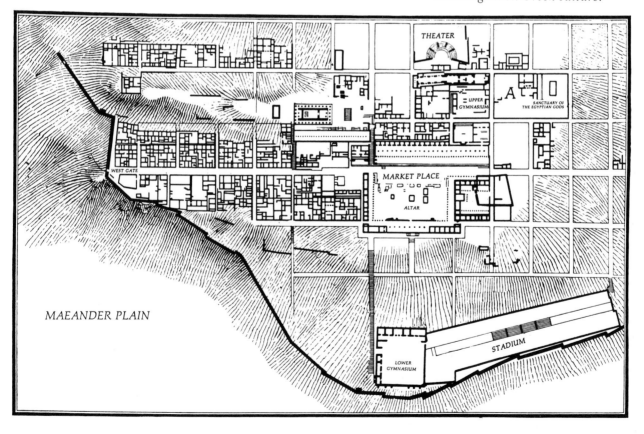

THEATER

UPPER GYMNASIUM

A

SANCTUARY OF THE EGYPTIAN GODS

WEST GATE

MARKET PLACE

ALTAR

MAEANDER PLAIN

LOWER GYMNASIUM

STADIUM

lar grid plans of the Romans were decidedly noncosmological. Cosa, an Etruscan fortress on the Italian west coast, which the Romans conquered and razed in 273 B.C., became the first Roman *colonia*. It was settled by 200 deported or imported families. The plan shows in a most graphic way the transition from the geomorphic tradition of the hillside citadel to the purely strategic empire link (*Fig. 177*). If it is agreed that a catalyst is an agent causing change in a substance without being altered by it, then Roman rule was the catalyst of urbanization. It transformed the traditions of building cities inherited from the Bronze and Iron Ages, and vanished from the world scene after 500 years of catalyzing. It is one of the remarkable facts about the Roman Empire that those who built and ruled it were not gradually absorbed by amalgamation with new, rising powers. During the third and fourth centuries, the Roman legions and their vast trains of dependents withdrew in perfect order from transalpine Europe, Asia, and Africa, and went home to die with their empire. The towns and cities they had built, and which numbered in the thousands, died with them. In Europe, the shape and organization of the Roman cities and towns were

Fig. 177. Cosa on the southwest coast of Italy is the oldest Roman colonia. After the expulsion of the Etruscans in 273 B.C., the citadel was rebuilt and resettled with 200 transplanted families. Modern planners have calculated a high density of 220 persons per acre, with one-sixth of the town area occupied by roads (compared to one-third of today's Los Angeles). The astonishing aspect of Cosa is the appearance at the very beginning of Rome's world conquest of the Roman castrum plan, which would remain basically unchanged for 500 years, as the late Roman plan of Aventicum in Switzerland shows (Fig. 178).

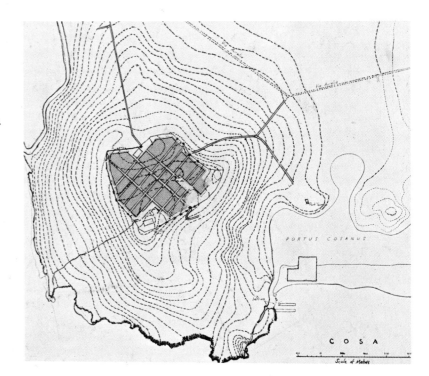

Fig. 178. The modular grid plan of Aventicum (today's Avanche) in Switzerland. Although founded almost 300 years after Cosa (see Fig. 177), it is based on the same principle of preconceived uniformity and regimentation. Surrounding the walled compound was the ager, *or* acre, *protected landholdings guaranteeing food supply and manpower. Its vast extent can be judged from a comparison with the contemporary Swiss village on the left side of the squared* castrum. *Roman plans in conquered territories were like stamps put on the raw skin of animals ready for slaughter.*

recovered from under a thousand years of medieval deposits when expanding national interests, international economics, and secularization of learning and the arts called for a new form of the city at the first dawn of the Renaissance.

The speed and thoroughness with which indigenous populations abandoned and destroyed the Roman towns is astonishing, if one considers that they inherited a ready-made environment of municipal organization, defenses, homes, spacious public buildings, heating, sanitation, and paved roads. The fact that indigenous societies rejected all these gifts, after sharing for hundreds of years in their benefits, could teach a thing or two to the computer planners of rational standardization. Roman military settlements and frequently even privileged administrative and commercial municipalities were abandoned and destroyed after the fall of Rome—or even before—because their layout did not respond to ethnic traditions, and because they expressed in tangible symbols the very essence of Roman colo-

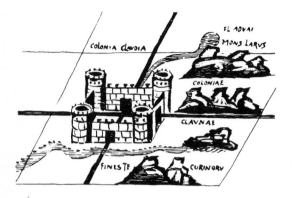
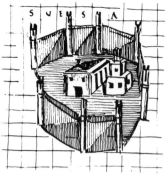

Fig. 179. The Roman castrum, in three presentations from the Roman manuscript Corpus Agrimensorum Romanorum of Hyginus Gromaticus, in the ducal library, Wolfenbüttel, Germany. The grid town as tie-knot for the Roman Empire's roads is clearly shown, as is the exurban modular pattern of centuriation, or land surveying.

nialism. This essence was "a decent minimum standard" for the conquered that would enable them to perform effectively for the ruling families who administered the provinces at a spectacular profit for the empire. Beyond that, the unvaried sameness of each *colonia* symbolized a corner of the earth that was forever Rome (*Fig. 178*). Public architecture was pared down to standardized designs, like those for United States post offices and State capitols, and distributed according to rank. Forum, temple, and public bath were minimum equipment for *oppidum* and *castrum,* the market and garrison towns. The accolade *municipium* and the coveted status *colonia regis* entitled the bearer to a basilica, a theater, and a triumphal arch in addition. It is amusing how the art of color photography tries to persuade modern readers that the deadening identity of Greek temples and Roman city remains is a glorious architectural experience. In reality, the sunsets and natural landscapes, not the architecture, provide the visual sensations. Thousands of Roman urban foundations were interchangeable parts in the Roman state machinery. Like steel cables, the Roman roads that spanned the empire held these parts together. The general Germanicus boasted that he could ride from Cologne to Alexandria without leaving Rome.

The illustrations in the Roman codex *Corpus Agrimensorum Romanorum* of Hyginus Gromaticus (*Fig. 179*) show the method by which uniformity of settlement and rural environment was achieved. This method was *centuriation*. All conquered land was divided into units based on the circumference a cooperative ox could plow in one day. Then the *gromaticus,* deriving his name from his instrument, the *groma* (*Fig. 180*), surveyed and subdivided the land into lots, which were distributed among the soldiers of a *centuria,* a company of 100 in a Roman Legion (*Fig. 181*). The absolute equity in lot sizes and homes, the schematization of movement through the town, and the total absence of varied monumentality in public buildings have been praised by today's great teachers as the basis of an ideal future environment.

As the basic cellular unit of that larger unit, the street, the dwelling-house represents a typical group organism. The uniformity of the cells whose multiplication by streets forms the still larger unit of the city, therefore calls for formal expression . . . The unification of architectural components would have the salutary effect of imparting that homogeneous character to our towns which is the distinguishing mark of a superior culture . . . The concentration of essential qualities in standard types presupposes methods of unprecedented industrial potentiality, which entail capital outlay on a scale that can only be justified by mass production.*

In a civilization like Rome's, which expressed the wealth and independence of its ruling class in extravagantly free-form

* Walter Gropius, *The New Architecture and the Bauhaus* (Cambridge, Mass., 1937).

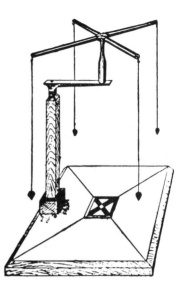

Fig. 180. Model of a Roman groma, *or surveyor's instrument, with movable plumb lines, used to survey conquered territory. From Charles Singer,* A Short History of Scientific Ideas to 1900 *(1959).*

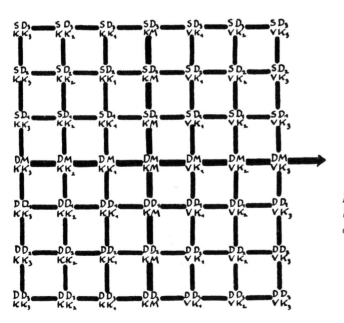

Fig. 181. A unit of thirty-six land parcels, subdivided by the groma *of the* gromaticus *from a piece of ground circumplowed in one day by one man with one ox.*

183

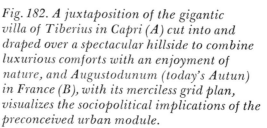

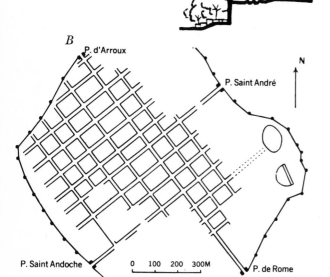

Fig. 182. A juxtaposition of the gigantic villa of Tiberius in Capri (A) cut into and draped over a spectacular hillside to combine luxurious comforts with an enjoyment of nature, and Augustodunum (today's Autun) in France (B), with its merciless grid plan, visualizes the sociopolitical implications of the preconceived urban module.

public buildings and villas (*Figs. 182A, 182B*), the discrimination and contempt for hirelings and serfs was expressed in the modular grid towns built for them.

It was this tradition that inspired European rulers to reconstruct Roman blueprints in the bastides of the Middle Ages. In France, the English defended their claims to the Pas de Calais with garrison towns, such as Monpazier; and the French king, in Paris, tried to hold in check both the feudal barons and the freedom-loving citizens of the eternally rebellious south by planting Aiguesmortes and Mirande (*Fig. 183*). A characteristic example of the bastide as coercive power center is Carcassonne (*Fig. 184*). In 1262, the citizens of this ancient fortified city with a commanding position over rich land and almost impregnable defenses rose in revolt against the centralized power of the French monarch St. Louis. They were betrayed to the royal army and forced to build their own prison town across the river Aude.

The colonization of East Prussia by the Germans and the subjugation of Italy by the Hohenstaufen emperors produced the same gridiron castrums as in France. The pattern was everywhere the same. Although most bastides are still on the map, none of them ever developed into major cities. Like deformed children, they had too many crippling defects. Among the

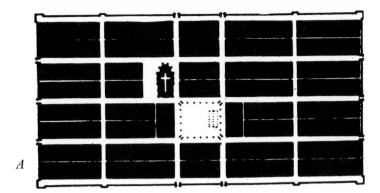

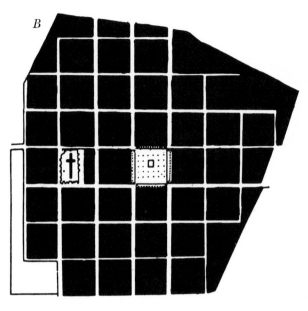

Fig. 183. *Characteristic bastides of the power struggle between centralized monarchies (England and France) in France. Monpazier, founded in 1284 (A), and Mirande, founded in 1285 (B). The arcaded central plaza and the rigidity of the grid would serve as prototypes for most colonial foundations in the Americas.*

deficiencies were lack of free trade, an open society, competition spurred by social and economic inequality, self-chosen contact with the world at large, and intellectual independence. All this inhibited the urge to change and to expand. It should be remembered that many of the New Towns and new capitals of the twentieth century were forced into the same bastide pat-

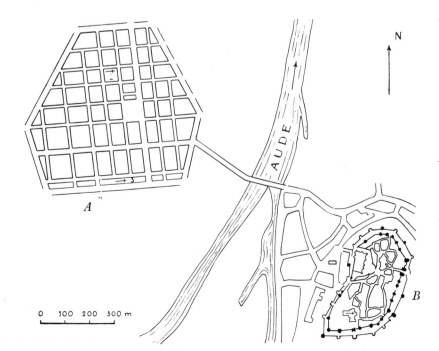

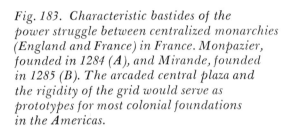

Fig. 184. *In 1262, after rebelling against unbearable taxation in money and in war recruiting, the citizens of Carcassonne, betrayed to the royal armies, were forced to abandon their impregnable fortress town (B) and to build their own prison bastide (A).*

tern and crippled by the same anti-urban handicaps, although the historical lesson has been glossed over with the promise of democracy.

It was the historical tragedy of the New World that the establishment of the first cities across the ocean occurred in the sixteenth century. The heedless admiration of the Renaissance for "classical achievement" can be well enough explained as rebellion against the regressive and constrictive collectivism of the medieval church and the closed guild system of the self-sufficient medieval city. But neither Spain, France, the Netherlands, nor Portugal sent out with their conquistadores and missionaries contingents of humanists who would mitigate the coarser aims of acquisition and exploitation by establishing

Fig. 185. Despite many earthquakes, the Plaza Mayor in Cuzco, Peru, still conveys the colonial core of the Spanish cities built according to the Law of the Indies.

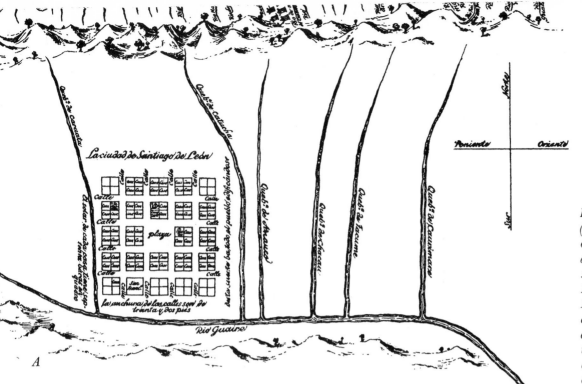

A

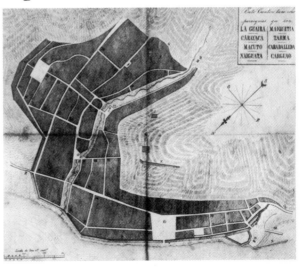

B

Fig. 186. Caracas, Venezuela (A), founded as colonial image of the power of Madrid, has a pure gridiron plan which still hampers its development. La Guaira (B), founded in 1600 as a seaport, has an expandable linear street plan and an excellent topographical adjustment. It did not fall under the Law of the Indies.

Renaissance culture. Instead, the administrators at home found in the newly translated Roman treatises of Polybius on land centuration and in those of Vitruvius on anything pertaining to a preplanned standardized urban environment, easily generalized rules on how to force the new lands into a uniform pattern. Between 1523 and 1573, the Spanish crown promulgated the city-planning directives known as the Law of the Indies. According to its directives, the Roman forum was resurrected as the central Plaza Mayor, surrounded by an arcade in the tradition of the Roman portico (Fig. 185). The cathedral facing the plaza took the place of temple or basilica, and in due course the bull ring would make its appearance in the precise shape of a Roman arena. The provincial caste system of the Roman colonies was strictly maintained. Only governors, officers, and clergy could own real estate, which excluded the natives and the merchant class from active participation in the progress of the city. This hangover from antiquity has accounted for centuries of economic and cultural stagnation in Latin America, creating the fatal gap between the economies of North America and Latin America. The juxtaposition of Caracas, the capital of Venezuela, with its port, La Guaira, repeats the story of the authoritarian grid and the commerce-generated orthogonal plan

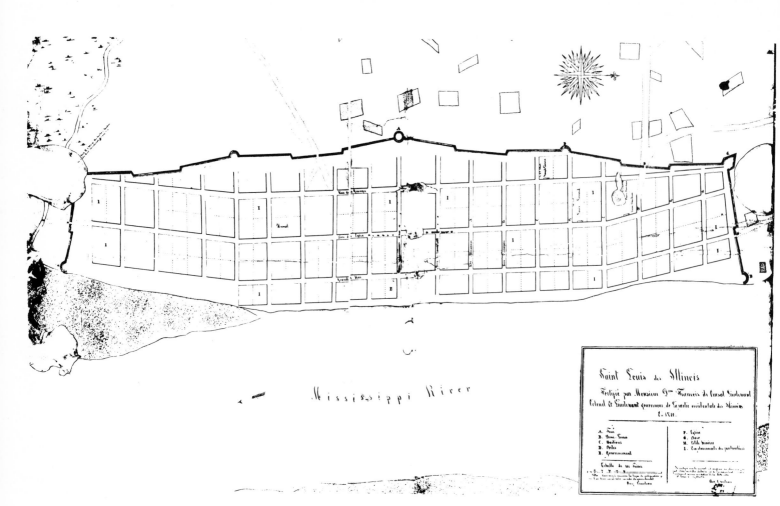

Fig. 187. Plan of the French fortress
town of St. Louis on the Mississippi
River, showing the characteristic grid
plan that was the stencil clamped
over a whole continent.

(*Figs. 186A, 186B*). The arrow-straight *autopistas* sliced in
desperation through the choked block dividers have done little
to alleviate a stagnant planning pattern whose ideological influence has not yet been liquidated.*

North America succumbed later to the Roman plague. Spanish presidio founders in California and New Mexico and French
fortress builders along the Great Lakes and the Mississippi Valley furnished prototypes which were avidly and fatally copied
(*Fig. 187*). But it is worth while to review briefly the exceptions
to the rule, because they bear out the central assumption of this
book that concepts rather than rationalizations generate city

* Richard M. Morse, "Characteristics of Latin American Urban History,"
American Historical Review, January, 1962 (with an excellent bibliography
about individual colonial cities of South and Meso-America).

plans. Quebec, founded by Samuel de Champlain in 1608, and capital of New France after 1663, is a fine geomorphic-concentric *Stadtkrone* city (*Fig. 188*). The Upper and Lower Towns are separated by a precipitous drop that would have inspired the King of Pergamon with an even finer ring of acropolis terraces than he built in Ionia. In the dour north of a traditionless continent, the French managed a bold citadel on Cape Diamond and a chateau for the French governor on Dufferin Terrace, floating 200 feet above the junction of the St. Lawrence and the St. Charles rivers. The cathedral, founded in 1647, provided the concentric focus for a wreath of parochial churches, because it was a major concern of the second- and third-generation colonizers to convert Indians and be created a bishopric, much to the detriment of the original commercial and territorial intentions of the founders of Quebec and Montreal.

Fig. 188. Quebec, capital of New France, a stately exception to the gridiron plague imported from Spain. Like a child with refined upbringing, having lost little of its well-conceived origins, it still is the handsomest Stadtkrone *in the New World today.*

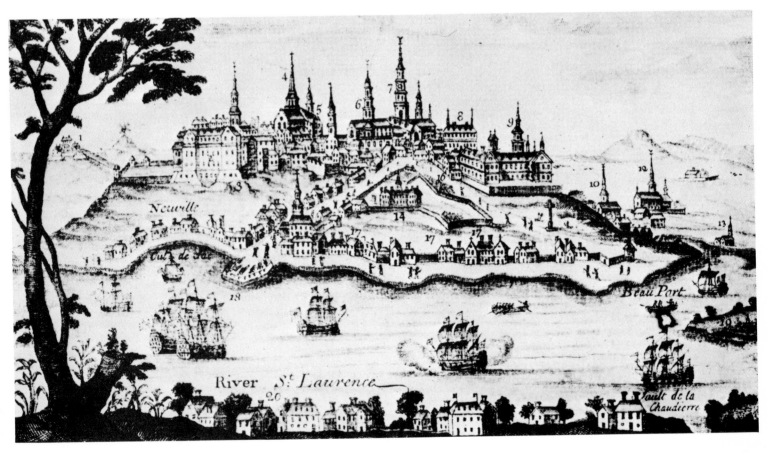

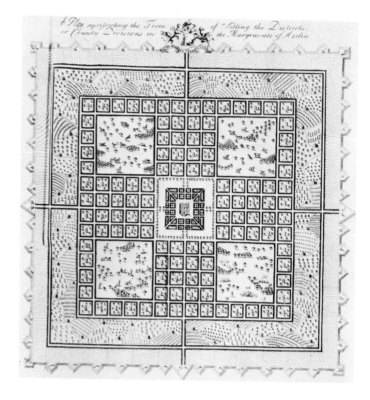

Fig. 189. Never executed, this first regional plan in America, the Margravate of Azilia, was planned in Georgia in 1717 by an English nobleman who saw himself as the overlord of a whole province, which would be subdivided into 250,000-acre regions with smaller and smaller quadratic subdivisions. The region was to be inhabited by several thousand families and surrounded by a bastioned wall, in the way that the Khwarizm people had built wall cities 2,000 years before.

The other geomorphic-concentric planning project in North America was much more original and much less successful. The Margravate of Azilia, laid out by the land grantee Sir Robert Mountgomery in 1717 (*Fig. 189*), would have been the first regional plan since Seleucus had conceived the Seleukis 2,000 years before (see *Fig. 102*). Under this plan, a considerable part of what is now the State of Georgia was to be surveyed into equal squares of twenty miles or 250,000 acres. The inhabitants were to live in three different habitats: in a concentric capital city where the castle of the Margrave—Mountgomery—was to be surrounded by large house blocks with interior garden courts; in an outer fortification belt, working two-mile-square "fee-farms" and the land of the Margrave; and on farms—116 in each province—of 640 acres each. There were four provincial forests for the benefit of the province and a greenbelt around the central city "to keep city and country separate."

A synthesis of the other two archetypal urban concepts—orthogonal-modular and orthogonal-linear—was Savannah, also in Georgia, founded in 1733 by James E. Oglethorpe. From his past as an army officer under Prince Eugene of Savoy, he carried the plan of the Renaissance army camp into the wilderness of America (*Figs. 190A, 190B*).* It is a nice proof of historical continuity and of conceptual identity that Oglethorpe did what the Romans had done when they conceived of the castrum plan. They too had used their camps as prototypes of a modular, uniform, and coercive planning pattern. Oglethorpe—certainly without historical knowledge—was equally inspired by the modular order of military planning. He systematized the camp layout by dividing his new city, which originally had a boundary of 2,115 by 1,425 feet, into six blocks, each centered by a market square of 315 by 270 feet. The house lots were a narrow 60 by 90 feet, divided from each other by 22½-feet-wide lanes and 75-feet-wide traffic roads. The density of the inner city was compensated for by garden and field lots of five acres. Each householder had an option to acquire a 40-acre farm on the city outskirts. A hundred years later, Martin Schreber, a school-

* Turpin B. Bannister, "Oglethorpe's Sources of the Savannah Plan," *Journal of the Society of Architectural Historians*, Vol. XX, No. 20 (1961).

Fig. 190. Savannah, Georgia (A), as planned by James E. Oglethorpe in 1733. A successful general, Oglethorpe applied the principles of the army camp (B) to plans for a colony where Protestants and destitutes could find refuge. In his American utopia, Oglethorpe surpassed the military colonies of Rome by transforming the camp squares into planted plazas and by introducing, earlier than anywhere else on the continent, streets of varying width, ranging from the center thoroughfare to pedestrian ways between the oblong lots.

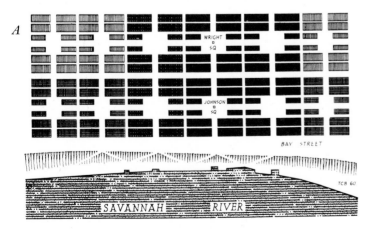

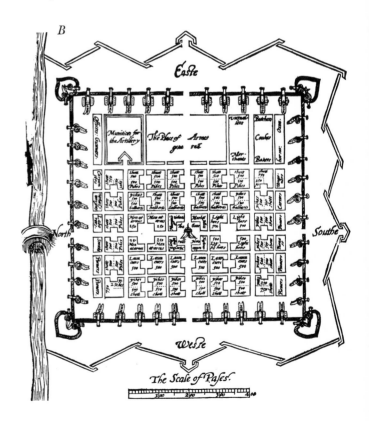

191

teacher in the German city of Leipzig, saw a solution for the suffocating density of the industrial city in precisely such garden-plot allotments which, though smaller than those of Savannah, have survived to this day as *Schrebergärten* surrounding all larger German cities. They helped to retain a sense of local identity and bourgeois pride in the social stratum of factory workers and service personnel, and saved millions from starvation during the destruction of cities in World War II.

But in general, the "New World" failed disastrously to conceive, much less to embody, a progressive vision of its urban environment. To the founding fathers, land was a commodity to be sliced, weighed, and sold to the highest bidder. "Buy the acre, sell the lot," was a slogan not of the late twentieth but of the early nineteenth century. It would take 200 years for the fugitives from millennia of urban tradition to acquire "city sense" and by that time—our own—the damage had been done. State capitals (*Fig. 191*) and mill towns (*Fig. 192*) were all plotted alike, by the same speculative greed that

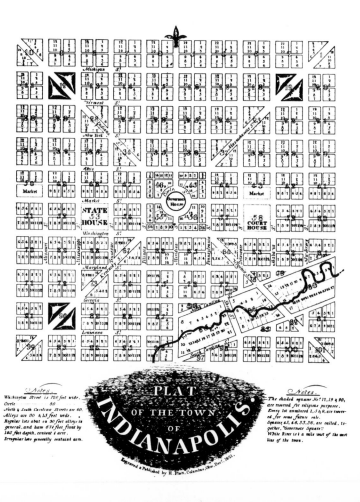

Fig. 191. Despite the four diagonals which were introduced in the 1821 plan of Indianapolis in honor of L'Enfant's capital, the plan of this state capital is no more than a modular grid, killing any incentive for decent residential or commercial architecture.

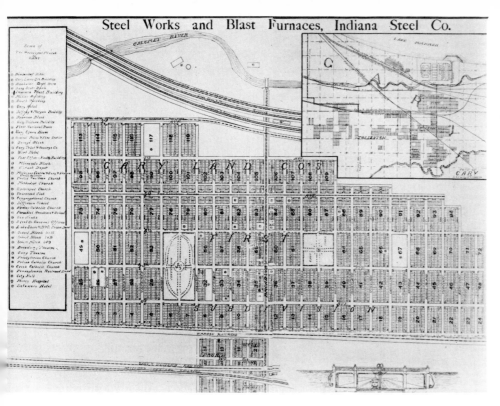

Fig. 192. As late as 1907, Gary, Indiana, owned by the Gary Land Corporation, was laid out as a choking minimum grid.

had motivated a Roman surveyor to plot the most exploitable spots in Nubia or Austria.

There is a "plan" by Thomas Jefferson, from 1792, for the new National Capital at the Potowmack (*Fig. 193*), which is the perfect illustration of his famous dictum, "I view great cities as pestilential to the MORALS, the HEALTH, and the LIBERTIES of man." While he could not hold back the Industrial Revolution, which would destroy his dream of "a happy land of tillers and artisans" (to which one might add the 180 slaves

Fig. 193. Thomas Jefferson, the guiding spirit of Federal architecture as classical revival, who believed that dormitories in the proportions of antique buildings would make better men of college students, proposed the plan below for the new capital of the nation he had helped to found. If the most educated and refined intellect of the United States knew nothing about the laws and influences of man-made environment, then the ignorance of lesser city founders cannot be a surprise.

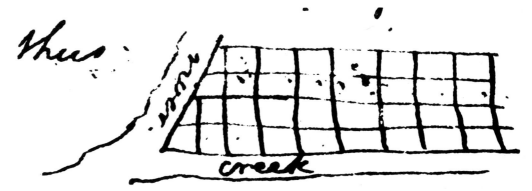

193

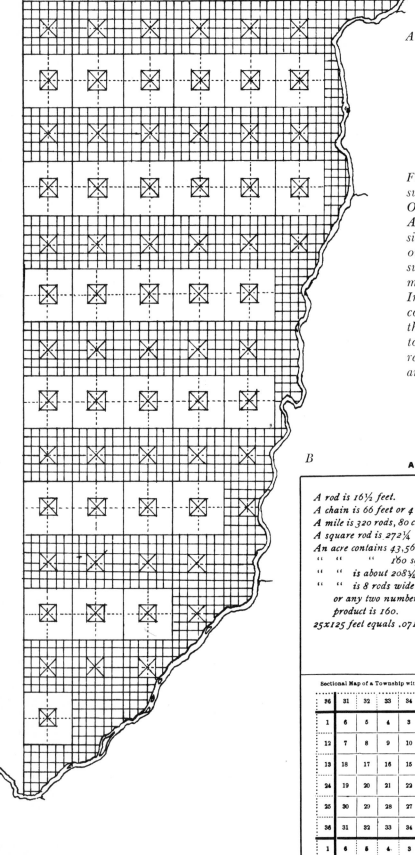

A

Fig. 194. Map (A) of the first townships surveyed in Ohio according to the Land Ordinance passed by Congress in 1785. A rigid land division (B) provided six-square-mile townships, one-square-mile (640-acre) farms, and subdivisions reserved for state, municipality, and veterans of the War of Independence. A bird's-eye view of the country from coast to coast still reveals the grid clamped over the natural topography, as if the boundary requirements of cities, villages, farms, and open land were all the same.

B

A SECTION OF LAND — 640 ACRES.

A rod is 16½ feet.
A chain is 66 feet or 4 rods.
A mile is 320 rods, 80 chains or 5,280 ft.
A square rod is 272¼ square feet.
An acre contains 43,560 square feet.
"   "   "   160 square rods.
"   "   is about 208¾ feet square.
"   "   is 8 rods wide by 20 rods long, or any two numbers (of rods) whose product is 160.
25x125 feet equals .0717 of an acre.

	10 chains.	330 ft.
80 rods.		5 acres. 5 acres.
		5 ch. 20 rods.
20 acres.	40 rods	10 acres.
	660 feet.	10 chains.
80 acres.		
	40 acres.	

CENTER OF SECTION.

20 chains. · 1,320 feet.

Sectional Map of a Township with adjoining Sections.

36	31	32	33	34	35	36	31
1	6	5	4	3	2	1	6
12	7	8	9	10	11	12	7
13	18	17	16	15	14	13	18
24	19	20	21	22	23	24	19
25	30	29	28	27	26	25	30
36	31	32	33	34	35	36	31
1	6	5	4	3	2	1	6

160 acres.

40 chains, 160 rods or 2,640 feet.

that maintained his bucolic paradise), Jefferson helped to instill in Americans, by his persuasiveness and his prestige, a contempt for the cities they built. In the cities of Europe and Asia, the urban lot was worthless unless the building erected on it gave it value and dignity. In America, the urban lot was from the beginning a speculative commodity and the building on it a temporary shelter and income. Ruth Benedict tells in her anthropological study of the Blackfoot Indians how an exceptionally serene chief explained the cheerful resignation in his impoverished lot.

The Great Spirit . . . has punished the white man with a far more terrible curse than he could visit on my people. He has condemned him to buy and sell the land on which he lives.

The rebirth of Roman colonialism finally came full circle when the Continental Congress, urgently in need of funds, faced the problem of disposing of a whole subcontinent. In 1785, a Land Ordinance was passed that surveyed the entire area of the United States into townships of six square miles (*Fig. 194A*) to be sold undivided. Blocks of thirty-six sections of one square mile (640 acres) each, were sold separately for farming (*Fig. 194B*). This was the same basic land module as in Azilia and Savannah. There was a provision that in each township Lot No. 16 was to be reserved for a school. On a huge midwestern tract, one-seventh of each township was to be allotted to veterans of the War of Independence in lieu of pay—precisely as Alexander and the Romans had done two thousand years before.

America thus lives on a giant gridiron imposed on the natural landscape (and the cities) by the early surveyors carrying out the mandate of the Continental Congress.*

That mandate from Rome rather than from the Continental Congress, was the inspiration of the city planners who dedicated their efforts to an elimination of all architectural frivolity and to the application of a scientific urban order. CIAM, the Congrès Internationaux d'Architecture Moderne, was founded in 1928 by a group of well-known modern architects. They developed a basic CIAM grid to serve as matrix for the replan-

* I acknowledge most gratefully the stimulus and factual information concerning the origins of American urbanization found in the monumental work of John W. Reps, *The Making of Urban America* (Princeton, N.J., 1965).

195

Fig. 195. Barcelona, replanned by José Luis Sert according to a 400-meter (1,300-feet) module applied to identical ten-story-high curtain-wall units, arranged in accordance with Le Corbusier's Cartesian system. At right are Barcelona's old apartment blocks, separated by the Ramblas (tree-lined malls), business streets, and the pleasant plazuelas formed at road intersections by diagonal instead of orthogonal block terminations.

ning of thirty-six cities in many countries and climatic regions (*Fig. 195*). Man's urban needs were established as dwelling, work, communication, and recreation, denying 5,000 years of emotional identification of city dweller and power image. Although Chicago and London escaped the new urban fascism, Brasília, being new and traditionless, did not. The plan of its urban body (see *Fig. 146*) is according to its planner, Lucio Costa, a perfect example of CIAM principles. Forty-two superblocks in "the city of tomorrow," uniform in shape, layout, and orientation along the cross axis (*Figs. 196A, 196B*), are geared to an undeviating, one-directional communication pattern with dead corner intersections. Any Roman army camp commander would have been instantly at home.

It was Le Corbusier who first tilted the grid of his CIAM colleagues ninety degrees and dreamed of modular villages, thrust sixty stories into the air (see *Fig. 276*). After him came

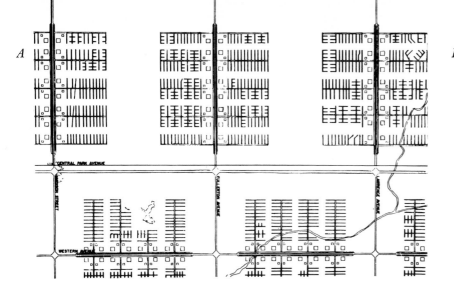

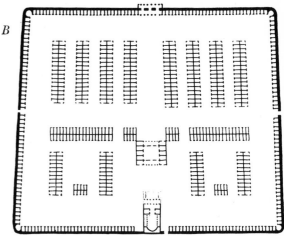

the "post-architectural" system makers whose plug-in, electronically controlled "total environments" (*Fig. 197*) await the system-controlled computerized office and factory worker at day's end with John Stuart Mill's 110-year-old Empirical Generalization that "given parts in given combinations must always act alike."

Fig. 196.
A) Ludwig Hilberseimer, superblocks for the replanning of Chicago (1940's).
B) Plan of a Praetorian castrum, a permanent camp of the Roman army. The similarity to the propositions of CIAM cofounder Hilberseimer should be evident.

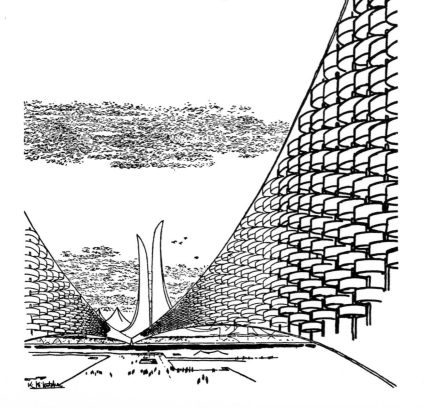

Fig. 197. Kiyonori Kikutake, City of the Future (1966). This vision by a member of the Japanese Metabolism Group envisions future communities as gigantic continuous hives composed of identical cells and operated by central electronic systems.

To understand the conceptual difference between the modular grid plan and the orthogonal-linear plan, it is necessary to understand the difference between traffic and communication. They are not identical! Traffic is a system of transferring people and goods through a given area by the shortest distance between origin and destination. Its planning is indifferent to the character of the area traversed or to the effect traffic has upon it. In the modular grid plan, streets correspond in width and length to the block module. They separate otherwise indistinguishable entities by providing the most direct routes of traffic. Communication, on the other hand, refers to the interconnection of human activities by means of streets and plazas. Their layout, connectedness, and delimiting architecture influence the life of people by providing a designed framework, qualified by tradition and aesthetics. In modern cities both traffic and communication exist side by side, but it is the communication plan that makes a particular city specific and memorable. The Ramblas of Barcelona, Piccadilly in London, the Champs Elysées in Paris, the Copacabana in Rio all create, through their interconnected shapes and spaces, an environmental scale that influences the attitudes of the inhabitants toward the city.

The emergence of an orthogonal-linear environment in the merchant cities of the Middle Ages had a significance quite different from the perpetuation of the triumphal-road concept described earlier. It shaped the physical image of the city in the likeness of the middle stratum of society which has, ever since, been the determining factor in urbanization.

Geomorphic, concentric, and modular grid plans survived and were initiated where the special characteristics called for this type of town. The orthogonal-linear merchant city gained ascendancy over all other planning concepts because it offered participation in the drive for power to the majority. From the eleventh century to the middle of our own, the planning of cities was dominated by orthogonal-linear concepts whose origins were Assyrio-Hellenistic.

In the Middle East and the Far East, the street as coordinating element of public life never vanished to the degree to which it was wiped out by the anti-urban invasions of the Dark Ages in Europe. There existed a good reason for the importance of a hierarchical street order. The ruler—Sheik, Shah, Mogul, Sultan, Caliph—was the owner and chief resident of the city. His interest in the commercial prosperity of his urban property was the reason for its existence. The antagonism between monarch and citizen was a purely European phenomenon, based on the feudal traditions of the Germanic tribes, which considered and still considers city life alien and depraved. This is borne out by the fact that the hostilities between Italian cities and the emperors erupted only when the imperial dynasties were German. The *suk* or bazaar street was the principal planning feature of the Eastern merchant center, just as the grand axis had been that of the Assyrian and Hellenistic empire cities. Like other urban and cultural features of the medieval Orient, the long, covered bazaar street was an adaptation by the eminently teachable Arabs of the Roman decumanus. This wide central road, always running north-south, had originated as the dividing line between the street blocks on each side, bisected by the cardo, or hinge, that ran east-west. In Roman cities classified as major capitals the cardo doubled as the royal road of triumph. A juxtaposition of the main axis of Ostia, the harbor city of Rome (*Fig. 198*), in the time of Augustus, and of Bukhara in Turkistan, refounded on an ancient city site by the Seljuk Turks around A.D. 830 (*Fig. 199*). demonstrates the shift in socio-economic structure from antiquity to Middle Ages, and from West to East.

Both cities were famous and prosperous trade terminals—Ostia as the port of Rome where all seaborne troops and goods had to land, and Bukhara as chief city of Transoxiana and as the intersection of caravan routes to Asia and Europe. Like Damascus, the most enduring Syrian trading post, Bukhara had the advantage of a fertile oasis surrounded by deserts, and from Damascus might have come the two-mile-long central bazaar street which is mentioned in the Bible as "The Street called Straight." The difference between the Roman linear city of Ostia and Bukhara is spatial. The builders of Ostia had learned nothing from Hellenistic urbanism. They strung their buildings "functionally" along the city axis, warehouses first and in greatest number, public baths next in number, because this was a sailor's and soldier's port where

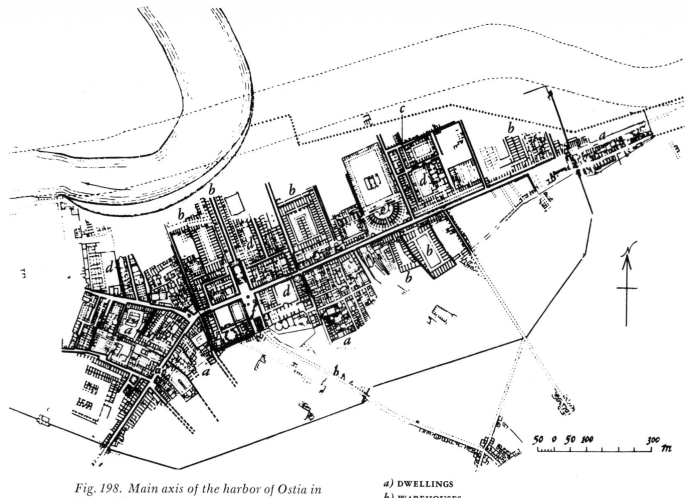

Fig. 198. *Main axis of the harbor of Ostia in Imperial times. The east-west decumanus was the main street along which all buildings— ceremonial, administrative, and commercial and residential—were strung like wash to dry. The unchangeable character of a port town is indicated by the fact that warehouses— meaning trading establishments (b)—take up the most space, followed by "bathing establishments" (d). Other elements on the plan are (a) dwellings, (c) barracks, (e) theater, (f) forum.*

a) DWELLINGS
b) WAREHOUSES
c) BARRACKS
d) BATHS
e) THEATER
f) FORUM

Fig 199. *The main axis of the central Asiatic town of Bukhara. Although the linear sequence of buildings is the same as in Ostia, two basic design features create a totally different environment. The arcading is maintained the full length of the street, re-creating the same unified, outdoor-room impression that had prevailed in the best Hellenistic cities. The other aspect was a continuous vista into highly imaginative courts of mosques and medreses, inviting the passerby to enjoy an interchanging experience of linear and circular spaces.*

"public baths" was a polite euphemism. Dwellings, those famous high-rise insulae whose sizable ruins still stand, were pushed together like boxcars at each end of the main street. The Seljuk masters of Bukhara and other famous caravan cities of Asia were not more virtuous or less materialistic than the Romans from whom they learned to build cities, but they knew that the main thoroughfare had to represent the self-image of a city. They placed their mosques, schools (medreses), palaces, and one gigantic, beautifully vaulted public bath in direct contact with the bazaar. To the Hellenistic tetrapylon (see *Fig. 105*), the four-columned intersection of the main axes, they gave an architectural spatial function. It was a mosque, but also a passage point and place of social gathering, as most early mosques were. There was a public park next to the covered intersection. Additional stalls for all the treasures of the Orient extended left and right along the cardo. The Great Palace on one side and the largest medrese and mosque in twin structures on the other gave to the "rotary" at the intersection the particular meaning of a choice of directions.[*]

The West had to wait more than 600 years for a modest renascence of the concept of communication lines as the basis for a city plan. In the eleventh century, large deposits of silver were struck in the Harz Mountains of northern Germany, suddenly increasing the flow of currency, which until then had been the exclusive possession of clergy and rulers. Only one aspect of the revolutionary importance of this silver strike for the history of Europe is usually conceded: payment in kind was gradually replaced by a limited circulation of coins, which liberated peasants and artisans from dependence on one location and stimulated flight from serfdom into the cities. The more far-reaching effect of the introduction of hard currency into European cities north of the Alps was the formation of a native merchant class. As in so many other aspects of civilization, the time gap between the Mediterranean and the Germanic cultures is startling. As far as we know, the first merchants were the Sumerians, who invented the two absolutely essential prerequisites of trade: the silver shekel and written contracts. With these two basic tools—portable, universally acceptable value, and protection of private property by universally applied law—they established the difference between the primitive trader, who exchanged commodities to satisfy

[*] M. A. Stein, *Caravan Cities* (1926–32).

his own needs and those of his immediate group, and the merchant, who converts commodities into hard currency, and the surplus value achieved in the transaction into investment capital. From the very beginnings of merchant cities—such as Byblos in ancient Syria, dating from about 3000 B.C., Lagash, or Loyang—two aspects distinguished the merchant from all other citizens: he was an internationalist, inclined to tolerance, liberalism in matters of race and religion and passionately dedicated to peace, since war has no respect for private property; and he was curious, the carrier of much "classified information."

These traits were basically unacceptable to the Germanic people of northern and western Europe, who believed in tribal loyalty, tradition, racial superiority, and in war as the natural occupation of man. Those among them who had followed the abbots and monks into towns that had accumulated around abbeys and the residences of feudal rulers, had been content with the ancient folkways, until the traders among them became merchants and the consequent rise in material wealth strengthened their self-confidence. This is how, a mere 900 years ago, Western Europe joined the civilized world, 4,000 years after Sumer. The new citizens petitioned their bishops and overlords for charters that would guarantee to the town a certain measure of its gains through artisanship and commerce. The civil rights drive of the late eleventh century spread like a fire from Le Mans in France (1069) to Worms and Cologne in Germany. It led to the famous League of Cambrai in 1076, by which several newly expanded merchant cities banded together for the fight to obtain city charters. The resistance of the princes and the bishops was fierce and the treatment of the citizens' leaders merciless. How much the introduction of currency had changed the economic structure in a hundred years can be seen from the actions of the citizens of Laon, who bought from the clergy for "a large sum of gold" a communal charter while their cruel bishop Gaudri was abroad. In addition, they paid the nobles to protect them if trouble should develop at his return. Trouble did develop, and the enraged bishop had to be appeased with another payment before the charter was ratified by King Louis VI in 1111. Needing ecclesiastic support for the Crusades, Louis intended to revoke the ratification and was paid 400 pounds in gold by the citizens of Laon to keep his word. But the bishop offered the monarch 700 pounds, and the Laon commune was extinguished in a

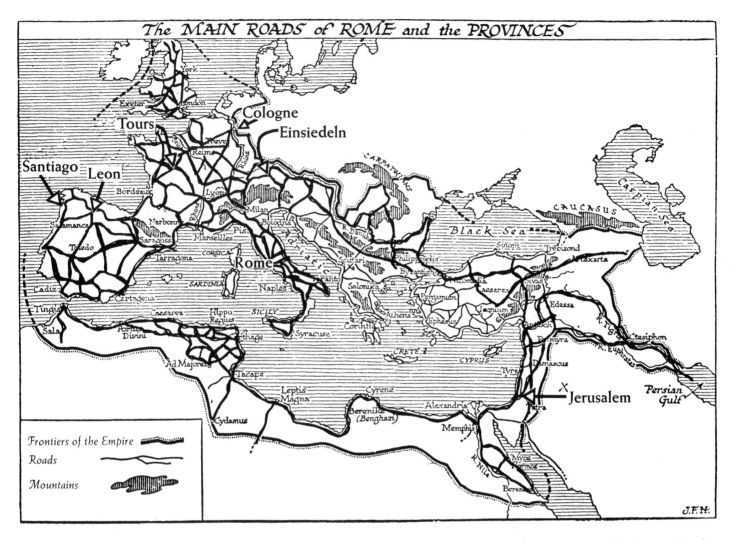

Frontiers of the Empire
Roads
Mountains

blood bath. . . . The church had become the greatest enemy of the people."*

Only the two most powerful weapons of Christianity, excommunication and penitential pilgrimage, prevented continuous civil war. Yet whole cities (Cambrai in 1206, Laon in 1213) were excommunicated, which, in an age with absolute faith in purgatory, was a high price to pay for civil liberty.

The other scourge for the sinner was the pilgrimage, which

*Arthur Kingsley Porter, *Medieval Architecture*, Vol. II (New York, 1909).

Fig. 200. Main roads of the Roman Empire at the time of its greatest expansion in the third century A.D. *As pilgrimages set the medieval population in motion, people traveled along the well-preserved highways of the legions to such famous shrines as Rome, Jerusalem, and Santiago de Compostela. Einsiedeln in today's Switzerland, Cologne, Canterbury, and Tours were famous starting points for the arduous trip through the sparsely-populated heart of Europe.*

203

Fig. 201. Woodcut of the great merchant city of Cologne, dominated by the towering church of St. Martin. Due to its river location and the particularly virile and cheerful disposition of its people, Cologne did not die after the withdrawal of the Romans who had bestowed exceptional favors on it as Colonia Regis Claudia. *Next to Lübeck, it became the most important "factory" of the Hanseatic merchant league.*

Fig. 202. The core of Cologne before its destruction in World War II. The orthogonal layout of the Roman portus (arrow) is still visible, its main space the bridgehead (a), where since Roman times all goods had entered the city. The great Gothic cathedral (b) never occupied a centralized position. It stands along one of four east-west thoroughfares, which since ancient times connected the river piers with the countryside and overland routes to Holland, Flanders, and France.

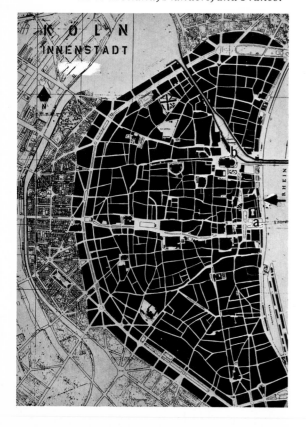

promised him salvation if he received absolution on holy ground. While Roman cities had long since disappeared or been built over by tight concentric towns, Roman roads were almost imperishable (*Fig. 200*). They now became the pilgrimage routes from England, Scandinavia, and Germany to the three great centers of Christendom: Santiago de Compostela, Rome, and Jerusalem. As anyone knows who has read his Chaucer or watched the miracle seekers of Lourdes, pilgrims are human. Their hope for salvation is matched by hope for adventure. In a just emerging profit economy, faith was fired by the innate trading instinct. The Church encouraged markets and fairs along the pilgrimage routes, and these soon attracted more pilgrims by displaying sacred relics brought back from the Crusades.

The Crusades were a predominantly French undertaking, in which all the main actors and events were directed by the French crown. The German emperors played an ambiguous role, and many of their feudal lords did not join in "the holy delirium," as the German chronicler Ekkehard von Aura noted disapprovingly. Among these noncrusading nobles who saw the opportunity for wider trade connections and an expanded living standard for the new urban populations were the dukes of Zähringen. Their dominion was a naturally wealthy and centrally located region in today's Switzerland and Baden, along the old routes from the North Sea and the Baltic Sea to the south. A duke of Zähringen had been prisoner in Cologne during one of the many local wars, and had learned much from the layout and prosperity of the ancient Roman *Colonia Regis Claudia,* whose incomparable location on the Rhine had saved it from abandonment and destruction (*Figs. 201, 202*). After his release, he founded Freiburg im Breisgau, supported by twenty-five prosperous "overland merchants" (1120), Murten, Rottweil (*Fig. 203*), and other markets. The dukes terminated their successful careers as city founders in 1191 with Bern, now the capital of Switzerland (*Fig. 204A*). The escutcheon of their

Fig. 203. Plan of the city of Rottweil, founded in the twelfth century as a commercial center by the dukes of Zähringen. The key feature is not the cathedral (1), but space—the elongated market which is left free of obstructions except for a covered market building (2). Wide parallel streets permit the arrival and departure of horse-drawn vehicles without endangering the market stalls and the crowds. The cross axis—which in Roman times would have been called a cardo, or hinge—is the administration street, accommodating town hall and guild houses (3, 4, 5). Together, the two main streets form the famous "Zähringer cross," symbol of the new era of linear merchant towns.

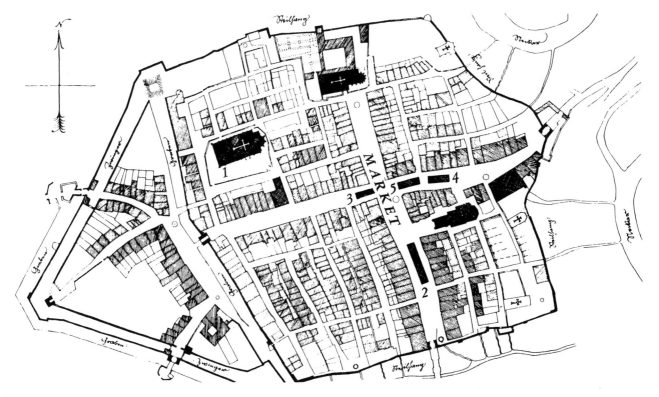

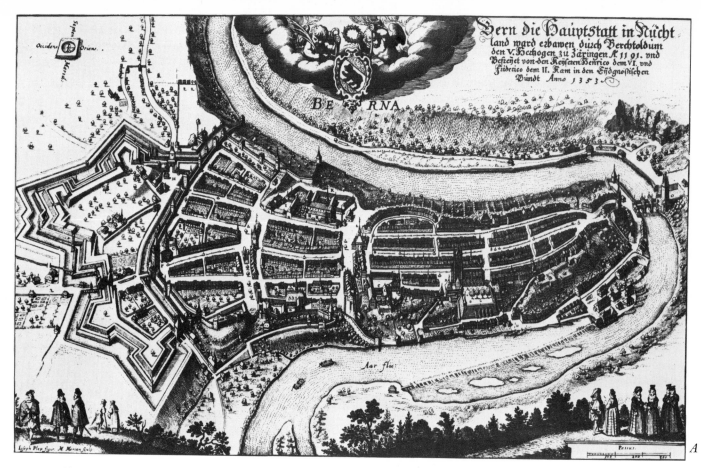

Fig. 204.

A) The Zähringer foundation of Bern, today the capital of Switzerland, which combines geomorphic adjustment to a unique site with an effective market-street plan.

house, which is also the grand seal of Freiburg im Breisgau, is reproduced on the jacket of this book.

The dukes departed radically from geomorphic and concentric town plans and instead emphasized the communication system as the determining factor of the plan. A wide market street took account of a development which the inventors of the wheel, some 4,000 years before, could have hardly foreseen. From its predominant use on war chariots and carriages, the wheel started to turn in the service of lesser humanity during the Middle Ages. The reciprocal relationship of roads and traffic started with the first market towns. Two lateral streets, parallel with the wide market street, were bisected by one or two crossroads, forming the "Zähringer cross," which permitted circulation of delivery wagons without disturbing the pedestrians in the market.

In the original Zähringer market centers, house lots and elevations were uniform. A few generations later, when the dukes had lost control over the foundations of their ancestors, deep

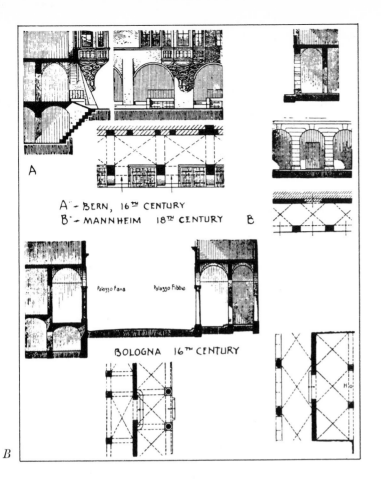

A - BERN, 16TH CENTURY
B - MANNHEIM 18TH CENTURY

Palazzo Fava   Palazzo Fibbio

BOLOGNA 16TH CENTURY

Fig. 204.
  B) Three characteristic arcade
sections and plans of post-Renaissance
cities in Switzerland, Germany, and
Italy.
  C) Market street (Kramgasse) in
Bern, Switzerland, with the Fountain
of Justice in the center.

arcades were put in front of the tall stone houses which were harmonious without being uniform. Bern set the example. Pedestrians today still move through deep arcades lined with shops of every description while the 64-feet-wide center lane is reserved for wheeled traffic (*Figs. 204B, 204C*). The artfully designed fountains, placed in the road center every 4,000 feet, once watered man and horse and should be, in due course, converted into gasoline pumps.

Freiburg im Breisgau was an exception among the Zähringer towns because it early acquired a cathedral and a university of outstanding quality that soon overshadowed its commercial importance. For the other Zähringer foundations and many market towns planned after their example, the church characteristically formed a spiritual center of its own, away from the commercial center.

The new communication network of streets for buying and selling formed connective tissue between the old introverted nuclei of abbey and cathedral. The wool merchants of Reims

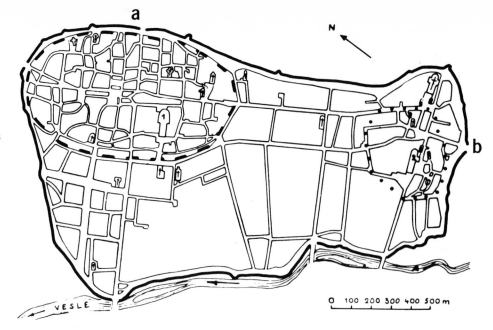

Fig. 205. Reims. The development of Reims characterizes the emergence of the linear merchant city. The ancient Roman-feudal bishopric (a) faced the hostile monastic abbey (b) across open land. As serfs moved away from the landed estates, and river traffic increased, they became self-sufficient artisans and merchants, filling the area between the antagonistic "heavenly mansions" with their homes and shops, and with an excellent access road system to the river. The result was a united front of cathedral (1) and abbey (2) against the new class of citizens who were forced to carry the main financial burden for the erection of the splendid coronation cathedral of the kings of France—archenemies of urban independence.

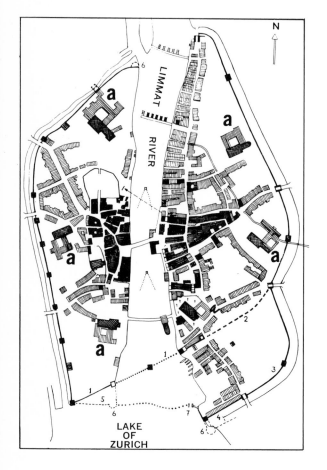

Fig. 206. Zürich, Switzerland, ca. 1300 A.D., a river town and important merchant center. The dark areas indicate the tight inner core with spacious quay and market spaces. The light areas are the burgher houses along the river. The monasteries (a) stood on open ground close to the outer defense wall, famous for its twelve towers.

had been particularly stubborn in their fight for a charter and were roundly condemned for their arrogance by St. Bernard. Despite their money and their handsome merchant town wedged between the feuding saintly administrators of monastery and bishopric, they were taxed out of their wealth by the kings of France who built the most elaborate of Gothic cathedrals on the spot where their ancestor Clovis had been anointed as the first King of France from a vial brought from heaven by the dove of the Holy Ghost (*Fig. 205*).

But roads were not enough to guarantee the growth of the merchant towns. They were costly to build, difficult to maintain, and open to attack by bandits and barons alike, who waylaid merchant caravans for loot or ransom. The heavy wagons could only cross rivers at fords or where the sturdy stone bridges of the Romans were still intact. The future belonged to cities that had a productive hinterland suitable for roads and connected to waterways for navigation. The Zähringer towns, exclusively designed for wheeled communication, never expanded into merchant cities. Instead, Zürich (*Fig. 206*) grew into the first city of Switzerland and central Europe. It combined a navigable river, usable lake frontage, and a flat hinterland for easy road approaches, rare in a country with the highest mountains in Europe. The bridges of Zürich (*Fig. 207*), like those of all Euro-

Fig. 207. Zürich, Switzerland, bridges over the Limmat and the quays. The bridge as communication link forms an integral part of the city, connecting rather than separating the two sectors of a city.

Fig. 208. Cleveland, The Flats (1878). In contrast to the civilized integration of bridges as essential communication links of urban life in Europe, American cities threw their bridges high into the air, to simplify the passing of ships without the spans having to be opened. Approach ramps cut brutally into the street pattern and created decayed areas next to the bridge structures, which could develop neither residential nor trade buildings because they were cut off from communication with the rest of the city. To this day, the worst slum lots of New York are in the shadow of the inaccessible bridges.

pean and Asian countries, are links of communication, road extensions from river esplanade to river esplanade. Unfortunately, North American bridge builders from the very beginning conceived of bridges as transportation machinery, unrelated to the communication system of the city, and remained indifferent to the decay of city life around their interminable approaches (*Fig. 208*).

Waterways had been recognized as determining factors of urban communication since Sumer and Assyria. When Leonardo da Vinci sketched an ideal city in the late fifteenth century it was composed of all the concepts that had gone into urban origins. His plan takes advantage of the river valley and the water highway. It is concentric, modular, and organized into an interior road system (*Fig. 209*).

The struggle between the Arabs and the Crusaders' kingdom of Jerusalem and Cyprus that lasted from 1100 to 1291 spelled the end of the Mediterranean as the highway of international trade. Sea routes became so unsafe and ports changed hands so quickly that inland waterways and northern seas gained in importance. In 1256, the representatives of north German river and seaboard towns met to found a coalition of mutual support and trade. The Hanseatic League, or Hanse, lasted till 1669, longer than any other urban league. The League's capital was Lübeck on the river Trave, several miles inland from the Baltic seaport of Travemuende. It was an advantage, sought by most of the cities of antiquity, not to be directly on the sea, since invaders and raiders usually arrived by ship. When gunpowder was invented, a hundred years after the founding of the Hanseatic League, a land barrier as protection against sea bombardment became even more important.

At the height of their power, the merchants of the Hanse ruled cities from Novgorod in Russia to the Steelyard in London, where the British crown was once kept in hock till a royal debt was repaid. Hanseatic armies waged successful wars against the kingdoms of Scandinavia, the Netherlands, the princes of Muscovy and Novgorod, and reflected the power of Germany

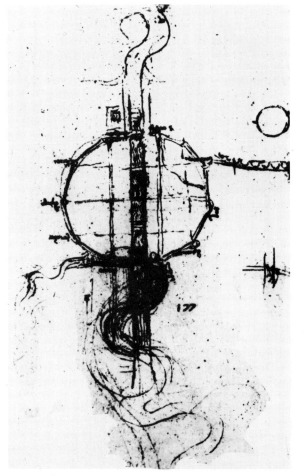

Fig. 209. Leonardo da Vinci, design for a river city, late fifteenth century. Leonardo combines all elements of urban origins: the concentric plan, the modular grid, the road communication system, and the highway of the river.

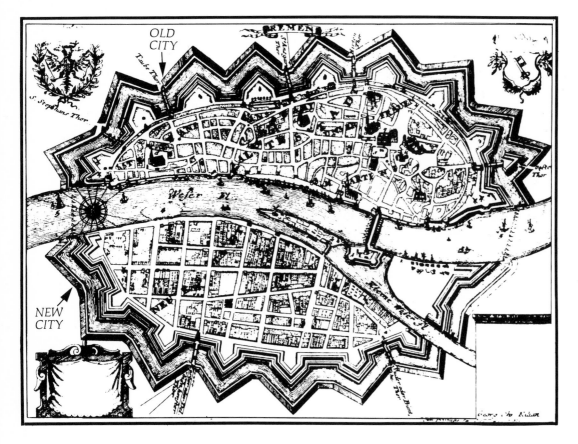

Fig. 210. Bremen in 1730. Bremen, after Lübeck the most powerful member of the Hanseatic League, is the last link with the Assyrian river-port cities, relying like these distant ancestors on the dual communication of road and water traffic.

more than the Holy Roman Empire, whose forces were constantly occupied in Italy. The basis of this vast power complex was exclusively urban and commercial, refuting the assertions that the twentieth century is more materialistic than previous times and that city life has replaced bucolic innocence. This hard-nosed concern with the acquisition and exchange of goods and the protection of profits expressed itself in the plans of the Hanseatic cities, of which Bremen and Lübeck are the two most explicit examples. They represent the high point of the linear orthogonal merchant cities and the last link with their Assyrian ancestors.

Bremen *(Fig. 210)*, shown here after M. Vauban had encapsuled it in the *système* of fortifications destined to be demolished 180 years after construction, is an Assyrian waterway metropolis. The remarkable aspect is the width of the main streets in the Old City, with Long Street as the seat of the powerful merchant houses, and the frequency of rectangular connective streets leading toward the loading quay on the river. In the seventeenth century, after the port of Bremen had silted up—the fate of many great historical ports—the harbor of Bremerhaven was founded; it is still the main point of entry from the New World to the Old. The New City across the river, replanned at that time, followed the orthogonal block system and the concept, so characteristic for merchant cities, that width and variety of communications is the framework necessary for the profitable exchange between man and man.

Lübeck (*Fig. 211*), which became the capital of the Hanse empire, was laid out in 1143. A linear orthogonal grid connected the center markets and merchant halls with the river Trave on all sides. A wide quay at the northwestern tip, pointing toward the sea, turned into a continuous esplanade along the waterfront. The center of Lübeck demonstrates that in the richest emporium of the north a balance-of-power agreement had been reached between the merchants and the clergy (*Fig. 212*). The Marienkirche, started in the twelfth century as an austere Romanesque cathedral of the Norman type, was covered in 1335 with a Gothic brick mantle to testify to the Hanseatic League's power over money and people. But instead of dominating the market place, the cathedral occupied a well-defined churchyard of its own, adjacent to, but not part of, the market place whose clothmakers' hall, city hall, and merchant exchanges occupied an area as large as the sacred enclosure.

In the thirteenth century, the expanding trade guilds of Paris remodelled the ancient concentric city core around the

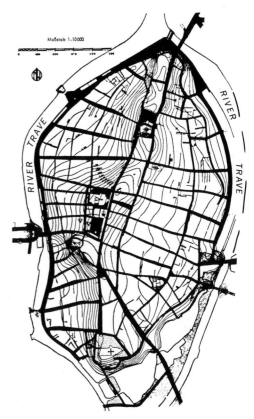

Fig. 211. Plan of Lübeck, Germany, laid out in 1143 as the future capital of the Hanseatic League. Two aspects characterize the merchant city: a total disregard for natural topography, because the shortest distance from the city core to the river piers is the only planning consideration, and the increasing width in roads and esplanades toward the outer limits.

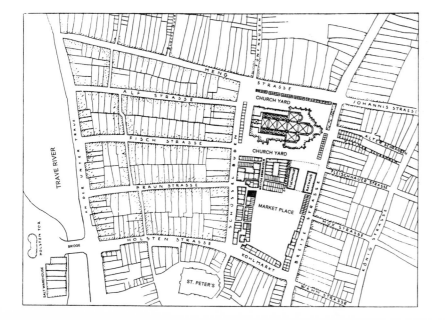

Fig. 212. Central district of Lübeck. The market, surrounded by guildhalls, town hall, and stalls, is separated from the churchyard as if to demonstrate the two incompatible realms of the material and the spiritual. The long, exceedingly narrow building lots are a special characteristic of Hanseatic cities. They give a maximum of houses the advantage of street frontage along the roads to the piers, and they allow for storage facilities in the back areas.

Fig. 213. *Medieval miniature shows the importance of quays and river to the commercial life of the city. Manpower, rather than draft animals, maneuvered the roads along the quays. At right, the figure of a traveler indicates the essential function of the river as an interurban highway.*

Ile de la Cité. to suit their needs. Along the Seine, spacious quays were constructed on which goods were loaded and received (*Fig. 213*). From there, traffic went along the Seine Valley to the English Channel and the North Sea. In 1517, Francis I, in continuous need of loans from the merchant bankers to

Fig. 214. *The port of Le Havre, constructed by Francis I in 1517. The black areas show the original harbor town with its strong emphasis on access streets and quays. White areas are eighteenth-century additions in uniform grid style.*

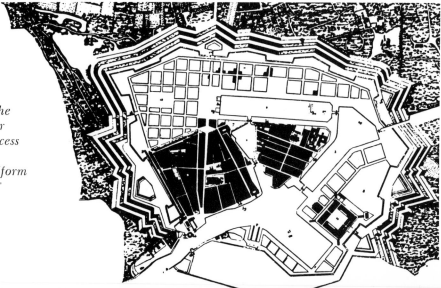

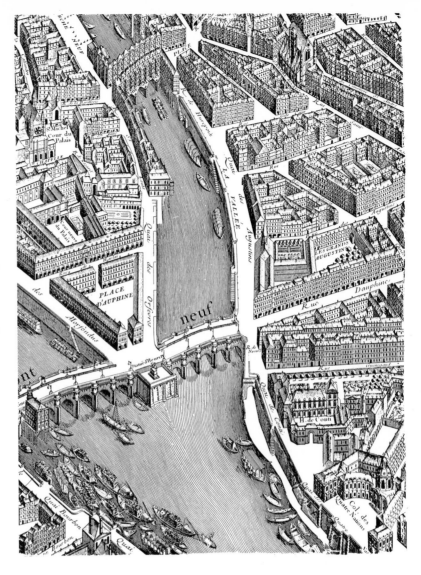

Fig. 215. The development of the Paris river quays shows the decisive shift in orientation from a concentric cathedral city, developed centrifugally outward from the Ile de la Cité, to a linear merchant city. In 1606, Henry IV had the Place Dauphine constructed. Its handsome row housing provided living quarters for civil servants and gave impetus to the speculative building boom that made Ile St. Louis and the quays the fashionable addresses of Paris.

satisfy his unfulfilled ambition for the conquest of Italy, founded Le Havre as a trade and military port at the mouth of the Seine (*Fig. 214*). Its plan is a characteristic street-oriented *portus* layout. Two generations later, in 1606, Henry IV built the first government housing project, the Place Dauphine, for civil servants and pensioners (*Fig. 215*). Paris became the birthplace of a decisive planning revolution that spread throughout Europe and North America and expressed for the first time the ruling influence of the commercial middle class. The innovations were: the designed transformation of the river quays into public esplanades with a high prestige and real estate value; the rise of speculation building projects on a large scale as

Fig. 216. Plaza Mayor in Madrid (1619),
133 by 102 yards. Residential buildings
assured their tenants preferred seats for
public spectacles. Deep arcades
provided indoor shopping, and high
archways connected the central square
with streets of access.

on the Ile St. Louis, which was leased from the crown in 1609
and developed by an entrepreneur, M. Marie; and the design
of street blocks as single buildings. The quays of Paris, which
became the location of high government offices and elegant
apartments, gave Paris an imperishable elegance. Speculation
housing for the nouveau riche merchant and manufacturer's
class prevented spotty renewal and achieved a hierarchy of locations that lacked democracy but fused architecture, communication, and real estate values into a lasting expression of free
capitalism.

In other capitals of Europe, the transition from royal residence to merchant city was characterized by a designed contrast,
within the street elevation, between the anonymity of residential blocks as one mansion and the unique religious or public

building. Residential design expressed the introverted privacy of family life and a new class consciousness, which based its cohesion not on land ownership or court positions but on wealth and international connections.

The Plaza Mayor in Madrid (*Fig. 216*), started by Juan Gómez de Mora in 1619, is a faithful replica of Henri IV's Place des Vosges in Paris, which might have aroused the envy of Mora's patron, Philip II. Here were held the big holiday fairs, the autos-da-fé of the Inquisition, the religious plays of Lope de Vega, and the corridas. Residents of the handsome, high-ceilinged apartments on the plaza had choice spectator seats in their windows. The Panaderia, administration center and public bread bakery, had its public character stressed by a conspicuous variation in design.

In England, French influence led after the Great Fire of 1666 to a rebuilding of residential streets according to the continuous elevation principle. Except in the luxury district of the resort town of Bath (*Fig. 217*), British streets lacked French style, till John Nash and his generation discovered around 1800 that high-class speculation housing pays off. London house lots were narrow (*Fig. 218*), 20 or 25 feet wide and 100 feet deep.

Fig. 217. Residential block, Bath, England, by John Wood, Sr. (ca. 1754). Despite its castlelike elevation, the three- and four-bay units are the façades of town houses. The psychological trick was the provision of a new merchant class with manor houses, the status symbol of British aristocracy.

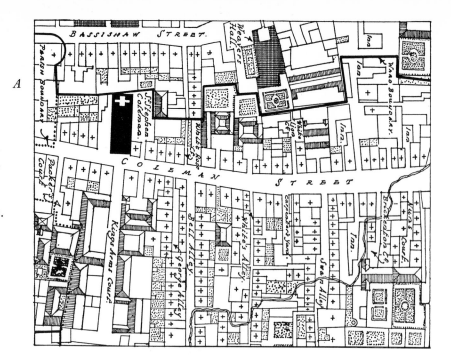

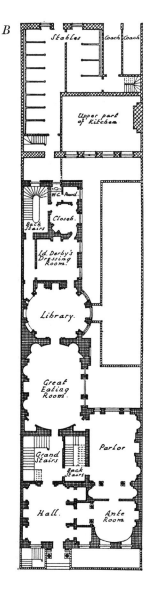

Fig. 218.

A) Section of London as rebuilt after the Great Fire (Ogilby map, 1677).

B) Lord Derby's house, Grosvenor Square, London.

Façades were built as one block unit, and the spaces behind were filled in according to the wish of the buyer (*Fig. 219*).

The concentric single-focused city-states had lost their ascendancy in the urban canon when the linear empire cities of world conquest replaced them. The orthogonal merchant cities lost their paradigmatic importance with the discovery of America. It is no small joke on man's greed for power over wealth and people that the conquest of a new continent, undertaken as a voyage to exploit the riches of Asia, resulted in the greatest economic disaster of Western civilization. Its main victims were the European merchants, who should have profited most from the new markets and the influx of precious metal, which they had established as international tender. In the cataclysmic clash between the ordained power of monarchs and the rights of ordinary men, they were the losers.

Neither Charles V nor his successor Philip II were raised to understand bookkeeping. The influx of eight million ounces of gold from melted-down Inca treasures, and an estimated twenty million silver ducats from the mines at Potosí in Bolivia in the first half of the sixteenth century represented a thirty-fold increase in the wealth of the Spanish crown. In reality, it was a revenue of diminishing returns. In contrast to the Portuguese monarchs, who did not share the transatlantic wealth with the merchants, the Spanish monarchs claimed only one-fifth of the American gold and silver, to encourage overseas discovery and investment. From this fifth, roads and towns had to be built; mercury had to be transported to the 12,000-foot peaks of the Andes, where it was needed to smelt silver. Governors and bishops built the lavish baroque palaces and churches we admire today, and the piracy of all non-Spanish nations, way-laying the gold and silver fleets, necessitated gigantic coastal

Fig. 219. Row housing, Park Row, London (early nineteenth century), was a pleasant variation of the French prototype, treating the street block as a single building.

defenses, such as the citadel of Cartagena. But the two main drains on Spanish economy were psychological. In an exact recasting of the tragedy that had wiped out Rome, the influx of wealth turned Spanish farms into enormous luxury estates and brought a steep decline in local agriculture, especially wheat farming. The easy gold of the sailors was easily spent and caused a disastrous inflation of prices. The precious metal coming with the galleons was worth less and less in Spain, and was drained off by import purchases from other European countries, notably France and England, where it was worth more and more. The sixteenth-century kings of Spain were still looking through the rear view mirrors of their minds at a feudal realm, where their incessant wars against France and Holland could be financed by imposing taxes, and borrowing limitless amounts for the royal treasury. Both sources of revenue were exhausted by 1550 and the great merchants, especially the two German houses of Welser and Fugger, were blackmailed into additional loans by being threatened with exclusion from the transatlantic trade. Their collateral was shares in the gold and silver of Peru, which they could not collect. As fleets sank or were robbed by privateers, and as interest rates soared, the situation of the Spanish crown became desperate. In 1557, Philip II suspended payments. He received one more gigantic monetary infusion from the great Italian merchant houses, the Medici, Orsini, and Pazzi, who hoped to eliminate their German competitors from the overseas developments. In 1576, the Spanish cortes declared the nation bankrupt. In the ensuing collapse of European economy, all great merchant houses went down. "Emperors, kings, and princes had killed the goose that laid the golden eggs."*

Spain never recovered from its paradoxical discovery of *El Dorado*. Deprived of their land, farmers took to raising sheep and goats, which made of Castile a treeless wasteland. The abject poverty of the people furnished Cervantes with the background for *Don Quixote,* and the New World with immigrants, who found in the exploited Indians the only sector of mankind worse off than themselves. The Spanish Main was soon ruled by Britannia. The proud and independent merchant cities of the Hapsburg empire shriveled under the stranglehold of mercantilism. The desperate move of governments to forestall "another Spain" vested the responsibility for balance of import-

* E. Oser (trans.), Ernst Samhaber, *Merchants Make History* (New York, 1964).

export trade with government rather than with free enterprise. It imposed tariffs on trade and neglected agriculture in favor of exportable home-industry products, creating in the process the new urban phenomenon of national capitals. As tightly controlled bureaucratic centers of mercantile power backed up by the new institution of a standing professional army, the capitals appropriated all wealth, influence, and culture to themselves. Without the internationalism of a prosperous merchant class, the self-sustained commercial city-states—Florence, Genoa, Venice, the Hanseatic cities in northern Europe, and the "unmittelbare Reichsstädte" (tribute-exempt city-states) in the south of Germany—sank into the same architectural and cultural provincialism as Barcelona and Seville. The main concern of capital-city planners was "the approach"—a monumental axis celebrating the resurgence of monarchic power.

It was suggested earlier in this book that cities, like human beings, form their character early in their existence and retain it despite exterior influences and peripheral variations. London had become a Roman trading post on a suitable Thames crossing in the first century B.C. Its reason for being was always the organization of continental trade and the distribution of goods, wealth, and people to the hinterland. In contrast to Paris, with its single nucleus of the cathedral on the Ile de la Cité, there never was a focal point in London and there is none today. From the beginning, London functioned through its road system and its bridges. Nothing came of Wren's plan to make the mercantile metropolis of Europe into a cosmological symbol (see *Fig. 136*). The sober "huckster mentality," as less prosperous Continentals would peg the English character, resisted the stellar straight jacket as stubbornly as it did the grand approach to the absolutistic residences. Rarely has one nation profited so blatantly from the misfortunes of another. The luck of Spain that sank with the Armada was bestowed on the little green isle, which turned within 150 years into the dominant European sea and land power. London grew proportionately. George Dance the Younger, who had followed his father as clerk of the London City Works in 1768, replanned the city as an interacting system of major thoroughfares and parochial "estates," in addition to planning the first double bridge over the Thames with roadways in opposite directions (*Fig. 220*).* A

* Map and data from Michael Hugo-Brunt, "George Dance the Younger as Town Planner (1768–1814)," *Journal of the Society of Architectural Historians,* Vol. XIV, No. 4 (1955).

Fig. 220. Plan of London, showing new residential developments and connecting main roads, as planned by George Dance the Younger between 1768 and 1814. His thoroughfares are not discontinuous, as so many of Haussmann's would be, but form a continuous connective system around the dense population centers. His double-roadway London Bridge, proposed in 1786, would have been a sensational improvement, anticipating the traffic increase of the nineteenth century, had it been realized. Map: Michael Hugo-Brunt.

comparison between Haussmann's road network (see *Figs. 143, 144*) and that of Dance reveals the entire difference between the Roman orbit plan and the merchant city plan. Dance ignored the royal palace and St. Paul's Cathedral completely as monumental vista points. All his roads were interconnected beyond the limits of the inner city, avoiding the discontinuous boulevards of Paris. Many of Dance's projects were not completed. The archaic proprietary laws of England, their 999-year-lease system dating back to Norman times, proved as frustrating in the eighteenth century as it was to reconstruction after World War II.

The orthogonal-linear merchant city plan survived vigorously only in the merchant cities of the Netherlands. Dutch merchantmen brought back huge profits from overseas exploration and a special skill in privateering. During the seventeenth century, the Dutch West India Company concentrated its operations on the Caribbean islands and ignored the exhausted shores of Spanish America. To supply the ships that brought cane sugar, tobacco, spices, slaves, and other highly desirable commodities to Europe, and to store and convert raw materials, the Dutch West India Company occupied the mouth of the Hudson River in 1618 and founded the port of New Amsterdam. It was the last of the merchant cities in the tradition of the Hanseatic League and the Protestant secularism of Renaissance Holland. In the course of 300 years, it was to turn, as New York, into the largest city on earth.

The concept Dutch urbanism bequeathed to its American offspring was grounded in trade competition, a high degree of specialization, and internationalism. When the Dutch West India Company bought, in 1626, a picturesque but topographically unsuitable island from the Manahatas Indians for sixty guilders worth of dime-store junk, the Dutch cities of Europe were at the height of their prosperity. We have been conditioned to see in Florence and Rome the epitome of Renaissance revival of art, learning, human liberty, and "the dignity of public places" through great architecture. As integrated urban organisms, the Dutch and Flemish cities of the sixteenth and seventeenth centuries surpassed most cities of Italy and France. Although there was a lesser concentration of individual genius, the general level of commerce, learning, the arts, architecture, and humanism was the highest in the world. Sciences, especially optics, botany, geology, and medicine, flourished at the newly created University of Leyden (*Fig. 221*). Leyden, a Roman foundation, became the great textile center of the Netherlands during the Middle Ages and Renaissance. Willem of Orange gave it the Netherlands' first university in 1575 as reward for the heroic resistence of the city against the Spaniards. Its medical faculty was soon the most progressive in the world. New Amsterdamers from Manhattan flocked there for training and established New York as the foremost medical center in the

223

new world. The plan of the city is remarkable for its use of the Old Rhine, which forms the natural fortification, the main *grachten* (canal) forking in two directions, and an interior ring. This tradition was brought to New Amsterdam and remained vital till the English successors of the Dutch filled in every foot of the original canals. Textiles, printing and publishing, goldworking, shipbuilding, painting, theology and philosophy, law and educational reform all flourished in Amsterdam, the Hague, Ghent and other cities. (There never was Dutch sculpture, which is an interesting reflection on the lack of stone and the diffused, nonmodulating light that prevails.)

The new outpost of Dutch culture on the Hudson, midway between Europe and the West Indies, was planned in the image of the mother city, Amsterdam (*Figs. 222A, 222B*). The determining factors were communication lines to the sea and the two rivers, and an option for orderly growth beyond Wall Street and its fortification. Within twenty-five years of the city's founding, the Hudson Valley to the navigable limits just beyond Fort Orange (Albany) has been annexed and surveyed, and a regular packet boat schedule established. After several destructive raids, the Mohawks, leaders of the Indian federation of the Five Nations, were brought into the fur trade by a peace treaty, and Dutch citizenship was offered to anyone who could pay eight beaverskins. By 1650, eighteen languages were spoken in New Amsterdam.

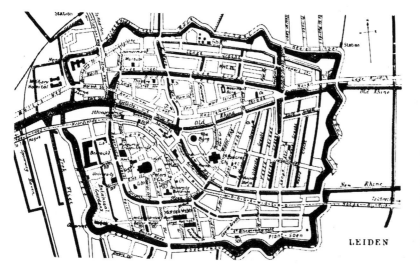

Fig. 221. Plan of Leyden, Holland. All linear communication depends on interior waterways formed by the waters of the Old Rhine, which has been spliced, like a cord, into a multistrand road system.

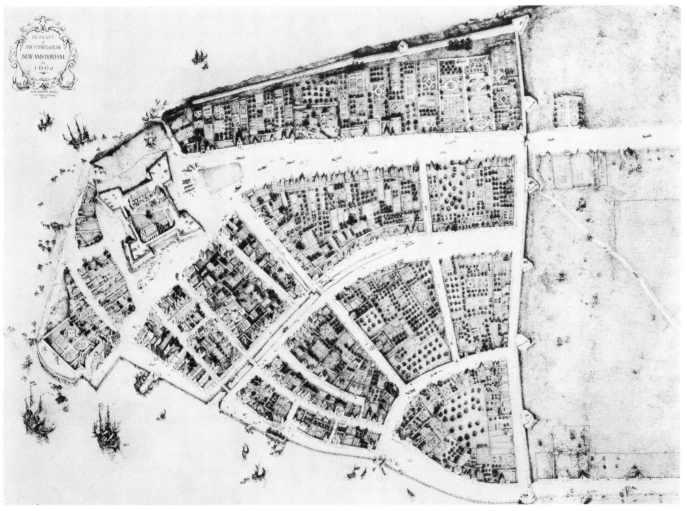

Fig. 222.

A) The city of Amsterdam, as it developed between the Middle Ages and the eighteenth century. The two determining factors are regulated development and a preconceived canal network, which is the regulator of the city to which all buildings adjust.

B) New Amsterdam in 1660 showed the influence of the Dutch mother city in an orderly plan of clearly delineated superblocks and wide roads serving traffic to the quays and the agricultural hinterland. The ample gardens were land reserves that permitted increased density without outward sprawl.

A

B

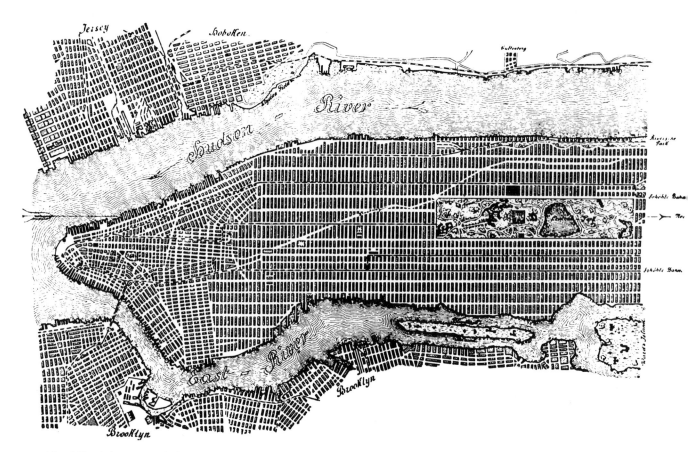

Fig. 223. The Commissioner's Plan for Manhattan Island, (1811). It ignored all topographical features and the aesthetic-recreational value of a continuous waterfront. Yet, when all criticism has been leveled, the question remains: what else could anyone have done with a shelf in the ocean, two and one-half miles wide and eighteen miles long, whose population was determined to concentrate the economic affairs of the world market on one spot?

From a city-planning viewpoint, the wisdom of the city corporation consisted in leasing rather than selling building sites, to control the size and quality of buildings which, from the beginning, were predominantly in brick rather than in the customary colonial wattle, daub, and clapboard construction. Despite grumbling about lack of housing, the corporation mapped city expansions very slowly, to keep real estate values high and centralization dense. The first substantial extension beyond Wall Street was called Montgomery Ward, in gratitude to a governor who had accepted a substantial bribe to grant the city a self-governing charter that gave it a freedom not shared by any other city in the Americas. The character of Manhattan can be assessed from the way in which the Dutch reacted to the demand of the British fleet to surrender in 1664. Governor Peter Stuyvesant tried frantically to raise sufficient wampum, the shell and pelt money still current in the absence of hard metal, to repair the dilapidated fortifications. But the burghers stalled, bickering for the enormously profitable rum concessions as a collateral. They finally decided to make their own terms, stipulating a guarantee of their trading freedom and a joint British and Dutch city council for a bloodless surrender. The governor, it is related, shattered his wooden leg in helpless fury on his desk, "although it was richly adorned with silver ornaments." After a brief resurgence of Dutch resistance, ordered by the European home government, the States General finally surrendered all claims to the impudent portus of the Hudson against a free hand in Surinam (Dutch Guiana).

The flight of British loyalists after the Revolutionary War dumped large parcels of the valuable expropriated Manhattan real estate into the lap of the city corporation, which up till then had played no role whatever in the affairs of the merchant corporations who ran the town. Between 1796 and 1811, the Commissioner's Plan was developed. In the subsequent fifty years, it was put into effect (*Fig. 223*). Although the modular grid plan was the rule of new town foundations, nothing had ever been attempted that equaled in brutality the grid stencil to be clamped over the cliff- and ravine-studded granite shelf. It consisted of 155 city blocks, drawn to a modular measure of 200 feet long and 100 feet deep and subdivided into ten house lots 20 feet wide and 100 feet deep. Streets were 60 feet wide, running east-west between the Hudson and the East rivers, and twelve avenues were 100 feet wide. They were irregularly spaced to bisect the east-west streets in a north-south direction, starting nowhere and ending in confusion in the ungridable fan shape of the old Dutch town. The argument for the excessive number of streets toward the waterfronts was the anticipated expansion of shipping and the need for commercial access. But shipping refused to be dislodged from its old moorings at the southern tip of the island, where ground was constantly gained by landfill. When the Vanderbilts put the railroad right into the middle of the city, the waterfronts—which had once been the reason for the city's being and the most exciting contrast to its sedate residential streets—turned into commercial slums, polluted and inaccessible (*Figs. 224A, 224B*). The mayor's residence (*Fig. 225*) facing the East River still shows that the esplanades of New York could have rivaled those of Rio de Janeiro, Nice, and Geneva if surveyor Kasimir Goeck had been capable of thinking of anything else except "the best way to buy and sell real estate."*

* I. N. Phelps Stokes, *Iconography of Manhattan* (1928, 1967).

A

Fig. 224.
A) New York
waterfront in 1870. The
broad piers and
commercial buildings
are a confirmation of the
city's origin and future.
B) New York
waterfront in 1966:
inaccessible, a warehouse
slum, and without any
visual connection with
the city.

B

Fig. 226. Manhattan's Broadway in
1899. There was no other direction
to go but up.

Although it must be conceded that the leveling of hills was necessary in the pre-motor age, when drays had to pull heavy wagons in ice and snow across the city, the "rape of New York" is an undeniable fact. A single diagonal street, Broadway, cut across the grid, and no spaces were allotted for parks, neighborhood squares, or even public buildings. Manhattan was saved from becoming merely another deadly grid town, bare of communication and architectural significance, by three factors. First, the natural linearity of an island two-and-a-half-miles wide and eighteen miles long, forced the avenues into verticality. With nowhere else to spread, they became communication links that made the expression "on the Avenue" synonymous with excitement and sociability (*Fig. 226*). The center avenues were architectural advertisements that changed with the times and presented to the city the image of Western progress. The second factor was New York's qualifications as a portus, which fulfilled the Roman specifications of international trade, banking, conversion of goods, learning, and art, whose practitioners sailed into the great harbor under many flags. The third and strongest factor that defeated the dead hand of the planning commissioners was the peculiar urban concept that New York-

229

Fig. 227. (above) Row houses, constructed from New York brownstone in Brooklyn Heights. Although they are fifty years younger than the ones shown in Fig. 228, the concept of residential unity and scale has been maintained.

Fig. 228. (right) The perpetuation of the French and British continuous elevation plan in Washington Square, New York, ca. 1832.

ers had inherited from their Dutch founders. Uninhibited by any "holy experiment" or "errand in the wilderness," they found their own remedies against monotony. From Georgian England they imported the unified block design that conceives of a street as one building. The attractiveness of these eleva-

Fig. 229. Central Park, Manhattan planned in 1857 by Frederick Law Olmsted on 840 acres and designed to offer every possible contrast to city life. The remarkable thing about Central Park is not its founding but its survival in a city with the highest per-square-foot land cost. From the J. Clarence Davies Collection, Museum of the City of New York.

Fig. 230. New York region, 1966. Despite its linear character as a typical merchant city, New York has grown into a modern equivalent of the ancient concentric city-states. Manhattan has assumed a Stadtkrone *character, symbolizing in the vertical towers of her skyscrapers the single focus of economic and cultural leadership.*

tions lay in the kaleidoscopic change from side street to side street, as if the speculation builders who put up these row houses knew that prosperous New Yorkers could not have tolerated the idea of living on a street identical with another (*Figs. 227, 284B*). This unity in variety was destroyed when speculation tenements appeared in the side streets. The so-called Old Law Housing Act (1867) had created the infamous windowless "passage rooms" between the front parlor and the kitchen; the New Law (1897) was based on the "dumbbell plan," stipulating a lightwell between building walls, and one toilet on each floor. But to this day the physiognomy of New York can be read from the planned contrast between unified side streets and the dynamic variability of the avenue elevations (*Fig. 228*). To alleviate the suffocating denseness of the 1811 grid plan, even the city's hard-boiled, money-greedy citizens were prepared to accept Frederick Law Olmsted's design for Central Park. They agreed to write off 840 acres of the most valuable real estate to create for their fellows "a lung, the redemption and the pride of the city," as its main promoter, William Cullen Bryant, called the huge green square in the heart of Manhattan when it opened in 1857 (*Fig. 229*). In the end,

Manhattan has triumphed over its planned strait jacket because its self-image is that of the last of the free merchant cities open to the whole world.

As immigration soared in the nineteenth century, and the surrounding Dutch villages became the residential base for the Manhattan work force, there occurred an urban phenomenon that has no equal in any other metropolitan development. The epitome of the orthogonal-linear merchant city, the island of Manhattan, assumed the single-focus function of the concentric city-states (*Fig. 230*). The four boroughs, Brooklyn, Queens, the Bronx, and Staten Island, developed no urban foci of their own. They were like the four quarters of the ancient cosmological cities, deriving their reason for being from the great symbol of the *Stadtkrone*. As the city turned into a region, the concentric focus of Manhattan gained in importance, controlling over 68 per cent of the region's wealth and less than 10 per cent of its territory.

It might be considered rank romanticism to look at the skyscraper ziggurats of Manhattan as an inspired temenos. Those who admit man's obsession with power over nature, wealth, people, and knowledge cannot deny the surrogate-religious significance of this tiny island for the Western world. Introducing in 1929 the Regional Plan which was a grandiose attempt to enhance that magic attraction of the regional nerve center, John H. Finlay said: "New York, not a New World city but an Old World city, sitting on the shores of the new with her back to it, and her feet in the ocean"; to which the English critic Reyner Banham added:

Old Futuropolis . . . . every block a flower bed bursting with architectural growth. . . . If Los Angeles is where the European visitor feels most lost, New York is where he feels most at home. . . . New York maintains grand old European traditions like pedestrianism and Socialism. . . . Everywhere else, more reasonable solutions have and will be found. Old Futurist dream-cities don't need reasonable solutions.*

The predestination of a city's historical development is particularly evident from the brief glance at three other merchant cities of the United States, which originated as urban personalities with higher, more sophisticated visions than the vast majority of colonial foundations. These three cities are Boston, Philadelphia, and Chicago. The Pilgrims who sailed in 1621

* *The Architect's Journal* (August 31, 1966).

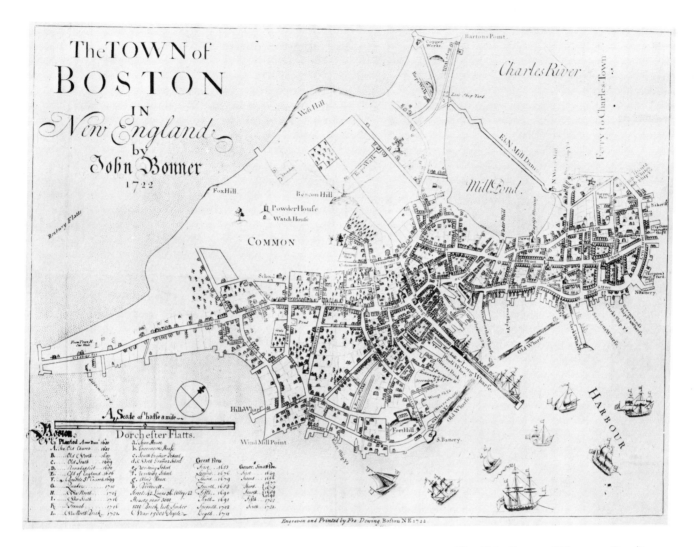

The TOWN of BOSTON IN New England by John Bonner 1722

Engraven and Printed by Fra Dewing Boston NE 1722

from Plymouth Harbor into Massachusetts Bay came into possession of one of the finest natural harbors in the hemisphere (*Fig. 231*). But they were as blind to its possibilities as an urban focus as they were to the needs of a merchant city. In one of the most peculiar experiments in Western history, the founders of Boston attempted to wipe out about 200 years of European development and revert in every aspect of their existence to the medieval standards of fourteenth-century England. A maze of winding streets, flanked by overshot half-timber houses, remained the butt of travelers' jokes into the nineteenth century. The chartered British company which ran Boston harbor as

Fig. 231. Boston 100 years after its founding showed the spotty development of a city with a civic focus. The Old Meeting House at the intersection of King Street and Cornhill was surrounded by a maze of narrow streets with timber houses that gave rise to incessant conflagrations. The city was "this fortress of God" which met "the hideous wilderness of an undeveloped continent. Bostonians denounced the prosperous Dutch for lechery and materialism, while the British Chartered Company, operating on Long Wharf, reaped profits that should have developed the city.

233

a highly profitable establishment, operated in the face of the fierce hostility of the townspeople, who retained a form of theocratic government that had been abolished in northwestern Europe with the granting of city charters in the twelfth and thirteenth centuries. The major north-south road ended abruptly at the city limits. The hinterland, so successfully opened up by the Dutch in their own region, was "a hideous wilderness," and its aboriginal inhabitants were vermin to be stamped out "by the wrath of a vengeful god."

The first printed account of the new England founded across the ocean appeared in 1654, written by Edward Johnson, with the title *Wonder-working Providence of Zion's Saviour in New England.*

The Lord with the waterspouts of his tender mercy has reduced the number of Indians in thirty years from thirty thousand to three hundred by disease and warfare. While this poor church of Christ grew to comprise forty-three congregational churches with seven thousand seven hundred and fifty members.

New York's population increased by 59 per cent between

Fig. 232. The beautiful park belt (shaded areas) developed by Boston in the 1880's did not remedy the chaos of its planless street system, but it offered relief to the shut-in citizens, who could walk from the Charles River to Franklin Park or relax in the handsomest Common in the center of a city. But parks did not abolish congestion or railroad tracks, which were pushed like ramrods through the residential areas.

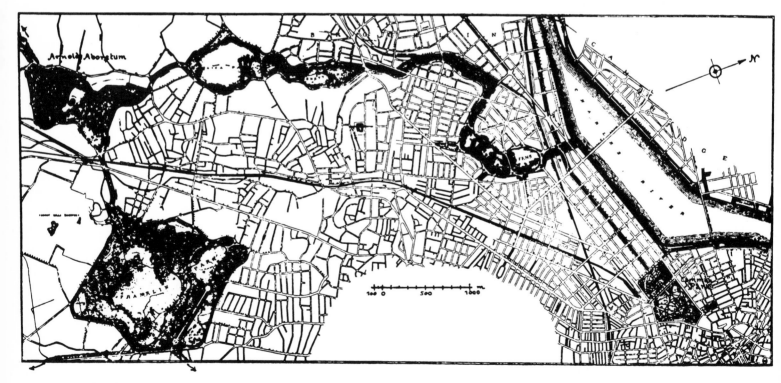

234

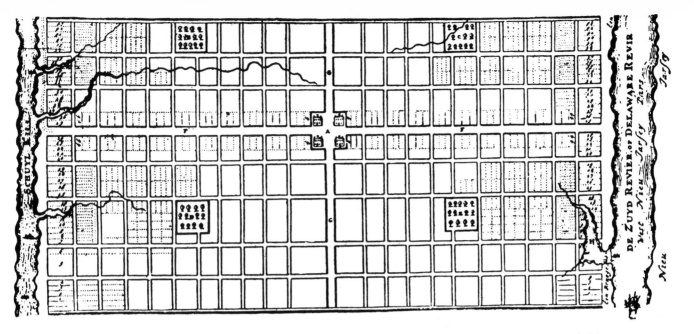

Fig. 233. Plan of Philadelphia, as drawn by Holme in 1682. The original blocks of 425 by 500 feet were cut up into eight minimum lots for two-story, one-family houses. Prohibited to succumb to "vain fashions," the core of the city displayed an undeviating plainness. The saving grace of the Holme plan was the four public squares defining each of the city sectors. Although the grid failed to provide a variation and hierarchy of streets catering to the need for differentiation and competition basic to merchant cities, the two broad main roads of Philadelphia served her well enough to accommodate artisan shops and British import houses, which were the backbone of Philadelphia economy. The other advantage Philadelphia had over Boston was the extent of the Penn land grant, which included in the city development interchange with native and immigrant rural populations.

1710 and 1740, despite yellow fever and a chronic water shortage; Boston's grew only 29 per cent and had, by 1790, fallen 12,000 behind the worldly upstart to the south. The substantial improvements Boston made in the late nineteenth century skirted the tangled mess of the city core, except for railroad tracks slicing through its approaches (*Fig. 232*). A remedy was sought in one of the finest continuous park systems in America, offering to the trapped city dweller the relief of Sunday walks along green pastures. But this did nothing for the commercial progress of the city, which changed its prejudices from religious intolerance to an exclusive caste system, and its preoccupation from Cotton Mather's hell and damnation to a productive interest in literature and learning.

William Penn founded Philadelphia in 1682, with a grant of land from the British crown which was so big that it was actually a province. His professed ideal was tolerance, in contrast to Massachusetts where three of his Quakers were hanged on Boston Bridge in the year in which the witches were burned in Puritan Salem. Penn's main concern was to safeguard his city of brotherly love against "the changeable nature of vain fashions" and to eliminate class distinctions as a handicap to a functioning urban society. On a one-by-two-mile rectangle between the Delaware and Schuylkill rivers, Thomas Holme laid out a plan of uniform 425-feet-by-500-feet plots, too large to prevent their being sliced into random strip lots, and too small to create orthogonal city sectors (*Fig. 233*). The plan's charac-

235

teristics were those of a medieval bastide (see *Fig. 183*). Charles Dickens, in his caustic *American Notebooks*, written in the 1840's, insisted that his face puckered into indomitable seriousness, his step became cautious and inaudible, and his hands folded over his stomach, when he walked down Market Street.

Despite a flourishing port, a world reputation for the superior craftsmanship of its workshops, and the nonconformism of its great adopted son, Benjamin Franklin, Philadelphia understood too late that the "plain spirit" of Quakerism, and the lack of arteries of communication to offset the traffic lanes of the grid, are fatal impediments to the status of a world port. We of the megacity age are constrained to see in each Philadelphia row house the urban significance of a Palazzo Massimi, but earlier centuries had less romantic views. Jefferson, John Lambert, and Mrs. Trollope all complained about the uniformity and drabness of Philadelphia and particularly about the "endless linearity" of its main streets. It was the particular tragedy of urbanism in America that the Philadelphia plan, through the city's prestige as a place of culture and virtue, became the prototype for all the lesser bastides, which did not even offer religious principle to justify monotony.

A city's parentage is its fate. With the exception of Hiroshima, no other city has been so radically torn down and rebuilt than Philadelphia. It is a game now played lightly in the United States, because no one believes in the *spiritus loci* as a generic characteristic. The ultimate plan for a new Market Street as crowning feature of a rebuilt Philadelphia, published by her famous city planner Edmund Bacon, displays a central axis whose relentless uniformity would be blessed by William Penn in his Quaker heaven (*Fig. 234A*). There are no frills of the design imagination playing spatial tricks that had delighted pedestrians of earlier truly urbane ages. It eliminates such silly romanticism as utilizing the broad Delaware as a termination point. A Miesian skyscraper rises from the reclaimed riverbank, crushing the old church steeples without eliminating the strait jacket of the past.*

Chicago has a special place in the history of architecture. It is the only American city which contributed an original design concept to the European heritage of man-made environment— the Chicago school of skyscraper architecture. Without the work of William Le Baron Jenney, John Holabird, Daniel

* See Bacon, *op. cit.*

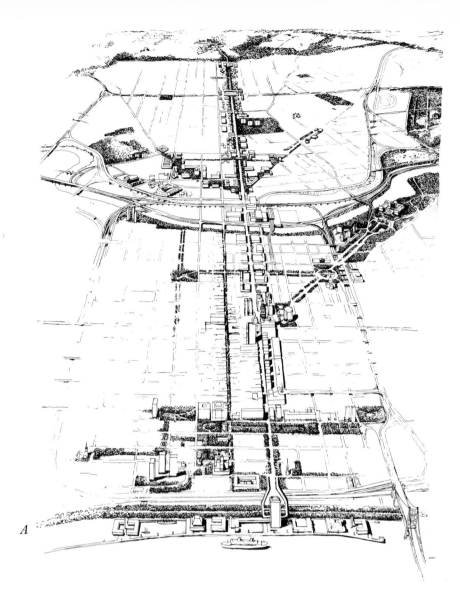

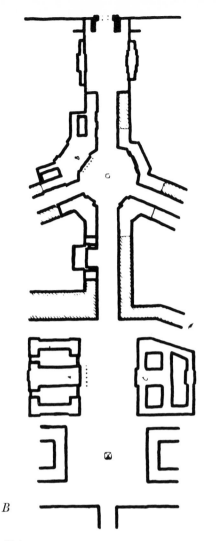

Fig. 234.

A) Perspective of the rebuilt main axis of Philadelphia, Market Street extension, as published by city planner Edmund Bacon. The relentless canyon offers no visual interest, no contrast between street and plaza, which are all planning tricks that had been known to city builders since Hellenistic times. A super skyscraper blocks the natural asset of the Delaware River landscape.

B) A detail from the eighteenth-century plan of Karlsruhe, Germany, reminds us of the concern with spatial-architectural interrelationships that had prevailed before city planning became a specialized profession, divorced from architecture. The two axes—historic Karlsruhe and ahistoric Philadelphia—tell the whole story of European and American urbanism.

Burnham, Louis Sullivan, and Dankmar Adler the high-rise steel-cage and curtain-wall construction might have developed elsewhere much slower and aesthetically in a much more compromising way. The Chicago school shared with the other reform movements of the nineteenth century a total indifference to city planning. The new towers were plugged into the standard gridiron plan of the Loop, the business district of Chicago, without any consideration for their visual impact on their environment. They were self-sufficient triumphs of building technology.

Daniel Burnham, one of the most prolific contributors to the Chicago school, betrayed its goal of astylar functionalism when

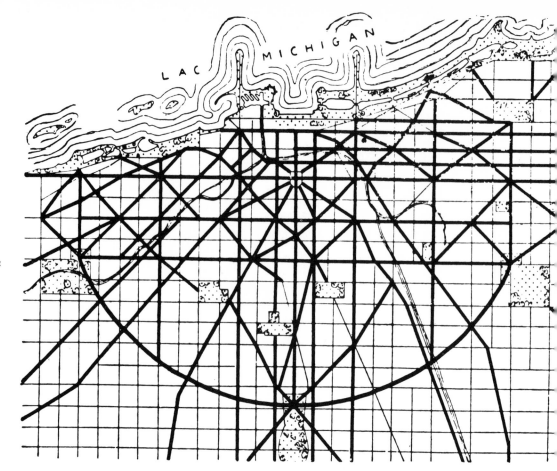

Fig. 235. Burnham's Chicago Plan of 1909 collided the ancient merchant-town tradition of communication as regulator of planning with traffic expressways to the suburbs. The result has been a flourishing commercial development along the lake and a steadily deteriorating inland city.

he inaugurated "Paris on Lake Michigan" as theme of the World's Columbian Exposition of 1893. His lathe-and-plaster Neo-Renaissance palaces, in the words of Louis Sullivan, turned American architecture back fifty years. Burnham was, however, the American urban planner who realized earlier than anyone else that automobile traffic and the expansion of cities toward the suburbs demanded replanning. He coined the expression "Mercantile Metropolis." In 1909, he published the Chicago Plan, a comprehensive scheme for the lakefront and public parks of the city and for a network of main traffic roads that made the efforts of Baron Haussmann look timid (*Fig. 235*). The hub of the road system was to be a civic center plaza (*Figs. 236A, 236B*) of gigantic dimensions, accommodating, in addition to the merging traffic of ten symmetrically disposed arteries, quasi-Hellenistic cultural institutions and a city hall that was a cross between the Pantheon and St. Peter's, fronted by an Egyptian

A

B

Fig. 236. Burnham's sketches (A, B) for the architectural treatment of his Chicago civic center, published a mere sixty years ago, are a grand finale to the origins of cities. Arcaded street elevations, a Roman Pantheon, Renaissance symmetry, Hausmann's bourgeois elegance, and a "Miracle Mile" of high-class retailing were brought together for the last time in a superimage of civic power. For his classical mirage, Burnham had to deny the architectural revolution he himself had done so much to bring about: the invention of the skyscraper.

obelisk. It is important to note that this radical scheme for the progressive development of the merchant metropolis combined two of the most incompatible planning concepts. It adhered to the via triumphalis and great entry scheme of Rome, arresting urban continuity and communication at the civic monuments in a static center. On the other hand, Burnham introduced the expressway cutting through the street system of the city, without any relationship or benefits to the city blocks. It was not only the rhetoric of Burnham's "think great" proposal that sold all major cities on the diagonal expressway system. The automobile had come and conquered, and the orthogonal-linear merchant city—living by architecturally-expressed street communication, human exchange, and environmental economical hierarchies—had started to decline.

6

The builders of cities were not marathon runners. They did not carry their faith in a man-made universe through history like a flaming torch without smoke. Uncounted urban foundations collapsed and died without having achieved either fortune or beauty, and many were born as stunted changelings, fitting no historical image and fulfilling no historical mission. Any history of urban origins must be filled with the finery, not the average dress man built for himself. In addition to urban failure, there was a continuous extrinsic force that worked against the city. Man is a split being. Five thousand years of urbanization have not been able to erase in him a secret or open longing to own a piece of native land, to work the soil, to be part of natural cycles and bounties, and to live as an individual free of the constraints imposed by a dense community.

Between urban mobility and land attachment there exists, however, a third area of human settlement, where the sharp artificial city lights and the diffused rural moon mix in a twilight zone. The German language calls this penumbra the *Weichbild,* or soft image, of a city. Modern urbanese has chosen to call it satellite development. A satellite is defined as an obsequious follower if he walks on earth; a satellite orbiting in outer space is a small, opaque body of low intensity, close to, but not part of, a stronger entity, to which it is bound by a common source of energy.

City satellites are clusters of buildings that belong neither to the city nor to the village, partaking of the open land and vestiges of nature, but dependent on an imitation of city life for survival (*Fig. 237*). Satellites or, as we shall call them, exurban clusters, have existed since the beginning of cities. Though born with the main urban bodies and circling them as moons circle the planets, they are harder to illustrate in the continuity of urban origins than main city types, because they have left few archaeological traces. They had no monumental buildings whose foundations could be excavated, and they had no street system defined by public structures and plazas. Most important, they left no documentary evidence to perpetuate their existence in history. By way of explanation, it must be assumed that the future excavators of Western culture will spend untold post-Guggenheim grants speculating on what made New York run. The bogus farmhouses of the Levittowns, strung on long "lanes" without beginning or end, will have vanished without a trace. It is only by sheer coincidence, usually at the off-center beginnings of an archaeological dig, that we have any evidence at all of the antiquity of the exurban cluster. We could let it go at that, as all previous historians have done, if this minor aspect of community building had not suddenly assumed an influence on the future of cities that is as revolutionary as was the emergence of the concentric concept after the geomorphic, and as was the shift from the hierarchical to the merchant city.

Clusters appear outside concentric cosmological cities in the Bronze Age for socio-economic reasons. The temple-and-palace economy of the city-state was geared to the exclusive benefit of one city alone. Commerce was exchange, not trade for profit as defined earlier. The traveling priest or the envoy of the king secured the best possible deal for commodities needed. The Aztec *pochteca,* an armed traveling royal merchant, must have

Fig. 237. Bird's-eye view of the new satellite landscape developing outside all major American and European cities. Featureless clusters of one-family houses—their "design" derived from European farm cottages—are strewn over the landscape, midway between the big city that furnishes income and the shopping center that furnishes a ready-made standard of living.

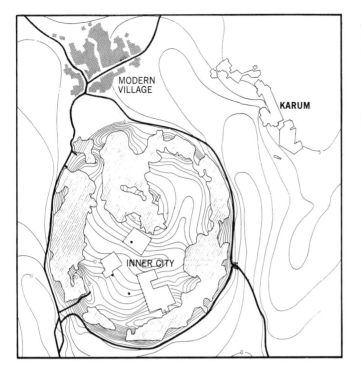

Fig. 238. The karum of Kanesh in Anatolia, one of the oldest known Assyrian trading posts, from the second millennium B.C. Thousands of clay tablets recording transactions and accounts were found on location. Excavations have shown an unorganized maze of adobe walls, without any focus on a sanctuary or a permanent palace. From Tahsin Ozgüc, An Assyrian Trading Outpost.

Fig. 239. Outside the tightly self-contained feudal community of Mycenae a group of buildings appeared during excavation, one of which had been obviously the establishment of an oil merchant. The Assyrian karum had found its way from Asia to one of the oldest European cities. From Joseph W. Alsop, From the Silent Earth: A Report on the Greek Bronze Age (1964).

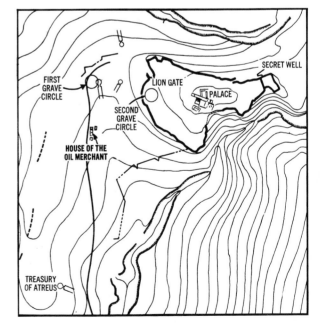

been the last survivor of this ancient institution. Early in the second millennium B.C., there appeared a different type of trader, the foreign merchant who was, as far as our present knowledge goes, an Assyrian—long before his race would make a bid for world domination. A few thousand years later, St. Jerome expressed public opinion when he sighed: The merchant pleases God only with difficulty. The usefulness of the merchant's mission soon became apparent and created an ambiguous reaction of the community to the traveling salesman that has lost none of its sting. Itinerant merchants, the "foreign people," had to stay outside the city walls because they were the roving ears and eyes of antiquity bound by no local loyalty oath. They were vital for supplying merchandise and the news of the world at large, carriers of ideas and skills and of strategic and political changes, all of which might be betrayed to enemies of the city. In the first urban age, the Assyrians were the "foreign people." Their karums form irregular clusters on the flanks of circular Anatolian fortress towns (Fig. 238), and their loosely strewn trading stations have been found along the coastal routes that connected the Indus Valley civilization with

243

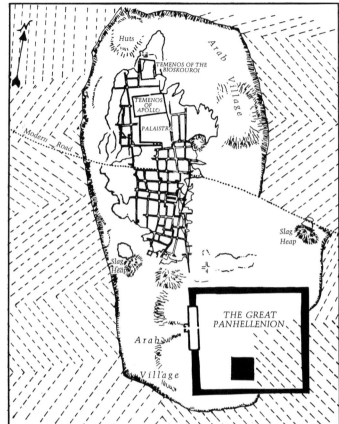

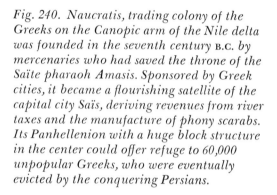

Fig. 240. Naucratis, trading colony of the Greeks on the Canopic arm of the Nile delta was founded in the seventh century B.C. by mercenaries who had saved the throne of the Saïte pharaoh Amasis. Sponsored by Greek cities, it became a flourishing satellite of the capital city Saïs, deriving revenues from river taxes and the manufacture of phony scarabs. Its Panhellenion with a huge block structure in the center could offer refuge to 60,000 unpopular Greeks, who were eventually evicted by the conquering Persians.

Mesopotamia.* In Mycenae, the House of the Oil Merchant well below the citadel indicates an exurban trade settlement (*Fig. 239*). The Assyrians were followed by the Phoenicians, after whom the Greeks became the typical foreign traders. Daphnae, their military outpost in Egypt, was destroyed, but they assumed a new role in the *karum* of Naucratis (*Fig. 240*), which served the Egyptian delta city of Saïs. Sponsored and supported by nine Ionian cities, the Naucratians gradually dominated sea trade in Egypt and supplemented revenue from a river tax with the manufacture of phony scarabs for the credulous Egyptians. A central enclosure, the heavily walled Panhellenion, could, according to Herodotus, hold 60,000

* "Assyrian Trade Colonies in Asia Minor, From the Third Millennium B.C.," *Der Alte Orient,* Vol. XXIV, No. 4 (1925).

people and had a huge square-chambered stone building, which looks very much like a warehouse.

Satellite clusters developed faster during Roman world domination because the more stratified an urban society, the more rigid are its discriminatory laws. The *cives,* a strictly nationalistic hierarchy of military and administrative delegates from the capital, could not share the city they governed with the native inhabitants (*incolae*), who were expelled to the *vicus canaborum,* or land belt (*Fig. 241*).

The Assyrians and the Hellenistic Greeks acknowledged the commercial base of their urban growth and liquidated the hypocrisy of the exurban trade settlement in Babylon and Alexandria. The Christians and Moslems inherited from Rome not only Roman law, and the influence of "Romanesque" architecture, but also adopted many of the prejudices of imperialism, tolerating people of other races and other faiths but excluding them from all civil rights. Cairo (*Fig. 242*) was founded as al-Fustat in A.D. 640 by Amr, a general of the Omayad dynasty, where he had pitched his tent (*fustat*) at the conquest of Egypt. In 969, Gohar of the Fatimide dynasty made excellent use of the cliffs above the river to construct a citadel. The Moslem city

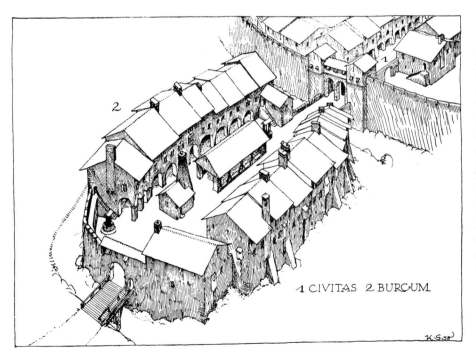

1 CIVITAS 2 BURGUM

Fig. 241. Even in the lonely outposts of Roman power along the frontier that separated today's West Germany from the eastern barbarians, Roman soldiers and administrators were strictly segregated from the native population. Civitas and burgum *were not only two different social worlds; they also told the long history of the semitic Mesopotamian city meeting and clashing with the Germanic anti-urban* burg. *From Gruber,* Gesicht der Deutsche Stadt.

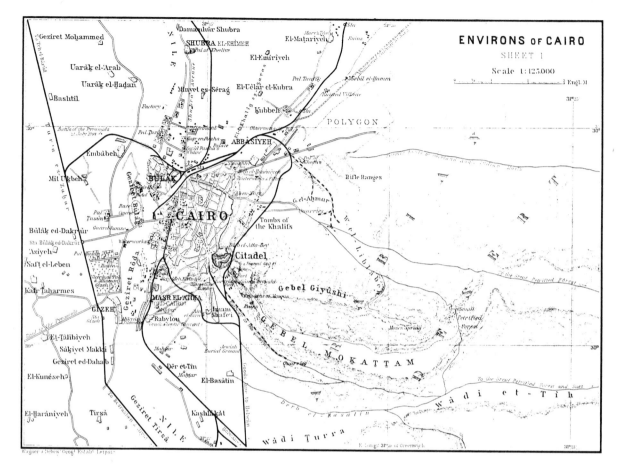

ENVIRONS OF CAIRO
SHEET 1

Scale 1:125,000

POLYGON

EL-CAIRO

Citadel

Gebel Giyûshi

GEBEL MOKATTAM

Wàdi et-Tih

Wàdi Turra

Fig. 242. Nineteenth-century plan of Cairo showing Old Cairo (Masr el-Atika) and New Cairo below the citadel.
Across the branch of the Nile is Bulak, the quarters for Jews and Christians, who were excluded from the Islamic city and became prosperous river merchants and artisans.

of Old Cairo developed to the south opposite the ancient Egyptian village of Giza. Jews and Christians were prohibited from living in the old or the new city, which sprang up at the foot of the citadel. They were assigned to an old village called Bulak, on the Nile, where they became highly successful merchants and artisans, free of Moslem restraints. As late as 1895 Baedeker's guide book refers to the Bulak "merchants of distant lands, including the Arsenal and stores of Messrs. Cook and Son." Their prosperity derived from a strategic location on the road to Bulak Island in the Nile, which became the playground of the British Colonial Set. This pattern of the split settlement is endlessly repeated—from Samarkand to Damascus to Delhi.

The oldest medieval cities accumulated around monastic strongholds after the Great Migrations had wiped out the

246

remnants of Roman colonization north of the Alps. Their plans distinguished sharply between the town of the bishop around the cathedral, and the town of the merchants and artisans. In St. Gallen a wide market was conveniently placed directly outside the monastic settlement (*Fig. 243*). If the trade was a public nuisance, like that of the tanners who worked with carcasses, acid, and noisy, pounding hammers, the cluster might form a miniature town of itself.

The Crusades had been intended as the death blow delivered by the flower of European chivalry to the abominable Arabs. As it worked out, the knights were civilized by their contact with oriental culture and carried back, together with their loot, urban concepts of great importance. Among them was the institution of the hospital and the almshouse as civic responsibilities. No other religion has made charity such a central article of faith as Islam. In a purely religious confederation that never had a unified state system, the giving of alms, both as tax and as voluntary deed, distributed social responsibility among the heads of households. The Seljuks—a Turkish people who in 300 years conquered their way from Central Asia across

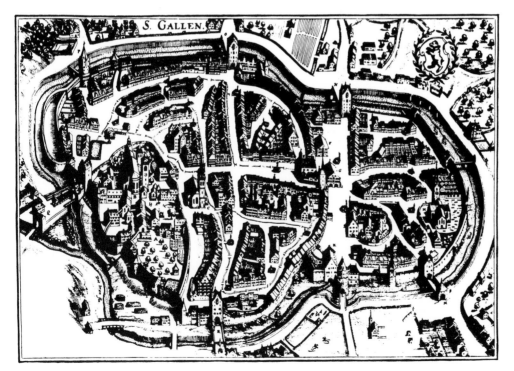

Fig. 243. St. Gallen, Switzerland, founded by Charlemagne at the end of the eighth century A.D. *The monastic foundation (left) is clearly marked off from the merchants' and artisans' town (right). The link between the heavenly and the material world is the town hall in the center of the wide market.*

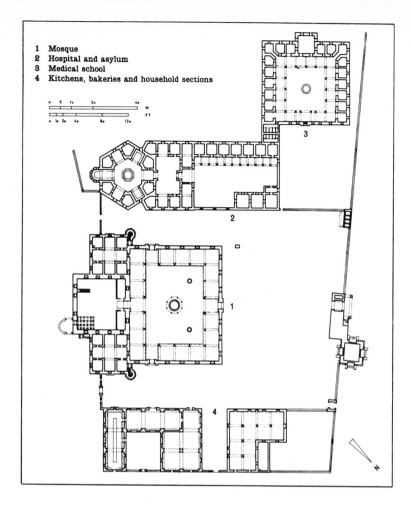

1 Mosque
2 Hospital and asylum
3 Medical school
4 Kitchens, bakeries and household sections

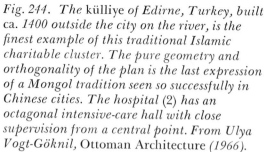

Fig. 244. The külliye *of Edirne, Turkey, built ca. 1400 outside the city on the river, is the finest example of this traditional Islamic charitable cluster. The pure geometry and orthogonality of the plan is the last expression of a Mongol tradition seen so successfully in Chinese cities. The hospital (2) has an octagonal intensive-care hall with close supervision from a central point. From Ulya Vogt-Göknil,* Ottoman Architecture *(1966).*

Anatolia toward Constantinople and the Mediterranean—refined what must have been a very old pattern into a new concept of the cluster. The külliye (Fig. 244) was a self-contained charitable establishment sometimes built by a sultan but more often donated by a rich citizen. Its sole purpose was social service.

Fig. 245. The Beguinages of Holland and Belgium carried the charitable cluster into the cities. They were founded in 1170 by Lambert Le Bègue as charitable institutions for the scores of widows and children of crusaders who did not return from the Holy Land. The close association with the Moslem world during this period permits the conclusion that the Beguinages were inspired by the külliye.

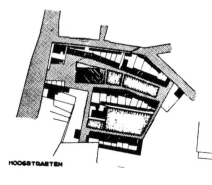

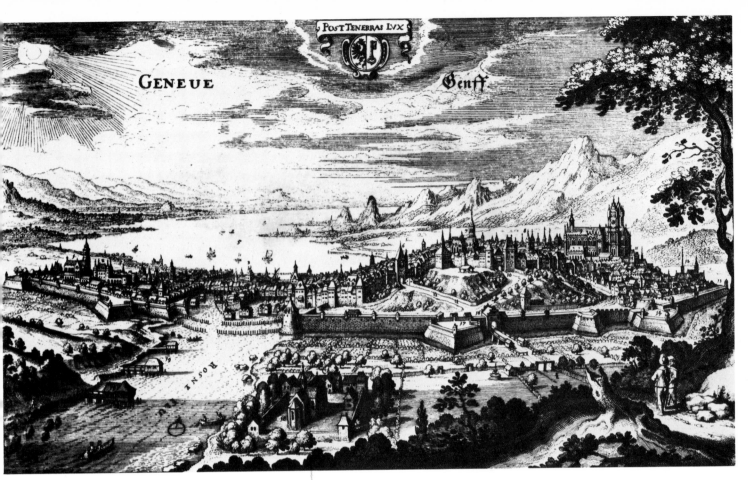

GENEUE   Genff

POST TENEBRAS LVX

Fig. 246. Merian's engraving of Geneva, Switzerland, about 1600. The small religious foundation in the foreground, a lepers' hospital run by monks, is characteristic of the exurban cluster that prevailed into the seventeenth century.

Each *külliye* contained a mosque, a hospital and insane asylum, an alms kitchen, and, in some of the largest ones, a medical school and a hostel. The one in Edirne dates from *ca.* A.D. 1400 and was situated outside the city on the river, and enclosed by a wall.

The influence of the *külliye* concept can be traced most directly in the Beguinages (*Fig. 245*). The Beguines formed a group of lay women that had its origin in the appalling number of wives and children who were left destitute by men who did not return from the Crusades. In 1170, Lambert Le Bègue founded a charitable institution in Liège that was soon known by a variation of his name. The Beguinages spread throughout Flanders, Holland, and northern France. It is significant that with the Beguinages the charity cluster invaded the city. Disreputable vagrants in roadhouses and on fairgrounds had shared urban ostracism with the sick, the aged, and the poor in exurban religious settlements provided by the equally unwelcome mendicant monks (*Fig. 246*). Now alms quarters appeared within the city walls.

249

Perhaps it was with these prototypes in mind that the fabulously wealthy banking and trading house of the Fuggers in "Golden Augsburg" planned the Fuggerei (*Fig. 247*). In 1514, they built an introverted cluster of fifty-three attached houses, surrounded by a wall and closed off from the splendid Renaissance city by three locked gates. Mile End Trinity Ground in London (*Fig. 248*), built in 1680 by Christopher Wren to house the widows and orphans of seamen, resembles a Protestant Beguinage. Like a cathedral close, it withdraws from the linear uniformity of London streets.

The social stigma attached to the cluster, whether outside the city gates or inside, found its strongest expression in the Jewish ghetto. Originally the term had merely implied the streets where Jews lived in medieval times. In some of the old imperial cities of Germany and Poland, it had been a term of privilege, since Jews had been invited by monarchs as financial advisers, scribes, teachers, and mathematicians. This did not prevent pogroms

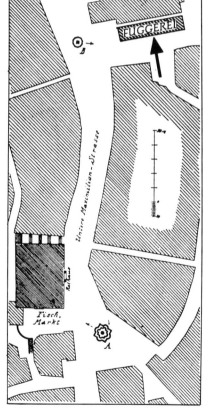

Fig. 247. The Fuggerei, a charitable housing development founded in 1514 in Augsburg by the merchant dynasty of the Fuggers, changed the tradition of placing socially undesirable or unsuccessful groups outside the city limits. The cluster was turned away from the linear main street of the great merchant city (see insert plan) and its single gate was locked at night. The social cohesion of the medieval city had received its first rupture.

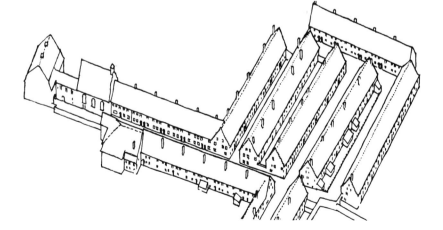

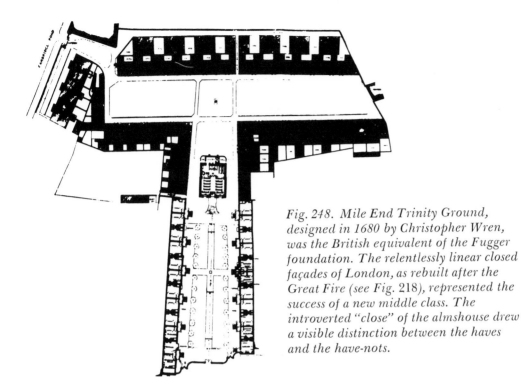

Fig. 248. Mile End Trinity Ground, designed in 1680 by Christopher Wren, was the British equivalent of the Fugger foundation. The relentlessly linear closed façades of London, as rebuilt after the Great Fire (see Fig. 218), represented the success of a new middle class. The introverted "close" of the almshouse drew a visible distinction between the haves and the have-nots.

and persecutions, leading in Spain and in England to total expulsion of the Jewish population; but those who remained in their old cities were free to move, to trade, and to teach. The Counter Reformation brought back not only the Inquisition and autos-da-fé, but a revival of accusations against the Jews dealing with ritualistic atrocities. In 1555, a papal bull proscribed any proximity between Jews and gentiles, thus creating the ghetto as an outcast community enclosed by walls, whose gates were locked at night and on Christian holidays (*Fig. 249*).

One has only to read *The Merchant of Venice* thoughtfully to understand that the ghetto was not altogether a place of humiliation, but also a place of pride and identification. The synagogues of Poland, dating mostly from the sixteenth and seventeenth centuries, were the tallest and most beautiful edifices in the rural towns and symbolized to the Jews their chosen destiny and their superiority over the host country.

Though the ghettos disappeared during the nineteenth century, the cluster concept did not. It expanded with the spread of the Industrial Revolution. The dirtiest and noisiest indus-

Fig. 249. *Two examples of walled ghettos in eighteenth-century Poland. (a) The ghetto of Kalisz was one of the most secure and thriving Jewish communities till the German invasion in 1939. It had a famous soaring synagogue (6), and wide market (5), and the only four-story houses in the city because the wall did not permit expansion. The ghetto of Kasimierz (b) was the result of Jewish expulsion from the capital city of Cracow after a severe conflagration in 1495, which was blamed on the Jews. Again synagogue (4) and market place (3) dominate the plan. The weakness of the segregated cluster lay in its vulnerability to attack by rioters. This doomed the Warsaw ghetto in 1943 and is still the peril of the Negro ghettos of America, as the Watts riots in 1966 demonstrated.*

tries had to move to the city outskirts, just as the more obnoxious crafts had to do in the Middle Ages. They were followed by company housing, whose ugliness conscientiously kept pace with the factories. This produced the ragged edges of American and European industrial cities (*Fig. 250*), followed by the commercial clusters along highway approaches.

The other nineteenth-century development that promoted clusters was the extension of welfare programs from care for the needy, sick, and aged to the building of whole charitable communities. Some seventy-five years ago, industrialists in England and Germany had become convinced by the theories of John Stuart Mill and Thomas Huxley that poverty was not divinely decreed, and that it was harmful to business. In 1887, the Lever

Fig. 250. A cluster of laborers' dwellings in the stockyards section of Chicago in 1931 is characteristic of careless and anti-urban land use, which creates a new type of ghetto.

family invested part of their soap fortune in Port Sunlight on the outskirts of Liverpool (*Fig. 251*). It is probably the earliest clustered community in which the street system is completely unrelated to buildings. Houses form independent insulae, which have no orientation toward each other or toward the city center,

Fig. 251. Port Sunlight, a company-financed garden suburb for 600 families, built in 1887 by the soap kings, the Lever brothers of Liverpool. The plan is the first realization of a cluster scheme consisting of introverted, unaffiliated neighborhoods, still the basic blueprint in 1967. The other pace-setting trend was a bogus medievalism in the design of houses that was symbolic of the reactionary trend away from dynamic urbanism.

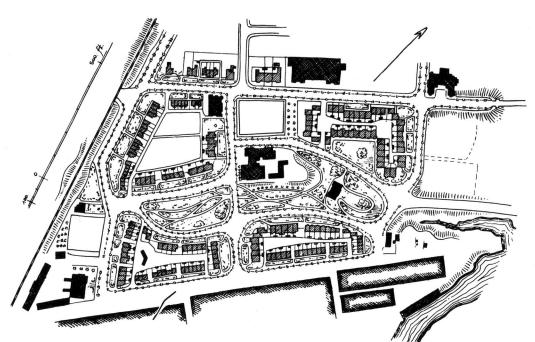

253

which is isolated in a hilly park. Six hundred families were provided with cottages in Early English Gothic style, and a young generation of community builders were provided with one of the most enduring prototypes. The ammunition dynasty of the Krupps in Essen emulated the soap dynasty by building Margarethenhöhe and Dahlhauser Heide for preferred Krupp employees, switching on patriotic grounds from Early English to overshot half-timber in their home design.

It is quite instructive to look at the replanning of Shoreditch (*Fig. 252*), one of the worst slum areas of London—undertaken in 1890 by the newly formed London County Council as its first project. Of 5,719 persons displaced, 5,524 persons were rehoused in their old neighborhood, a record seldom equaled by subsequent urban renewal projects. Shoreditch represents the urban versus the romantic mood. In contrast to Port Sunlight, it retained the relationship of row housing to the streets; it provided a focal point for the community in the Arnold Circus, with greenery and benches for evening gatherings, and ample yard play-space between the house rows. The future, however,

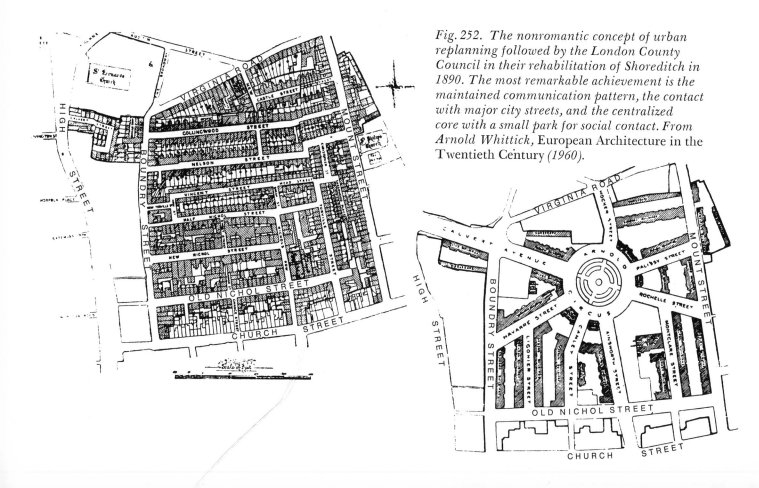

Fig. 252. The nonromantic concept of urban replanning followed by the London County Council in their rehabilitation of Shoreditch in 1890. The most remarkable achievement is the maintained communication pattern, the contact with major city streets, and the centralized core with a small park for social contact. From Arnold Whittick, European Architecture in the Twentieth Century *(1960).*

Fig. 253. Letchworth Garden City, planned by Parker and Unwin (1903) covered 4,500 acres for a planned population of 32,000, of which 1,500 acres were to be built up and 3,000 acres retained as permanent greenbelt. After World War II, the town had only 15,000 inhabitants.

belonged to the romantic followers of Ebenezer Howard. His centralized cosmological schemes (see *Fig. 76*) did not provide urban prototypes but furnished the confused vocabulary of country and city magnet, meeting (at point zero, we believe) in the suburban fringe area.* Raymond Unwin, a wealthy London architect, planned and built Letchworth (*Fig. 253*) as a non-profit corporation venture, designed for 32,000 people but housing less than 15,000 forty years after its beginnings. Hampstead Garden Suburb and Welwyn Garden City followed, with a medium density of ten families per net acre, living in tiny medieval farmhouses around dead-end lanes.

* See Ebenezer Howard, *Tomorrow: A Peaceful Path to Real Reform* (1899).

255

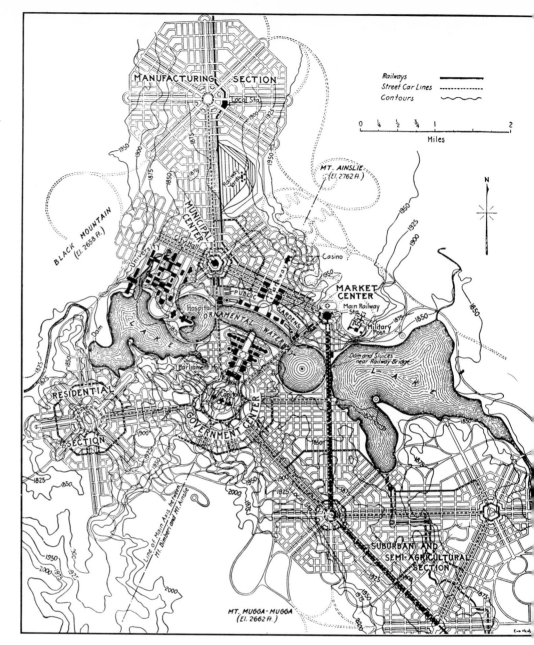

Fig. 254. Plan for Canberra, the capital of Australia, by the Chicago architect Walter Burleigh Griffin, collaborator of Frank Lloyd Wright. Although construction began in 1913, in 1964 the city's population was 32,000, a fraction of the number for which its 939 square miles were set apart. The discontinuous garden city is no magnet for an urban population seeking employment and success through the interaction of industry, economy, and learning.

Unwin was the great inspiration for the Continent and America. His prolific writing, especially his popular book *Nothing Gained by Overcrowding*, inspired Walter B. Griffin, the Chicago architect and collaborator of Frank Lloyd Wright, to submit a plan to the competition for the new Australian capital of Canberra which won first prize (*Fig. 254*). Automobile roads as ligaments between the nucleated satellite bodies were built,

256

but the muscle was very slow in developing. Against Griffin's intentions, plenty of greenbelt space is left around each satellite, and no overcrowding can be reported because less than 50 per cent of the projected population has materialized. It is an amusing sidelight on the unoriginality of the human mind that in 1785 an enlightened governor of Nova Scotia, Joseph Desbarres, tried a similar scheme when he founded Sydney, Nova Scotia, as "a haven of new hope" for loyalist refugees from the United States, and as the future capital of the Maritime Provinces (*Fig. 255*). Industry, coal mining, and agriculture were to have separate but interconnected clusters. Sydney failed as a capital. Its plan was lost in a sprawling gridiron company town.

Unwin's satellite diagrams quickly spread among the clustering faithful. Patrick Abercrombie, who was knighted for his efforts,

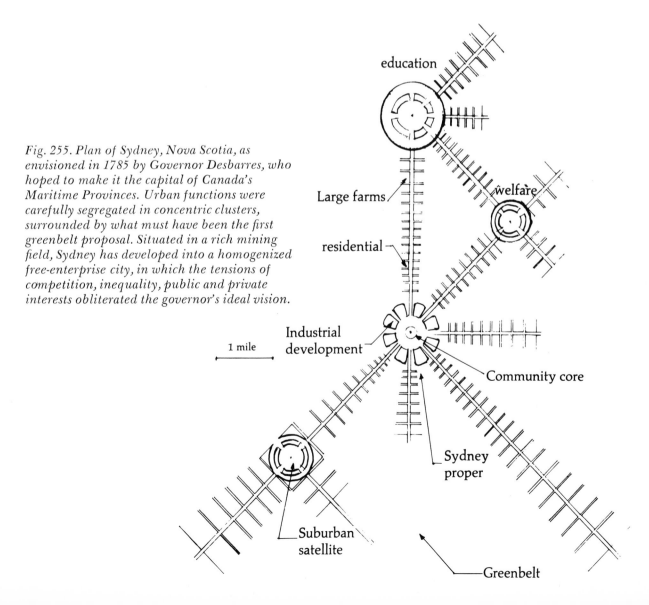

Fig. 255. Plan of Sydney, Nova Scotia, as envisioned in 1785 by Governor Desbarres, who hoped to make it the capital of Canada's Maritime Provinces. Urban functions were carefully segregated in concentric clusters, surrounded by what must have been the first greenbelt proposal. Situated in a rich mining field, Sydney has developed into a homogenized free-enterprise city, in which the tensions of competition, inequality, public and private interests obliterated the governor's ideal vision.

wove the cutest daisy pattern from pure cluster philosophy (*Fig. 256*). Eliel Saarinen, a Finnish member of the Deutscher Werkbund, wrote the first in an unending row of books dealing with the growth, decay, and future of the city. His remedy was an actual, not a metaphorical, urban explosion (*Fig. 257*), whose fragments would hopefully rearrange themselves, like magnetized steel shavings, into appealing star patterns of small communities, pledged not to undo each other's greenbelts.

There is a consistent pattern to the numerous reform movements originating in England during the nineteenth and twentieth centuries. They are based on excellent diagnoses of existing shortcomings, while proposing solutions that are romantic and regressive. It is easy to connect this trend with the ancient tradition of British isolationism, the smallness of physical area, the denseness of settlement, and the absence of diversified urban societies. Only London had an urban tradition and therefore set the standard for the rest of the country, a standard of overcrowding and lack of centralized planning. The cosmological cities and charitable paternalism of the Utopians have already been mentioned; Ruskin's medievalism and Morris' return to handicraft and cottage industry, and the Ebenezer Howard school of a rose-covered cottage in every marriage contract, could find a certain response in a society that yearned to be an island unto itself.

The transplantation of these very special environmental ideals into America by ardent proselytizers who played into the hands of the most ruthless profiteer, the speculative builder, is less explicable and excusable. The British inheritance of hatred of cities, having very ancient roots in the Anglo-Saxon and Indo-European tribal past, irrevocably influenced the former colonies. American urban reform took—and takes—its cues from Britain. Patrick Geddes, a Scot, conformed to the insular model by offering, around 1910, excellent analytical insights and research methods for the crowded, brutal, and ugly cities of India. Neither he nor his most faithful American disciple and commentator, Lewis Mumford, reflected on the fact that these conditions were the result of a nonindustralized society, just as the fearful conditions of seventeenth- and eighteenth-century London and Paris had nothing to do with capitalism, factory production, building technology, and the automobile, which Geddes and Mumford blamed for all urban ills. City deterioration in India and elsewhere was, as it had always been, the result of city attraction, which Geddes and Mumford's mentor, Ebenezer

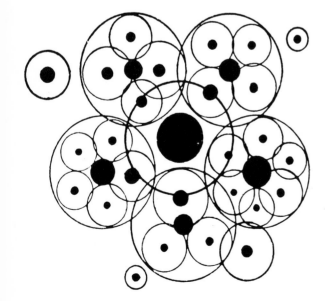

Fig. 256. Sir Patrick Abercrombie's decorative schematization of core city and clustered satellites.

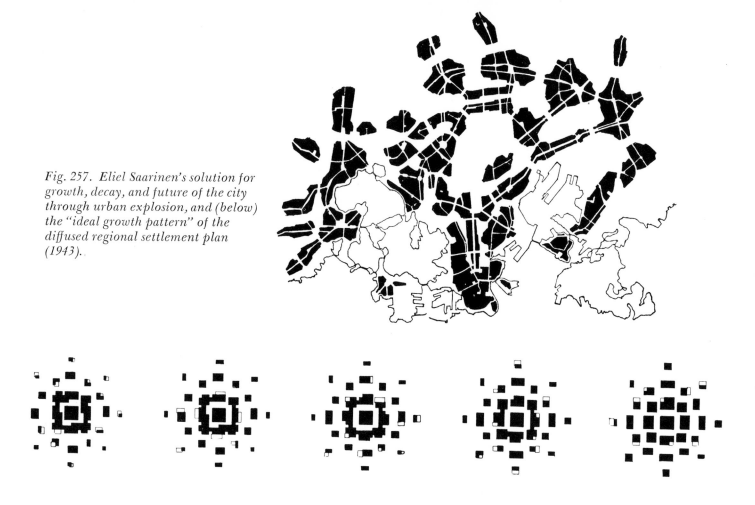

Fig. 257. *Eliel Saarinen's solution for growth, decay, and future of the city through urban explosion, and (below) the "ideal growth pattern" of the diffused regional settlement plan (1943).*

Howard, had so correctly analyzed and so incorrectly resolved. With unbelievable naïveté, the Geddes-Mumford school tried to solve the problem by declaring this urban attraction morally wrong. The straight transplant of the Ruskin-Morris ideology, which had so blatantly failed to change anything at all in the cities of England, is a suggestion made in dead earnest by Henry Wright in 1926 to the Commission of Housing and Regional Planning for the State of New York (*Fig. 258*). In a society whose entire economic and social structure is based on the two foundations of private property and freedom of decision, Wright proposed to "withdraw" the permanent population of the Adirondack region in northern New York State; to return the entire region to wilderness and recreational state parks; and to settle the "withdrawn" population, together with a maximum number of big-city refugees, in neatly spaced towns along the Hudson and Mohawk valleys, "limited in size, set in prosperous agricultural land, and serviced entirely by automobile highways." Mumford coined the expression "etherialized" urbanism for the Geddes-Wright concept which, taken in its semantic

259

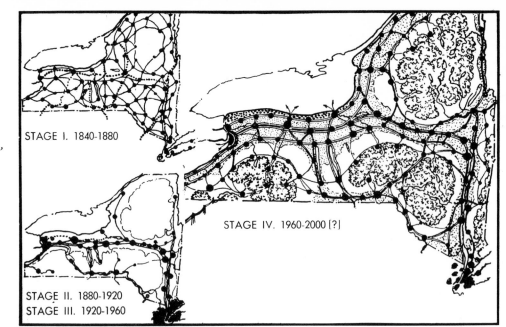

STAGE I. 1840-1880

STAGE IV. 1960-2000 [?]

STAGE II. 1880-1920
STAGE III. 1920-1960

Fig. 258. The regional plan for New York State by Henry Wright (1926) proposed "the" withdrawal of the permanent population from the Adirondack Mountains region." Not only was the absurdity of this proposal in a free-enterprise, land-speculating society never challenged; it earned for its promoters an almost saintly reputation. From Lewis Mumford, The City in History (1961).

meaning, means diffusion of matter into a celestial state of weightlessness.

As a beginning, Wright, Clarence Stein, and Mumford—with the backing of a New York speculative builder, who had made a fortune on Park Avenue, created Radburn, New Jersey, which was dependent for survival on New York City; Chatham Village, dependent on Pittsburgh; Baldwin Hills Village, dependent on Los Angeles; and Greenbelt, Maryland, dependent on Wash-

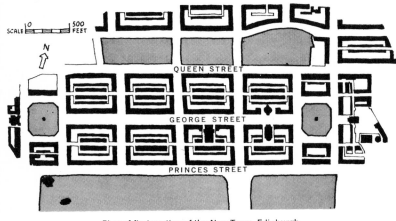

SCALE 0 500 FEET

N

QUEEN STREET

GEORGE STREET

PRINCES STREET

Plan of first section of the New Town, Edinburgh.

A

Fig. 259. In his book New Towns for America (1957), Clarence Stein, partner of Henry Wright, claimed that his Radburn and Baldwin Hills (B) plans derived from James Craig's Edinburgh plan (A) from 1767. The comparison is as fallacious as it is instructive. Craig retained linear communication within the city. His public nodes are planned, both spatially and architecturally. His house elevations are continuous and of fine detailing, in the most contemporary style of his day, and no phony village analogy denies the city.

B

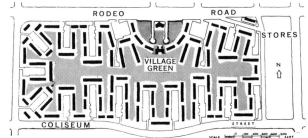

RODEO ROAD

STORES

VILLAGE GREEN

N

COLISEUM STREET

SCALE 0 100 200 300 400 500 FEET

Plan of Baldwin Hills Village to the scale of the plan of New Town, Edinburgh.

Fig. 260. Site plan development of tenement houses in Manhattan: (A) three Old Law plans with windowless bedrooms and two New Law plans, after housing law of 1887, with improvements in lot width, access, and ventilation. (B) First low-cost housing project (1877) by Alfred T. White in Brooklyn started trend toward inturned cluster planning but retained the street block. (C) Stuyvesant subsidized housing project, built in 1945 by the Metropolitan Life Assurance Co., New York, inaugurates total disregard for the existing street lines. Built for 24,000 people at a density of 600 persons per net acre, it provided totally inadequate, sunless, and congested play areas.

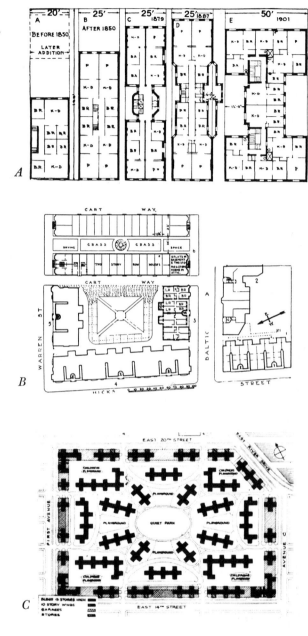

ington (Figs. 259A, 259B). It became fashionable not to discuss architecture any longer and to substitute awakened social conscience as justification for the new "villages," which were liberating the lower middle class from the shackles and iniquities of the city. Jefferson's declaration of urban hatred confessed by liberals, segregationists, and speculators alike, had become a national creed.

But cities don't die from human hatred. They are impervious to the emotions of their inhabitants. They have to be destroyed physically in order to disappear. This destruction started inconspicuously when the first municipal housing projects were constructed (Fig. 260). In keeping with a law of urban origins that asserted itself without the knowledge of the planners, low-cost housing projects turned their bleak backs to the streets, retaining pieces of tattered lawn in front to simulate garden courts (Fig. 261). A few scattered blotches of minimum housing expanded after World War II into a determined effort to cover every available site, regardless of its context within the city plan, with housing towers, guaranteed to waste no public funds on design and to return to the builder 23 per cent of his invested capital (Fig. 262). The recipients of public housing lost contact with the social life of the city. So far, the genesis of the cluster had been quite logical as an expression of inferior status in the hierarchy of human settlements. This changed when the lowly cluster was invested with an architectural pedigree.

Western culture can always rely on the Germans to amalgamate and abstract the original ideas of others. Kant's logic is the abstract of Locke's empiricism and Spinoza's ethics, and Hitler's National Socialism was the systematization of Mussolini's Fascism and Lenin's Bolshevism. The Deutscher Werk-

261

Fig. 261. Stuyvesant Town in Manhattan from the air, showing the destructive character of undesigned buildings, abnormal density, disregard of the existing orthogonal planning pattern, and lack of interior green spaces, which would have been the only excuse for a mid-city cluster.

Fig. 262. New York City housing development on a high bluff above the Bronx River demonstrates the continuation of the "social cluster" as stigmatized by separation from both the city and the landscape.

bund was founded in Berlin in 1907 by a group of architects and artisans on the initiative and under the leadership of Hermann Muthesius. As an attaché at the Imperial German Embassy in London, he had systematically studied all aspects of English residential architecture and had published his observations in a four-volume work, *The English House*. The Muthesius-inspired philosophy of the Werkbund was a combination of aggressive German nationalism, rampant under Kaiser Wilhelm, and a systematization of English design reform, from William Morris and his arts-and-crafts movement to Ebenezer Howard and the garden cities. The offspring of this curious union of interests were the German *Heimatschutz* and the German *Heimatstil*, the first a pioneering step toward the preservation of indigenous landscape and buildings, the second a return to the village community. At the outskirts of big cities factory worker and clerk could, at least on Sunday, regain contact with their native land. So the program said. While the English garden cities and their later American offspring had been content with providing low-cost houses at generous mortgages, German housing developments inclined heavily toward *Weltanschauung*.

Fig. 263. *Hellerau near Dresden (1909), first of the Werkbund settlements, planned and designed by Riemerschmid and Tessenow. The emphasis was on* Heimatstil *(indigenous style) and standardization, simulating the old German village units.*

The earliest one, Hellerau, near Dresden (*Fig. 263*), was planned and built in 1909 by two Werkbund charter members: Richard Riemerschmid and Heinrich Tessenow. They clustered high-gabled stucco cottages around the dance academy of Jaques-Dalcroze, a French apostle of eurythmic movement, yoga breathing, and meatless diet. The *Heimatstil* went down with the monarchy at the conclusion of World War I in 1918. It was replaced by *Sozialer Wohnungsbau*—welfare residential build-

Fig. 264.
  A) Clustered romantic housing scheme (1923), by Zabel.

  B) Low-cost housing project, Frankfurt (1923), by Ernst May. The continuity of a street system has been completely abandoned. Roof terraces were a new feature in subsidized housing, showing Le Corbusier's influence.

A

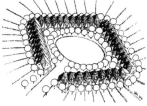

B

Fig. 265.

A) *Plan of the Werkbund exposition, Stuttgart-Weissenhof, and the names of the invited architects. The project still stands as a self-contained cluster on the outskirts of the city. Plan and supervision: Mies van der Rohe.*

B) *Plan of Roehampton Lane Estate in London, developed by the London County Council in the 1950's as a number of free-standing Unités d'Habitation in the concept and architectural design of Le Corbusier. His hope for Vertical Villages, suspended between the sky and "unviolated verdure," was here more closely realized than anywhere else.*

ing—in keeping with the social-democratic Weimar Republic. The generation of architects who came into their own after 1920 considered it an essential point of professional ethics to concentrate on social housing rather than on the design of individual monuments. Ernst May, advocate of rational building methods, introduced cluster housing in Frankfurt am Main (*Figs. 264A, 264B*). Bruno Taut built Britz and other tightly clustered low-cost housing groups. Walter Gropius built Dessau-Toerten while he was director of the Bauhaus, and, in Holland, J. P. Oud and others followed the German prototypes. All these efforts were combined in 1927 at the Werkbund Building Exposition in Stuttgart-Weissenhof (*Fig. 265A*). Under the guidance of Ludwig

Mies van der Rohe, each participating architect contributed one or two characteristic dwelling groups, which were combined into a suburban cluster. This plan became the prototype for all the New Towns that sprang up after World War II. Roehampton-Alton at the outskirts of London (*Fig. 265B*) was the first much hailed British housing scheme; and of the wreath of suburbs around Stockholm, Vallingby is the most publicized. They all are the offspring of Werkbund-Weissenhof.

Twenty years after the founding of the Werkbund, most of the architects had published extensive treatises on the concepts underlying their work. The claims made for the new architecture of the 1920's were surprisingly uniform: functionality, economy, rationalization of structure, qualitative excellence, denial of all artistic individuality or regionalism, and—most essential—standardization to ensure easily mass-produced units. This serialization, supported by an increasing use of mass-produced building components—cement blocks, standardized doors and windows, prefabricated bathroom and kitchen units, and standard modules for room sizes—was in complete accord with the Werkbund program, which had introduced the DIN standard, an anagram of *Deutsche Industrie Norm* (German industry standard) for building materials and industrial design. The CIAM Town-planning Charter summarized it all in the thesis, "Only in the field of town planning will modern architecture find true expression and a wide field for discovery of new solutions."

While Hermann Muthesius was the brilliant organizer and propagandist of the Werkbund program, Peter Behrens was its best-known designer, known chiefly for industrial buildings and product design. Gropius had been his assistant before opening his own office in 1909. Mies van der Rohe had worked there, and by his own testimony had fallen in awe before technology, which determined the entire direction of his long career. The third man in the famous trinity that emerged from a Behrens apprenticeship was Le Corbusier, who contributed two houses to the Weissenhof Exposition which were neither anonymous nor low-cost nor type-cast nor community-oriented but great individual design (*Fig. 266*). They still testify forty years after the event to the revolutionary influence he exerted on the latest act in the drama of urban origins.

Le Corbusier's contribution as a designer of individual buildings cannot occupy us here. It forms a self-contained history of

Fig. 266. Two residences by Le Corbusier at the Weissenhof Settlement near Stuttgart (1927). His contributions to the permanent exposition of modern planning theories was prophetic of the ambiguous role Le Corbusier was to play for the next forty years in the polemics between planning as social collectivism and designing as architectural art.

one aspect of his many-faceted genius. Le Corbusier's work as a city planner has a peculiar logic and continuity that encompasses in one lifetime the whole genesis of the cluster concept. In 1923, still under the influence of his work with Behrens, he designed a housing project for industrial workers at Pessac near Bordeaux (*Fig. 267*), which postulates three types of "taylorized houses." Each attached dwelling unit had its own roof terrace, duplicating, in Le Corbusier's theory, the ground it occupies on the earth. Forms were cubic and roofs flat—far removed from the German *Heimatstil*. Simultaneously with this experiment, which was actually built, Le Corbusier initiated a series of plans for entire cities, starting with the "City for Three Million People" (*Fig. 268*) and continuing with *La Ville Radieuse* and *Le Plan Voisin* for Paris. The City for Three Million is the first station in Le Corbusier's lifelong search "for the absolute measure that orders all things." The city core is still maintained: a vast terrace, raised above the main traffic lane, framed by eight 60-story-high cruciform skyscrapers for commerce and the pro-

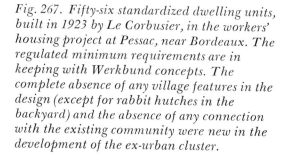

Fig. 267. *Fifty-six standardized dwelling units, built in 1923 by Le Corbusier, in the workers' housing project at Pessac, near Bordeaux. The regulated minimum requirements are in keeping with Werkbund concepts. The complete absence of any village features in the design (except for rabbit hutches in the backyard) and the absence of any connection with the existing community were new in the development of the ex-urban cluster.*

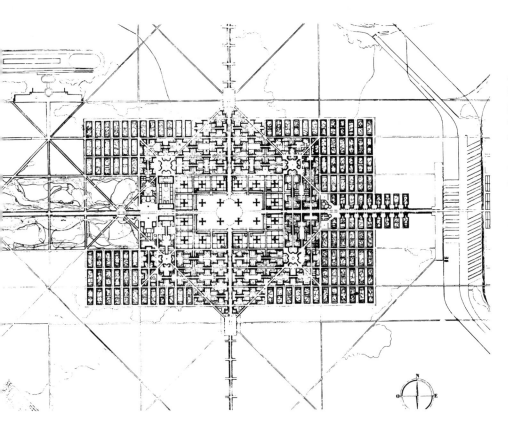

fessions. The surrounding city has an inner core of Cartesian skyscrapers in continuous slab formation, permitting wide, open courts. The outer area forms a rectangular grid of identical residential walk-ups built around a central court.

In 1934, in response to a commission by the Czech shoe manufacturer Bata, Le Corbusier designed Hellocourt (*Fig. 269*). From the centralized concept of ten years before, he had switched to linear planning. He arranged the factory and administration of the town along a combined railroad track and automobile

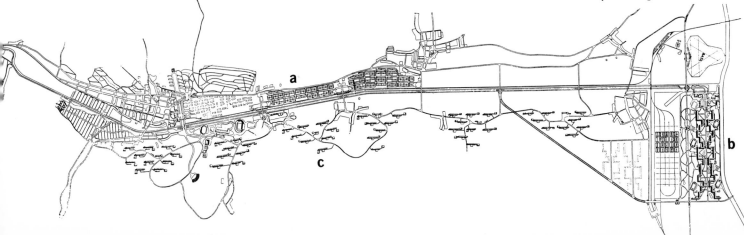

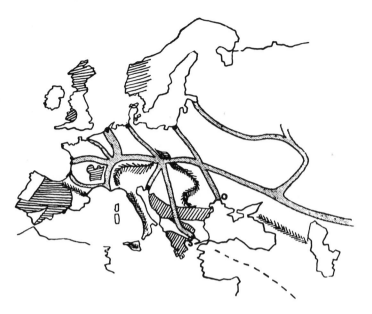

Fig. 270. *Instead of cities as irregularly expanding agglomerations, Le Corbusier and his Ascoral group suggested in the early 1940's a continuous built-up spine extending throughout Europe and possibly into Asia. The linear continuity of industry and urban housing was to leave the areas in between free for agriculture and natural landscape.*

expressway, and he placed the residential high-rise slabs in the landscape on the opposite side of the production center, serviced by curving secondary roads leading to the educational and commercial center. The Hellocourt plan was a more realistic application of a project, conceived for Rio de Janeiro in 1929. The expansion of the Brazilian capital was to follow the single line of a continuous street building, respecting the land by being raised on pilotis, and absorbing automobile traffic into a road placed on top of this highway city. By 1943, during the enforced inactivity of the war years, the two continuous road schemes had

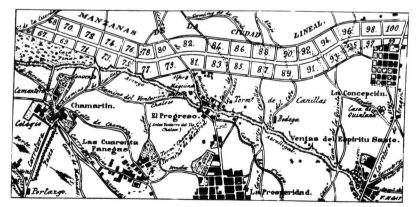

Fig. 271. *The Madrid entrepreneur Soria y Matta was one of the first to conceive of linear expansion as an extra-urban planning feature. His* Ciudad Lineal *(1892) has received undue immortality from historians because he couched his promotional intentions for the first Spanish streetcar line and telephone system—which he owned—in the abstract verbiage so beloved by planning theoreticians, in this case, "symmetry, sexuality, and progress."*

progressed into La Carte d'Europe de L'Ascoral, worked out clandestinely by a group of progressive Parisian architects (*Fig. 270*). Starting, naturally, in Paris, a linear city was to develop along a single spine reaching from western Europe to the Near East and sending off branch linear cities into northern and southern Europe. City centers were to be placed at defined intervals. The idea was not new. In 1892, Arturo Soria y Matta had founded the Madrid Company of Urbanization, for the construction of an endlessly expanding linear city (*Fig. 271*). "Symmetry, sexuality, and progress" were to be the benefits bestowed on the happy homeowners of the *Ciudad Lineal*. Animal vertebrae, vegetable cell growth, and brotherhood of man were also invoked by Matta to boost his urban revolution—in reality

Fig. 272. The realization of Soria y Matta's dream as it existed in 1966 could be more appropriately paraphrased as banality, profit, and overhead wires.

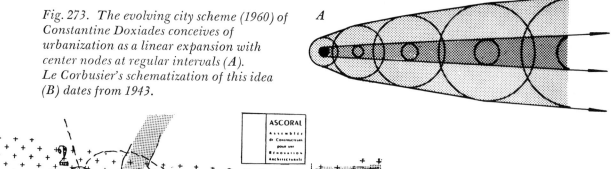

Fig. 273. The evolving city scheme (1960) of Constantine Doxiades conceives of urbanization as a linear expansion with center nodes at regular intervals (A). Le Corbusier's schematization of this idea (B) dates from 1943.

A

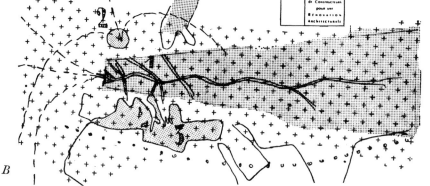

B

nothing but a propaganda scheme for the first streetcar line and the first telephone company in Madrid, which Matta owned. Today his *Ciudad Lineal* on the outskirts of Madrid has the streetcar and the telephone wires, but neither symmetry, sexuality, nor progress (*Fig. 272*). Long after Le Corbusier had abandoned Matta's inspiration and had moved on to the third and final step in his philosophy of urbanism, Constantine Doxiades discovered the precedents and developed his much publicized philosophy of the expanding center city (*Fig. 273*).

By the end of World War II, Le Corbusier had given up any integrated urban plan. In his two-volume work *Le Modulor,* he asked: "What is the rule that orders, that connects all things? I am faced with a problem that is geometrical in nature. I am in the midst of a phenomenon that is visual."

The answer was the Unité d'Habitation, a single high-rise residential unit, placed in the landscape, and removed as far as possible from both the city and the highway. The first one rose in 1949 on the outskirts of Marseilles, "a box of homes" with 360 units, based on a complicated calculation of the Golden Section applied to human measurements and an ancient algebraic progression, the Fibonacci curves. Identical units were built in Nantes, Strasbourg, and Berlin (*Fig. 274*).

The two driving motivations, which one might call obsessions, behind the step-by-step genesis of Le Corbusier's Urbanism were *The Ideal Social Norm* and *The Destruction of the City.* The town-planning charter of the Congrès Internationaux d'Architecture Moderne, whose main author was Le Corbusier, had included a resolution that "the course to be taken by all town-planning projects will be influenced basically by political, social, and economic factors existing at the time, and not by the spirit of modern architecture." The slabs and towers rising in Le Corbusier's ideal landscape from fields, meadows, hills, and valleys were "Vertical Villages." According to his highly poetic description, the family would assemble fifty or sixty stories above ground around the hearth as in olden times; the mother would prepare the meal, and the father would survey the unspoiled landscape from a 6-feet-wide loggia, which "Socrates would have envied." The essential aspect of each village was total self-sufficiency through shopping streets, kindergartens and elementary schools, and recreation areas on the rooftop.

The other compelling motivation of Le Corbusier's planning work, the destruction of the city, is less simple-minded in its assumed social benefits. The new twist was a rejection of the

Fig. 274. Drawings by Le Corbusier illustrate his ideal of Unités d'Habitation, or Vertical Villages placed in the landscape without any urban or communications context.

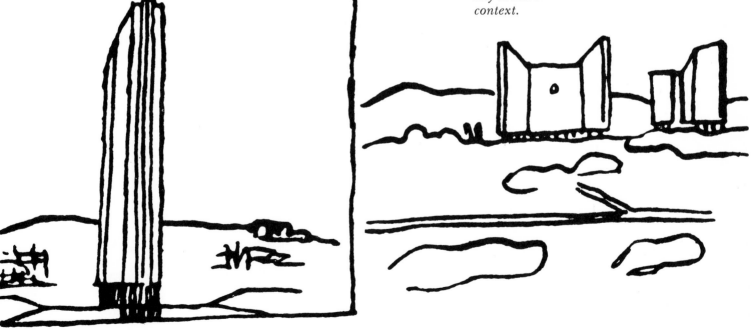

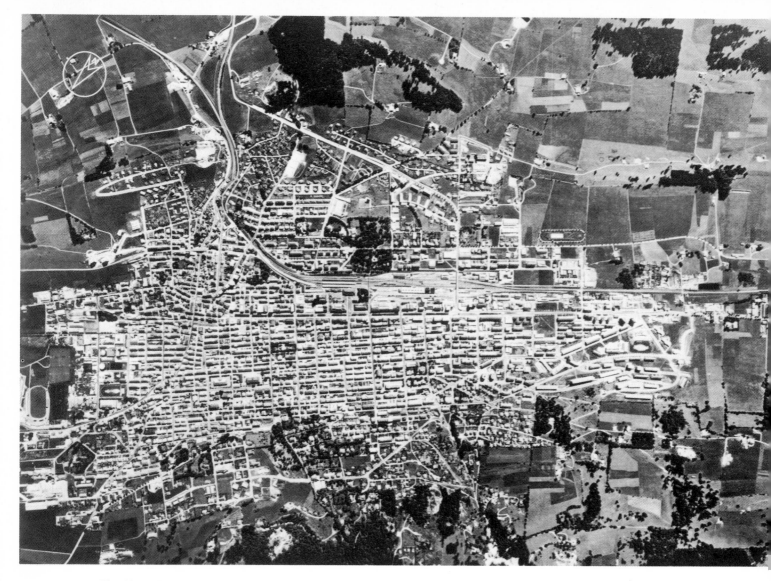

Fig. 275. Aerial view of La Chaux-de-Fonds, the small industrial town in Switzerland where Le Corbusier was born. Perhaps it was the relentless linearity and drabness of its streets that inspired in him hatred of the closed communications network that determines urban existence. Though Le Corbusier traveled over the world and his notebooks show a superb awareness of historical continuity, he never experienced the street as the riverbed of human existence. From Boesch-Hofer, Flugbild der Schweizer Stadt.

city as an essential historical factor, though it had still been recognized by the earlier reformers as the source of work and education. The target of Le Corbusier was the liquidation of the city as a compound social and architectural entity. Throughout his professional life, he worked tirelessly on the elimination of the ligaments that held the urban body together. It is a question for psychiatrists whether the relentless linearity of his hometown, La Chaux-de-Fonds, inspired him with this fierce hatred of the street (*Fig. 275*). "We must kill the street," he thundered at the ninth lecture of the Friends of the Arts in Paris on October 18, 1929. "We shall truly enter into modern town-planning only after we have accepted this preliminary determination."

The Vertical Village, with a density of 400 persons per net acre, of which only 12 per cent was covered, once and for all liquidated the

impenetrable web of streets, passages, houserows, courts . . . avenues or boulevards, adjoined by pedestrians, walks, traffic lanes full of noise and smell of cars, buses, motorcycles.

And, of course, people. They no longer had any need to tread the common ground, because above each Vertical Village floated *le sol artificiel*, the artificial ground, re-created 163 feet above the earth by the architect as a 438-feet-long and 78-feet-wide roof garden from which to contemplate but not contaminate the "green carpet" that separates them from the community of men. And in a final burst of triumph he wrote in *Propos d'Urbanisme:*

We have, of course, killed the corridor street, the street of any and every town in the world. Our dwelling houses have nothing to do with streets.

The influence of Le Corbusier was world-wide and decided the fate of city planning in the twentieth century (*Fig. 276*). No

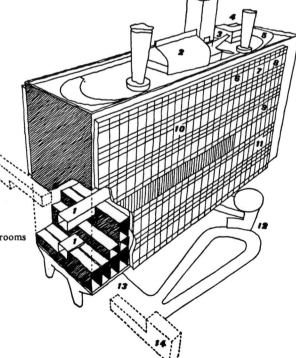

1. Internal thoroughfare
2. Gymnasium
3. Café and sun terrace
4. Cafeteria
5. Children's playground
6. Health centre
7. Crèche
8. Nursery
9. Club
10. Youth clubs and workshops
11. Communal laundry and drying rooms
12. Entrance and porter's lodge
13. Garages
14. Standard two-floor flat

Fig. 276. Le Corbusier's Marseille block demonstrates the effective contrast between a gridiron modularity in plan and elevation and the sculptural imagination of the "artificial earth" of the roof garden. From J. M. Richards, Introduction to Modern Architecture *(1961).*

Fig. 277. Airview of Detroit, with the cleared site of the future Lafayette Park in the center. The location contiguous to the downtown core and within the orthogonal street pattern is clearly visible. Photo: Lens-Art.

one paid attention to the warning he gave his CIAM collaborators against a rigid adherence to the charter principle that "we refer only to those who understand the social role of architecture, not to those who practice modern architecture as a fashionable hobby." At the 1938 CIAM congress, devoted to the exploration of universal minimum standards for living, working, and recreation, he burst forth in a protest of desperate intensity that climaxed in the confession:

The common effort at the hour of its birth comes from the hands of a single man who has accepted the responsibility. This man sends a message to the unknown, but to unknowns who he knows to be there and to listen, and to whom *feeling* and *art* are as necessary as bread and butter.

The bewildering productivity of a single creative imagination, experimenting with every conceivable possibility of man's place on earth, became a grab bag for speculative housing. In the United States, Mies van der Rohe, whose fame rests on his single-mindedness, developed from the stimulus of the Unités d'Habitation an Instant Architecture. By mixing the same basic module with the same skeletal grid, he produced the same "universal envelope" with the same space units, segregated from the city street by the same platforms and stilts. Apartment towers and office buildings became as interchangeable as the sites on which they were assembled. The Lafayette Park redevelopment project in Detroit, which started in 1955, is as good an example as any other. The area of 129 acres had been a "gray neighborhood" in the downtown section (*Fig. 277*) with a predominantly

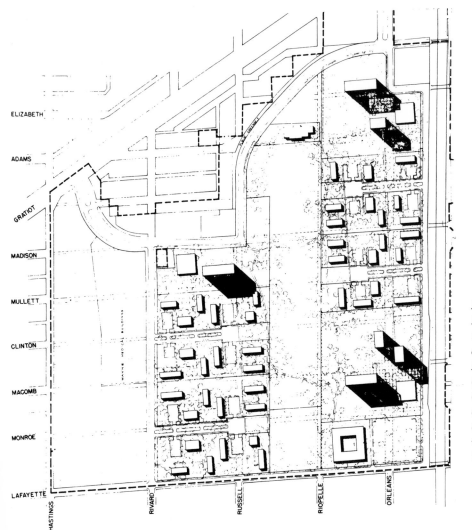

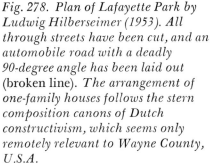

Fig. 278. Plan of Lafayette Park by Ludwig Hilberseimer (1953). All through streets have been cut, and an automobile road with a deadly 90-degree angle has been laid out (broken line). The arrangement of one-family houses follows the stern composition canons of Dutch constructivism, which seems only remotely relevant to Wayne County, U.S.A.

Fig. 279. Twenty-two story high-rise apartment building and town houses, with glass front and rear elevations, by Mies van der Rohe, Lafayette Park, Detroit (1957).

Negro population. Almost 2,000 families were "relocated" in a manner that caused the first of many such scandals. City-planner Ludwig Hilberseimer and architect Ludwig Mies van der Rohe were commissioned to design the project (*Fig. 278*). As they had done fifteen years earlier in the planning of the Illinois Institute of Technology, Mies and Hilberseimer paid homage to the constructivist ideals of their youth, by arranging a constructivist pattern that turned the narrow brick sides of the housing units toward the surrounding parkland and the glass fronts toward each other. The first building phase called for one twenty-two-story apartment building and 186 town houses, of which 162 were two-story height and twenty-four were one story with walled patios. Front and rear elevations were glass from roof line to groundsill, in accordance with Mies's pronouncement that "the curtain is the finest wall" (*Fig. 279*). The most un-Corbusier-like variation was the town house, which became the rage of the 1960's. I. M. Pei followed Lafayette Park with his combination of three Vertical Villages and high-priced, low-density villas in the Society Hill section of Philadelphia (*Fig. 280*), equally central to the core of the city as Lafayette Park and cleared of its low-income inhabitants with equal brutality. Le Corbusier's fluctuating experimental exploration became universal prototypes, losing in the process of popularization those features that had counterbalanced their urban destructiveness: relationship of building to the open ground, designed elevation, coloristic and textural variations in open loggias, and—to him most important—the roof terrace with the greatest possible freedom of sculptural form and recreational variety.

The effect of the introverted-court cluster on the orthogonal city plan will remain limited because the communication pattern is linear. Despite set-back and plaza-zoning laws, the block

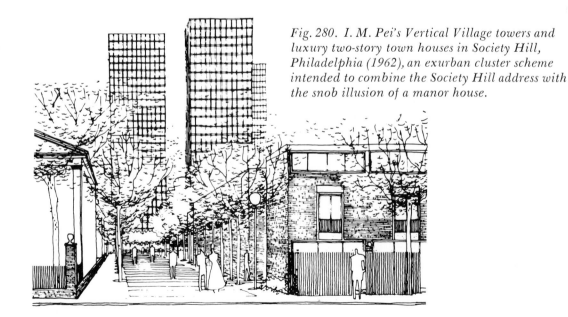

Fig. 280. I. M. Pei's Vertical Village towers and luxury two-story town houses in Society Hill, Philadelphia (1962), an exurban cluster scheme intended to combine the Society Hill address with the snob illusion of a manor house.

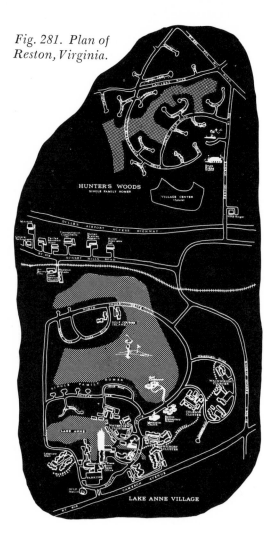

*Fig. 281. Plan of
Reston, Virginia.*

pattern must remain largely intact. Even cities like New York —which, in Mrs. Trollope's testimony from 1836, "have a rage to tear down what they have just built"—respect for sentimental reasons the public spaces that adjoin civic buildings and terminate main avenues. The impact of the cluster concept on urban origins can be properly assessed only in new extra-urban developments.

Reston, Virginia, is a persuasive example of where the cluster concept will lead city planning ideologically and practically (*Fig. 281*). It also proves through its promotion literature that the architectural pedigree acquired by the cluster concept some forty years ago has resulted in a sham ideology camouflaging a feeling of historical guilt. In a mockery of the crystalline logic of 5,000 years of urbanization, clusters of one-family houses, strewn over 7,400 acres of landscape, are advertised as "not a sub-division, a suburb, a small town, or an isolated city. Reston is a contemporary city, urban in character and open-spaced in design." If the visitor should balk at the anti-urban plan of seven village centers for 10,000 to 12,000 people each, with their own community centers for shopping, cultural, religious, social, and recreational facilities, but without any communication pattern whatever, he can look at a single skyscraper, forlornly rising on the village plaza in an attempt to provide vertical scale (*Fig. 282*). Columbia, another new community built between Washington and Baltimore on identical lines as Reston by "an evangelist of urban renewal," adds to the metropolitan claims of Reston the CIAMese cliché that its nine specu-

*Fig. 282. Apartment tower, Reston,
Virginia, Conklin and Rossant, architects
(1965). The failure of Reston to live up to
its advance billing as a new city expresses
itself visually in this vertical accent,
intended to provide contrast to the low,
one-family units. Were it not for its good
design, the tower would be an eyesore.
A skyscraper is an image of city power. In
Reston it achieves the opposite effect—it
proclaims that there is no city to justify it.
Photo: William Maris.*

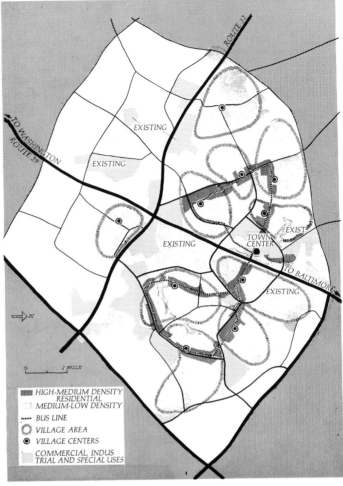

Fig. 283. Plan of the New Town Columbia, between Washington and Baltimore. The ordinary speculative cluster scheme is sold to the public as a saintly experiment in social altruism. Another parcel of open land has been despoiled with giddy village floats, while the location at the intersection of two expressways would have made the development of a high-density, multiple-occupancy form feasible.

lation villages are built "not for art, for business, for political or economic expediency. . . . It is to serve people" (*Fig. 283*). And, in deference to the London court stenographer who freed the suburban satellite from its ancient social stigma, the Columbia slogan promises: The Best of Town and Country. A new generation raised in the belief that mock village clusters are "the best" of urban life will have been duped out of the most uniquely human, inexhaustibly creative experience man has provided for himself: the duality between a man-made world of forms, spaces, and structures and an evolutionary nature, following different laws and producing a different beauty.

The financial difficulties reported for the Reston development at the close of 1967 might, hopefully, indicate a growing awareness among families refusing to move into nowhere that the developers' stereotyped insistence that "this is what the people want" is no longer true. The makers of man-made environment are at a crossroad. They can destroy the city as the matrix of man or renew it. The small survey of existing or planned building groups, forming the conclusion of this inquiry, is a hint at the options still open for the next link in the long chain that binds the past to the future through the image of the historical city.

7

OPTIONS: A CONCLUSION

OPTION: the exercise of a power of choice, an alternative.

A

Fig. 284. *The expanding urban world is faced with the paradox of disappearing environmental alternatives. City suburbs (A) differ from city centers (B) only through increased inaccessibility and the amount of wasteland left visible. Even latitudes no longer matter. The Pedregulho housing development by Alfonso Reidy on the outskirts of Rio de Janeiro could be on the fringes of Rome or Bombay, despite its elegantly curved main structure, which was abandoned before it was occupied. And the view into inside Manhattan proves again that it is not lack of available rebuilding space that forces suburban scatteration but lack of planned-site economy. What are the alternatives?*

B

285

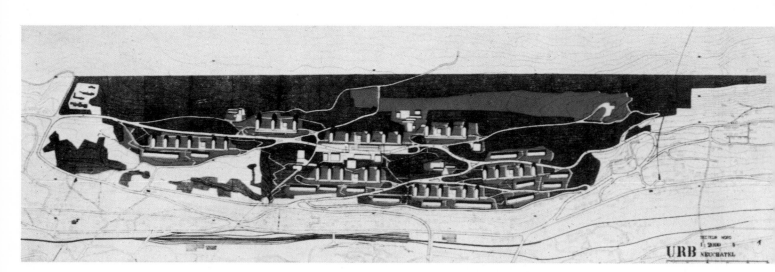

Fig. 285. Urban expansion of Neuchatel, Switzerland.
P. Waltenspuhl, architect and planner, in collaboration with the
Neuchatel Technical Services Administration. (Project start: 1961.)
A new city terrace above the ancient lake town is formed with a
minimum of site disturbance. Light gray areas on the plan are
landscaped grounds compensating for the lakeview, which only the
front slabs can enjoy. Dark areas are woodland. The excellence
of the project rests on the counterpoint concept of dense, linear
residential streets with natural environment.

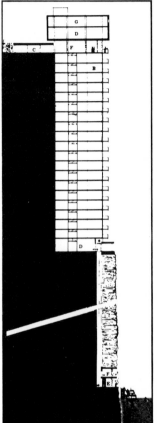

Fig. 286. Vacation town of Gozo, Island of Malta, Mediterranean. Julio Lafuente, architect and planner (1966). This is the newest version of the ancient rock ledges of Spain, the Italian islands, and Mount Athos in Greece—mountains honeycombed with dwelling caves. Man's habitation has been adjusted to the site and the site adjusted to man, who has replaced the hauling basket on a straw rope with an elevator shaft to sea level.

287

A

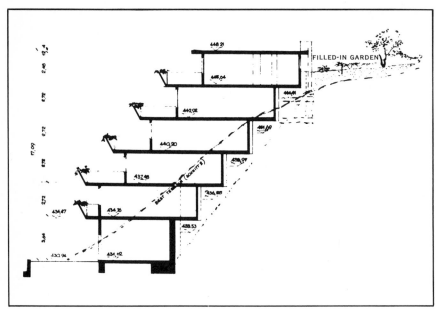

Fig. 287.

A) In 1961, architects Stucky and Meuli completed in Zug, Switzerland, a terraced housing project that excels in a combination of ancient local geomorphic traditions and contemporary formal and structural interaction. The demands of privacy and spatial economy, so often ignored in speculation housing, have been turned into assets. The canted horizontal terrace walls delineate with their sharp white surfaces the domain of each dwelling and emphasize through vertical repetition the urban aspects of high-rise density. Photo: René Hartmann.

B

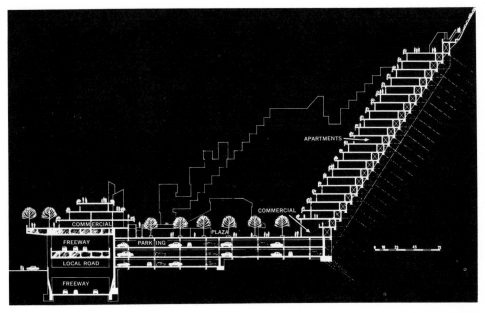

*B) Designed six years later by
architects Burger and Coplan for
the steep slope of San Francisco's
Telegraph Hill, this project expands
the Swiss concept into the dimensions
of a city sector. Moving traffic and
parking have been put below grade
on level ground, to make room for
a pedestrian plaza at the foot of
the house mountain, acknowledging
for the first time in San Francisco's
dismal urban history that here
one of the finest bays and most
grandiose vistas should be saved for
the citizens.*

Fig. 288. The winning design for the St. Giuliano sector of Mestre, opposite Venice, by Ludovici Quaroni and Associates, is a promising synthesis between a linear communication network and concentric focal points of commerce, administration, and especially recreation. The linear roads lead outward, toward the expressways and railroad, while the concentric, raised esplanades focus attention on the single asset of the town—the Adriatic Sea.

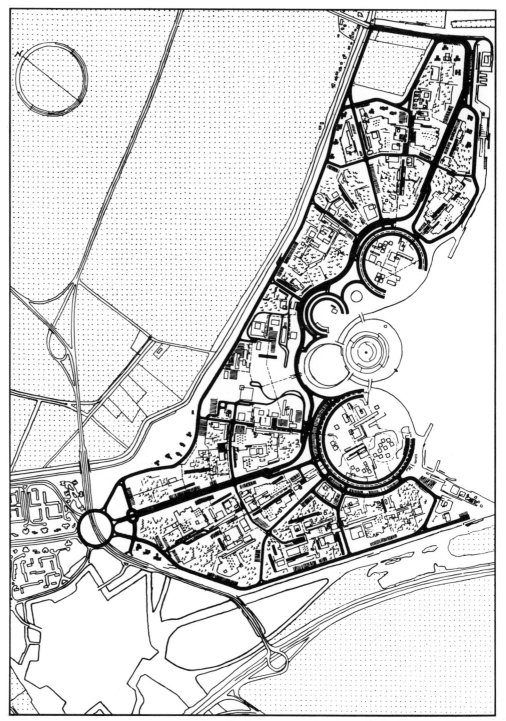

Fig. 289. Architect Konwiarz aroused a storm of protest and
sarcastic comments when his entry into the replanning competition
for the Alsterzentrum–St. Georg in Hamburg, Germany, was
published in 1966. This is astonishing, because the plan offers a
brilliant solution for the difficult contrast in historical and modern
scale. Instead of muscling their way into established street patterns
and blighting everything where their foundations are put down,
the megastructures of tomorrow assume a defining and protective
position. The traditional and the technological city act upon
each other by emphasizing to each its own.

291

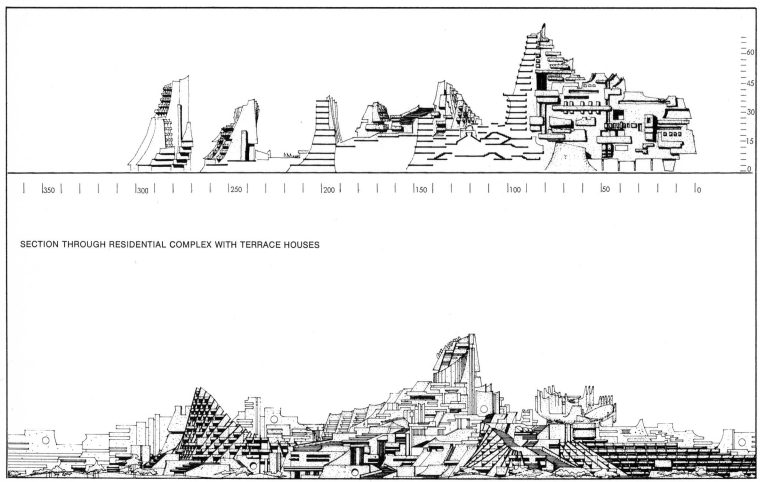

SECTION THROUGH RESIDENTIAL COMPLEX WITH TERRACE HOUSES

A

Fig. 290. Ratingen West, Germany.
Project for a new town, by Merete Mattern
and Associates (1966). This highly concentric Stadtkrone is planned for an area
where suburban scatteration from the
metropolis of Düsseldorf is threatening
the destruction of the countryside.
Constructed of poured concrete slabs
with suspended wall systems, a basic space
module achieves maximum variety by
twisting units around a vertical communication network of roads and elevators (A).

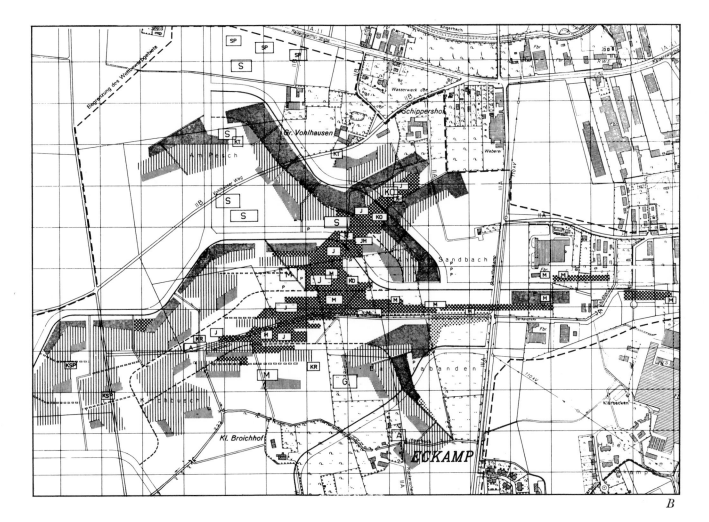

B

Shops (M), *playgrounds* (J), *and schools*
(S) *are repeated on various levels till the*
administrative center (KO) *is reached*
(B). *The basic principle of the project was*
the creation of a distinctive gestalt—an
urban personality—and the amenity of the
inhabitants being at no point more than a
ten-minute walk from any other point in the
city. For the surrounding land, it would be as
commanding a cityscape as the old cathedral
towns had been, while each living space
would partake of the countryside.

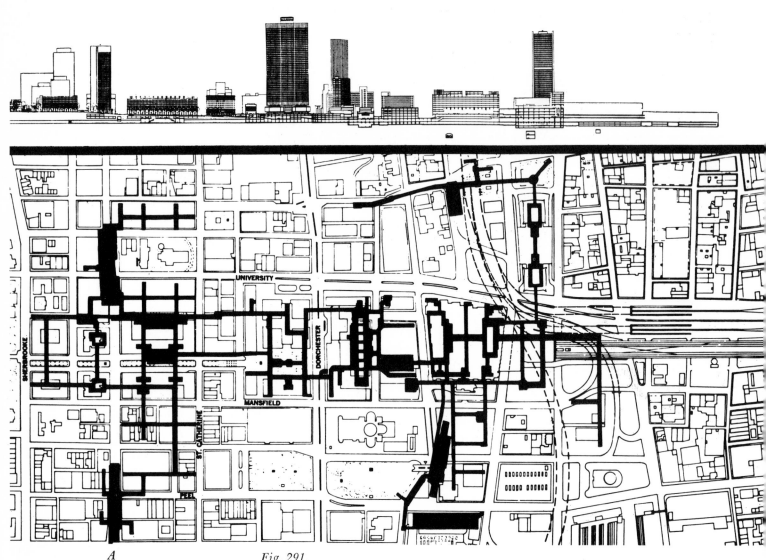

A

Fig. 291.

A) The master plan for a subterranean plaza system and communication network in Montreal, Canada, combines a subway system with shopping and recreation facilities, directly accessible from the station platforms. The plan frees the city from Canada's extreme weather conditions. Whether this new interpretation of the street as urban continuity will adversely affect the civic character of the most urbane and promising city on the North American continent remains to be seen. What is demonstrated is the achitectural concept of space, structure, and light as urban factors. Without the aesthetic gratification of design excellence, the subterranean city would lose its appeal.

294

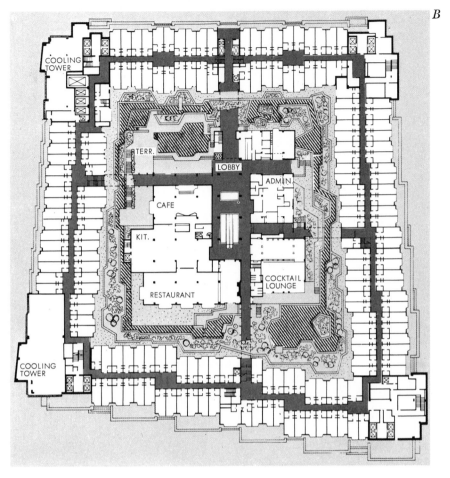

B

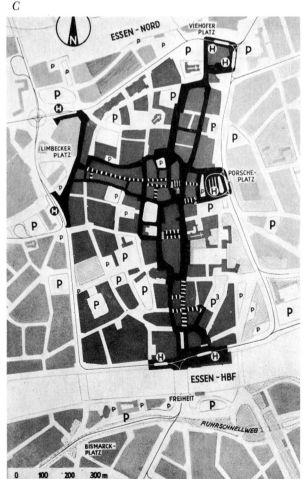

C

B) One of the new Montreal plazas, Bonaventure, by
Affleck, Desbarats, Dimakopoulos, Lebensold and Sise—
has an antispace, much as the Greeks postulated an
anti-earth. On top of the tall office tower sits a hotel,
whose rooms form a perfect city block with continuous
staggered elevations. The interior communication system
resembles that of the subway system, connecting nodes of
intense social, commercial, and residential concentration.

C) The core of the old merchant and manufacturing
city of Essen, Germany, as replanned after the
devastation of World War II, offers a third variation
of the linear city as pure communication. Surrounded
by ample parking spaces (P), the commercial center is
predominantly reserved for pedestrians. Black roads
indicate a combination of delivery routes and sidewalks;
black-white roads are arcaded shopping lanes. In
planning both street types, a unifying pattern
of large show windows and attractive graphic design
was adopted.

295

*Fig. 292. The Lower Manhattan Plan
Capital Project. Wallace, McHarg and
Conklin and Rossant, architects and
planners, produced in 1965 the first viable
plan for the rehabilitation of New York's
densest borough. The point of departure
was not a* tabula rasa, *as in other "urban
removal" schemes, nor a denial of the
growth-inhibiting boundaries of two rivers.
In a further development from the original
Dutch plan, the cross-island connections
and river embankments are restored to the
pedestrian. The plan fully understands the
difference between communication and
traffic, which is largely put below level.
Business and residential high-rise buildings
are closely interspersed—continuing a
specific Manhattan tradition (A). The Wall
Street Mall (B) serves here as a close-up of
the plan. Continuous street arcades,
landscaped plazas with fountains and
sculpture, and a careful grouping of
terminal buildings at each end of the mall
are straight out of the Hellenistic urban
vocabulary. The Roman heritage is the
affirmation of the* portus *that thrives on
power and money, on interaction of diverse
social elements, and on an actual and
symbolic outlook toward other continents.*

A

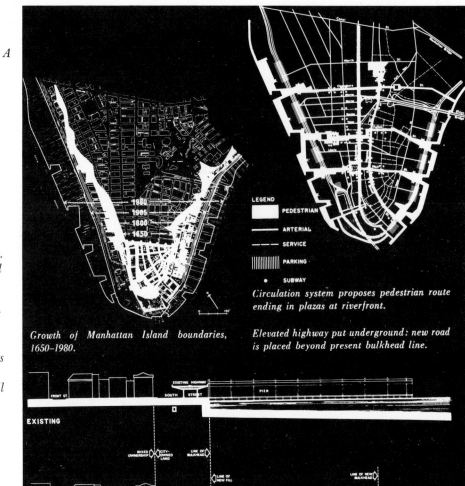

Growth of Manhattan Island boundaries,
1650–1980.

*Circulation system proposes pedestrian route
ending in plazas at riverfront.*

*Elevated highway put underground: new road
is placed beyond present bulkhead line.*

B

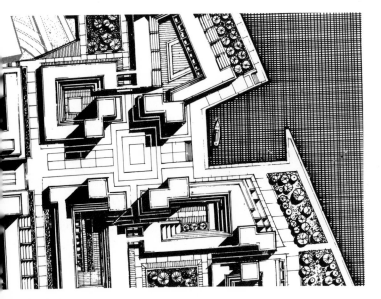

Fig. 293. *A linear city for Long Island, New York. Designed by McMillan, Griffis, and Mileto (1967). An urban road city operating on three levels. Above the subway—but covered by the pedestrian road—runs the automobile expressway. Above the pedestrian road rise bridges, connecting the terraced residential units with each other. The peculiar combination of privacy inside the apartments and neighborliness at visual and shouting distance is a Mediterranean tradition, which the immigrants brought to Brooklyn, Queens, and other typical first-generation parts of the big city. It has been revived here in a new key, which would open the old shabby thoroughfares to new vitality.*

Fig. 294. Project for a Graphic Arts Center, Manhattan. Paul Rudolph, architect (1967). The famous functionalists of the 1930's—Mies van der Rohe, Le Corbusier, Gropius, and others—tilted the ancient coercive grid 90 degrees and applied it to building elevations rather than to horizontal town plans. The structuralists of the 1960's have gone a decisive step further. They have retained the module but have freed it from the grid. The megastructure of the future will be a combination of prefabricated modular units and the city plazas above which they rise. The spatial uniformity of the dwelling "system" will be counteracted by an endless variety of river vistas and a response to the human predilection for movement in all directions. The urban justification of this unprecented concept will depend on the architect alone—on his ability to manipulate his modular raw material in such a way that it creates a new formal identity that does not repel but attracts.

A

B

Fig. 295. So far, only one architect, Moshe Safdie, has succeeded in actually constructing this new modular prefabricated verticality. Habitat (A), at Expo '67 in Montreal, despite its world acclaim is rarely understood or illustrated in its most creative urban context. Facing the main access road and the Montreal skyline, the modular units of Habitat present that same symmetry and continuity which tie the diverse forms of old cities into a harmonious entity. The left bank of Florence (B) and Safdie's west elevation share street-consciousness as the most essential factor of the anonymous urban cityscape.

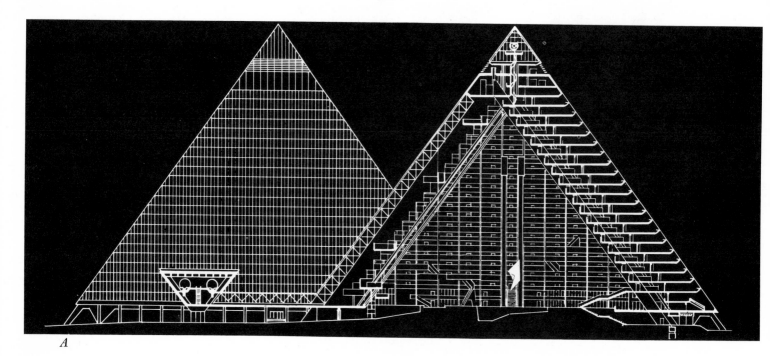

A

Fig. 296: *Pyramid housing cluster (A, B) for 2,000 people. Designed for Siberia by A. Schipkov and E. Schipkova (1967). Twenty-five-story-high hollow pyramids, with 579 apartments on twenty floors, provide completely regulated climatic conditions. The north wall of each equilateral pyramid is glazed, to permit interior lighting for the living spaces and for an extensive garden court with flowers, trees, vegetable beds, and birds the year round. The Schipkov pyramids, completely calculated and feasible, would create a unique regional architecture, adapted to Siberia's hostile weather and to no other place. They would also set an urbanization pattern that precludes sprawl, instant slums, and low densities. It would not provide for an open, competitive, highly diversified and specialized society. Marxism and urban society are as incompatible as urbanism and any other form of orthodoxy. From* Architecture d'Aujourd'Hui, *No. 134 (October, 1967).*

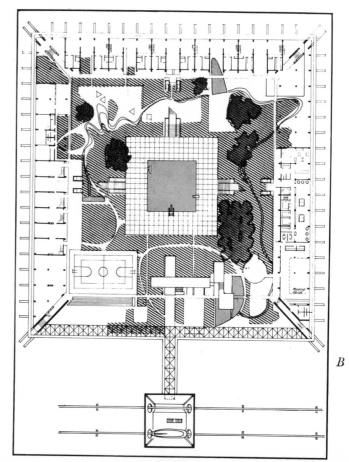

B

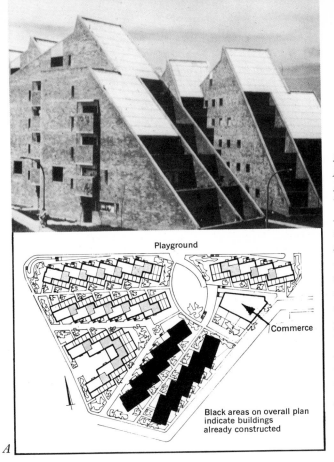

Fig. 297. *Low-cost housing project, Bogotá, Colombia. R. Salmona, H. Vieco, E. Zarate, architects (1966). The cliché "building for the people" loses its American connotation of ugliness and cheapness when applied to this cluster scheme in the process of further development. This is minimum-budget, maximum-design performance. A cohesive neighborhood is formed by continuous six-story duplex units, whose privacy is protected by deep terrace recesses and staggered elevation (A). Despite the development's location in the socially inferior* barrio *outside the amenities of the city, its interior street provides a closed urban feeling and the neighborly evening meeting place that is the psychological mainstay of Latin American communities (B).*

Playground

Commerce

Black areas on overall plan indicate buildings already constructed

A

B

301

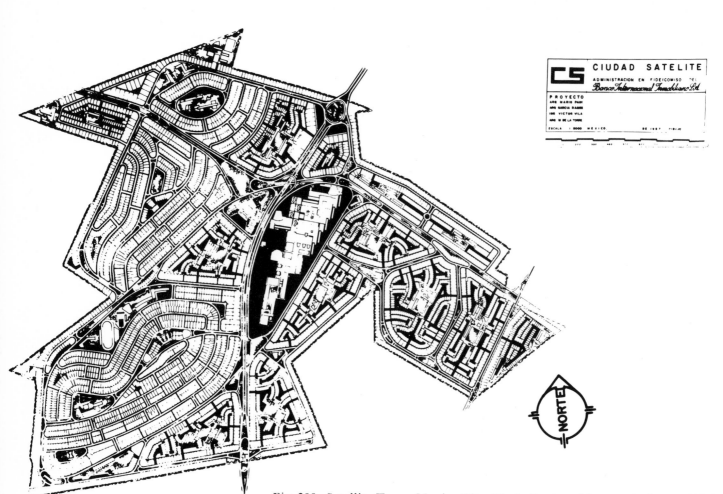

Fig. 298. Satellite Town, Mexico City. Mario Pani, architect and planner (1957). This plan for a new town on the outskirts of the Mexican capital is a curious hybrid scheme, only partially realized. The separate neighborhoods form self-contained clusters of modular units without over-all continuity; but the street pattern is linear, with a tight alignment of houses that is reminiscent of the casa mura *tradition of the colonial city. The roads follow the contour lines of a hilly site, adjusting the building alignment to natural conditions. This geomorphic element is also decisive for the placing of the town center, which rises in successive terraces like a pre-Columbian acropolis. If such a scheme could have been implemented with architectural excellence, it would have been a synthesis of all the ancient concepts of city-building developed on three continents. The failure to achieve this syncretic quality is as significant of our times as an architectural success would have been for earlier periods. The significance lies in our confirmed insecurity, in our lingering knowledge of what a planned urban environment should be, and in our denial of this knowledge in a world dominated by the experimental transience of science and technology. The children born in these satellites are indistinguishable from those that have populated all prototypes, yet they are proclaimed a new race fitted for a new matrix shaped without ancestors by a computer. It is all so logical, so scientifically correct— except that the computer cannot be taught the meaning of urban environment.*

302

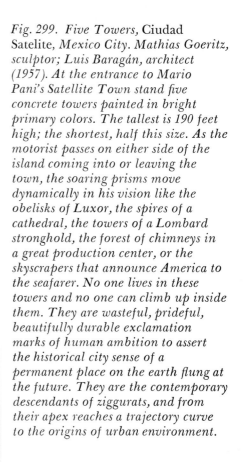

Fig. 299. Five Towers, Ciudad Satelite, *Mexico City. Mathias Goeritz, sculptor; Luis Baragán, architect (1957). At the entrance to Mario Pani's Satellite Town stand five concrete towers painted in bright primary colors. The tallest is 190 feet high; the shortest, half this size. As the motorist passes on either side of the island coming into or leaving the town, the soaring prisms move dynamically in his vision like the obelisks of* Luxor, *the spires of a cathedral, the towers of a Lombard stronghold, the forest of chimneys in a great production center, or the skyscrapers that announce America to the seafarer. No one lives in these towers and no one can climb up inside them. They are wasteful, prideful, beautifully durable exclamation marks of human ambition to assert the historical city sense of a permanent place on the earth flung at the future. They are the contemporary descendants of ziggurats, and from their apex reaches a trajectory curve to the origins of urban environment.*

Books of particular relevance have been mentioned in context with the cities to which they refer. Additional information can only come from library book lists and card catalogues. However, for the serious student of urban genesis there is no more relevant source of information than specialized journals. The freshness and authenticity of new knowledge gained from excavations, reconstructions, and scholarly research often gets lost in the long, tedious process of writing and publishing books. The following list is an excerpt of a vast field of specialized periodicals, which should be augmented by looking through the Periodicals card files of libraries.

GENERAL SURVEYS

AUZELLE, ROBERT. *Encyclopédie de l'Urbanisme.* Paris: 1950—.
Installments appear in irregular intervals and without detectable interconnection. Selected cities are thoroughly analyzed and documented.

EGLI, ERNST. *Geschichte des Städtebaues.* 3 vols. Zurich: 1959—.
Despite the German text, this all-inclusive survey of world planning history is comprehensible to all students because of excellent maps and plans.

GUTKIND, ERWIN A. *International History of City Development.* Vol. 1, "Urban Development in Central Europe." Vol. 2, "Urban Development in the Alpine and Scandinavian Countries." Vol. 3, "Urban Development in Southern Europe: Spain and Portugal." New York: 1964—.
An awe-inspiring enterprise whose future volumes will document the entire world history of cities.

HEGEMANN, WERNER, and PEETS, ELBERT. *The American Vitruvius.* New York: 1922.
As document of the *beaux arts* approach to the City Beautiful, and as comparative study of Western European and North American capital city development, this large volume has its place.

LAVEDAN, PIERRE. *Histoire de l'Urbanisme.* 3 vols. Paris: 1926–52.

The selection is confined to Western urban cultures but is especially valuable as a continuous record on French cities, from Roman times to the early twentieth century. Lavedan's *Les Villes Françaises* is available as a separate volume, paperbound.

RASMUSSEN, STEEN EILER. *Towns and Buildings.* Cambridge, Mass.: 1951.

A restricted selection of well-known cities, which is relevant because of the author's sensitive presentation of the interaction of plans and buildings.

TUNNARD, CHRISTOPHER. *The City of Man.* New York: 1953.

A leisurely, thoroughly humanistic interpretation of urban development as ideology rather than physical fact.

INDEX SYSTEMS

The following index systems should be consulted for periodicals and books:

Art Index

Book Review Digest

Chamberlin, Mary W. *Guide to Art Reference Books.* Chicago: 1959.

Columbia University Avery Architectural Library Index to Architectural Periodicals

Columbia University Library Book Catalogue

International Index to Periodicals

N.Y. Metropolitan Museum Library Catalogue

Reader's Guide to Periodical Literature

JOURNALS AND REPORTS

i) General, unspecified publications dealing with contemporary and historical plans

Architectural Forum (New York)

Architectural Review (London)

L'Architecture d'Aujourd'hui; with English summaries (Paris)

L'Archittetura; Cronache y Storia (Rome)

Journal of the Town Planning Institute (London)

Town and Country Planning (London)

Town Planning Review (Liverpool)

Urbanistica

ii) *General, unspecified publications dealing with historical*
    plans only
American Journal of Archaeology
Annals of Archaeology and Anthropology (Liverpool)
Antiquity
The Archaeological Journal (London)
Archaeology
Horizon
Journal, British Archaeological Association
Journal of the Society of Architectural Historians (also relevant
    to category *viii*)
National Geographic Magazine
Papers, Peabody Museum of Archaeology and Ethnology at
    Harvard University
Revue Archéologique (Paris)

iii) *Publications dealing with Prehistory, the Old World*
Asian Perspectives (Bulletin of the Far Eastern Prehistoric
    Association)
Bulletin, American School of Prehistoric Research
Excavaciones Arqueológicas en España (also relevant to category
    vi)
Israel Exploration Journal (also relevant to category *iv*)
Nordiske Oldskrift-Selskab (deals with Nordic archaeology; also
    relevant to category *vii*)
Praehistorische Zeitschrift
Publications, International Congress of Anthropology and Pre-
    history
Sovetskaia Arkheologiia (deals with Russian archaeology; also
    relevant to category *vii*)

iv) *Publications dealing with the Orient, Middle, and Near East*
Anatolian Studies
Annual Bibliography of Indian Archaeology
Armenian Review
Ars Orientalis
Artibus Asiae
Bukkyo Bijutsu: Quarterly journal of Buddhist art
Expedition, University of Pennsylvania
India: A review report on Indian archaeology
Indian Antiquary
Journal of the Society of Oriental Research (Chicago)
Museum Monographs, University of Pennsylvania

Oriental Art

The Phoenix: A monthly magazine for India, Burma, China, Japan, and Eastern Asia

Publications, Comité de Conservation des Monuments de l'Art Arabe

Publications, Japan Society of London

Publications, Royal Asiatic Society of Great Britain

Sinica: Zeitschrift für Chinakunde

Syria: Revue d'Art Oriental et d'Archéologie

Transactions, Society of Biblical Archaeology (London)

University Museum Bulletin, University of Pennsylvania

v) Publications dealing with Egypt

Journal of Egyptian Archaeology (London)

Publications, British School of Archaeology and Egyptian Research

Publications, Société d'Archéologie Copte (Cairo)

vi) Publications dealing with Greece and Rome

Egypt Exploration Society: Graeco-Roman Memoirs

Greek, Roman, and Byzantine Studies (Cambridge; also relevant to category *vii*)

Hesperia: Journal of the American School of Classical Studies at Athens

Journal of Hellenic Studies (London)

Journal of Roman Studies (London)

Papers, American School of Classical Studies at Athens

Papers, British School of Rome (also relevant to category *viii*)

Publications, Bibliothèques des Écoles Françaises d'Athenes et Rome

vii) Publications dealing with the Byzantine, Islamic, and Medieval

Ars Islamica (Ann Arbor, Michigan)

The Art Bulletin (also relevant to category *viii*)

Byzantion: Revue Internationale des Études Byzantines

Cahiers de Civilisation Medievale

Speculum: A Journal of Medieval Studies (Cambridge)

Transactions, Chalmers University of Technology (Gotenburg, Sweden)

viii) Publications dealing with the Renaissance and Baroque

The Burlington Magazine (London)

307

Journal, Warburg and Courtauld Institutes (London)
Marsyas
Mélanges, École Française de Rome
Renaissance News
Revue des Deux Mondes
Zeitschrift für Kunstgeschichte

ix) Publications dealing with North and South America
American Anthropologist: Selected papers
American Antiquity
The Americanist: Proceedings of the Congresses of Americanists
Archaeological and Historical Publications, Ohio State University
Ars Americana
Boletín del Centro de Investigaciones Históricas (Caracas)
Journal of American History
Publications in American Archaeology and Ethnology, University of California
Scientific American
See also all publications of the Museum, University of Pennsylvania, listed under *iv.*

*   *   *

In conclusion, it should be mentioned that general encyclopedias offer detailed information that supplies the essential knowledge of religion, mythology, political development, science, fine arts, and leader personalities in all known countries, without which cities are meaningless.

INDEX

Numerals in italic type refer to numbered illustrations.

313

Designed by Helene Berinsky
Printed by Halliday Lithograph Corp.
Bound by Montauk Book Manufacturing Co., Inc.

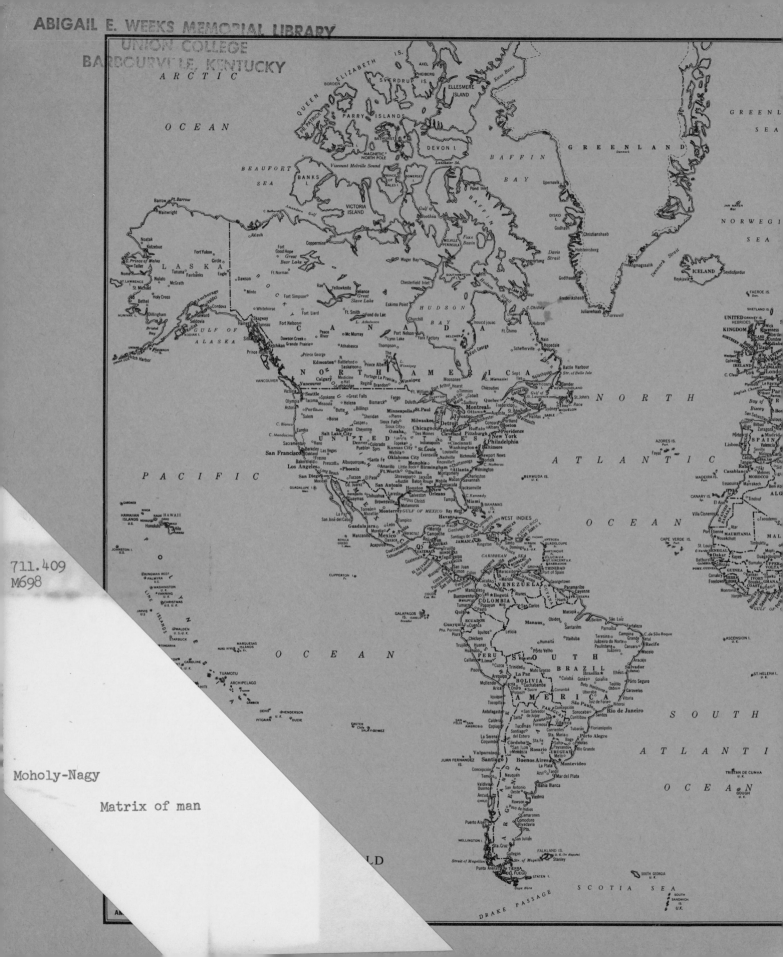